PRINCIPLES FOR SUCCESS

RAY DALIO

Avid Reader Press

New York   London   Toronto   Sydney   New Delhi

AVID READER PRESS
An Imprint of Simon & Schuster, Inc.
1230 Avenue of the Americas
New York, NY 10020

First Avid Reader Press hardcover edition November 2019

AVID READER PRESS and colophon
are trademarks of Simon & Schuster, Inc.

For information about special discounts for bulk purchases,
please contact Simon & Schuster Special Sales at 1-866-506-1949
or business@simonandschuster.com.

The Simon & Schuster Speakers Bureau can bring authors
to your live event. For more information or to book an event contact
the Simon & Schuster Speakers Bureau at 1-866-248-3049
or visit our website at www.simonspeakers.com.

*Jacket and interior design by Mark del Lima, Mio Yokota,
and Christina Peabody*

Manufactured in the United States of America

1 3 5 7 9 10 8 6 4 2

Library of Congress Cataloging-in-Publication Data is available.

ISBN 978-1-9821-4721-1
ISBN 978-1-9821-4725-9 (ebook)

To my grandchildren who are born and yet to be born. This book is for you (and for all others who find it useful).

You are on an adventurous journey called life.

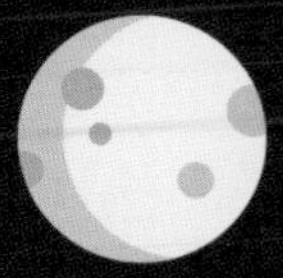

Because there's a lot ahead that you haven't yet encountered, you can't possibly know what it will be like.

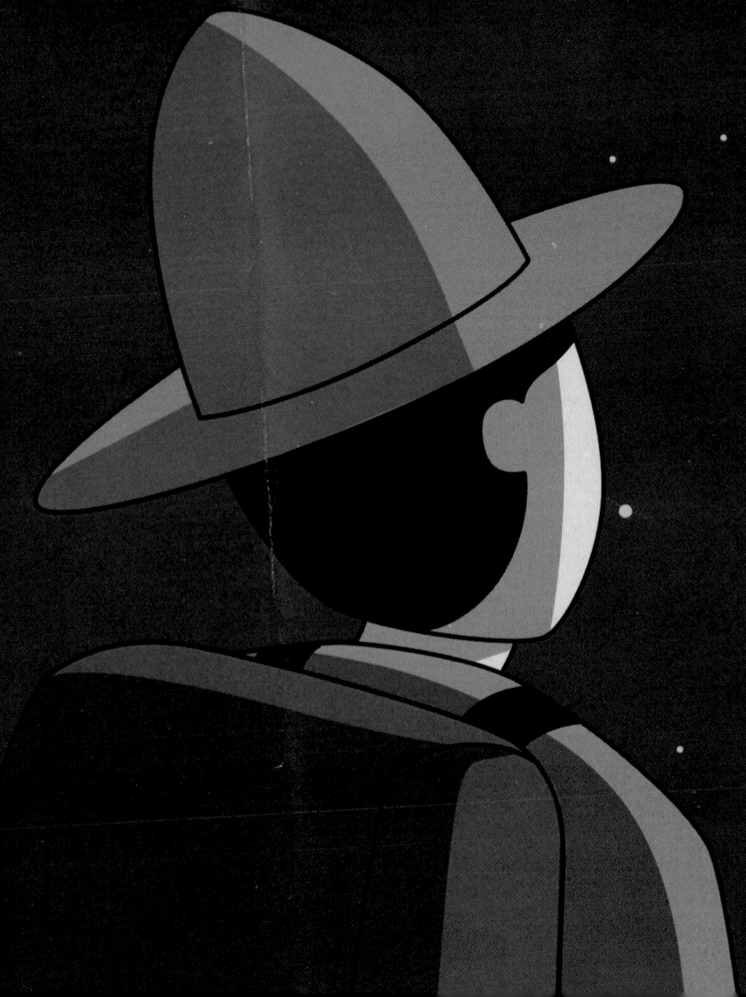

Since I'm near the end of that journey and have successfully navigated most of it, and because I care about you, I'd like to show you some of what you can expect and give you some principles that helped me and I believe can help you.

The most important things you need to have on your journey through life are good principles.

Principles are ways of successfully dealing with the realities that you will encounter.

They're essentially recipes for success.

Every successful person has principles that make them successful.

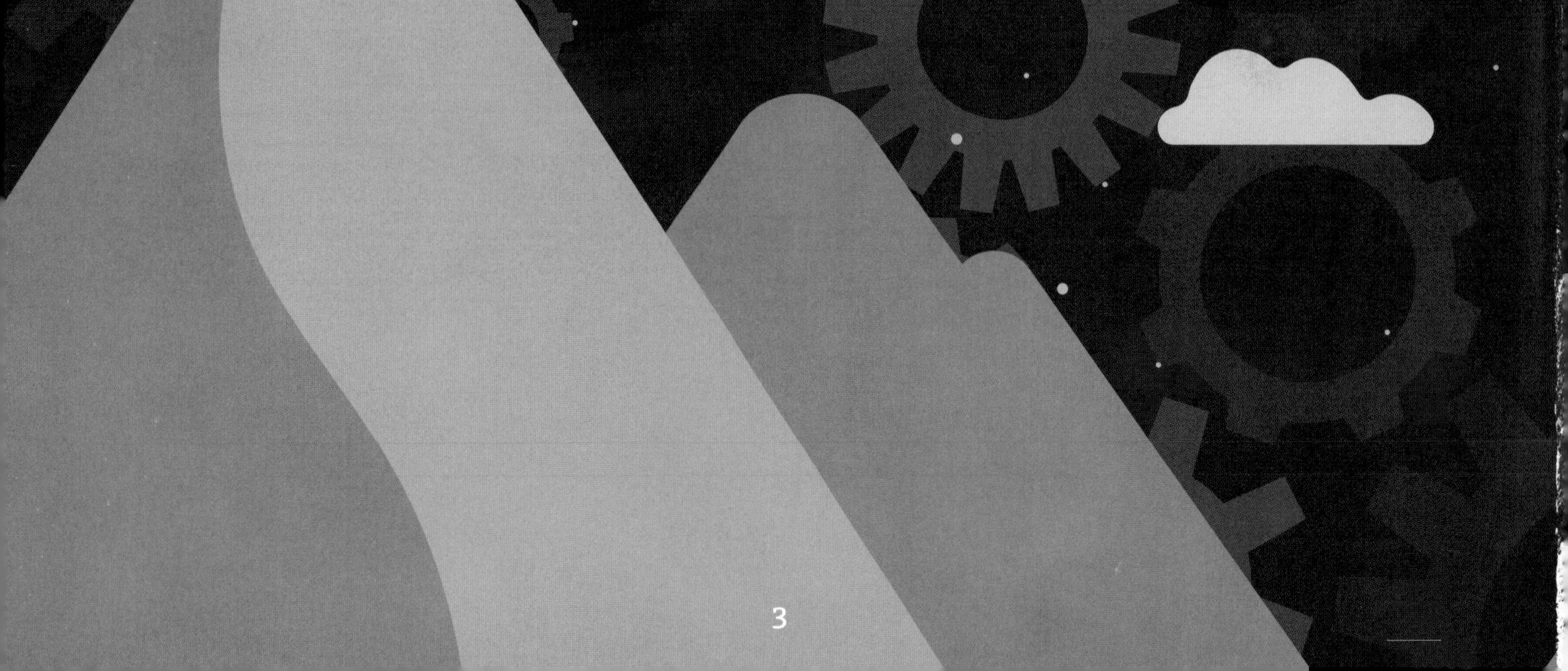

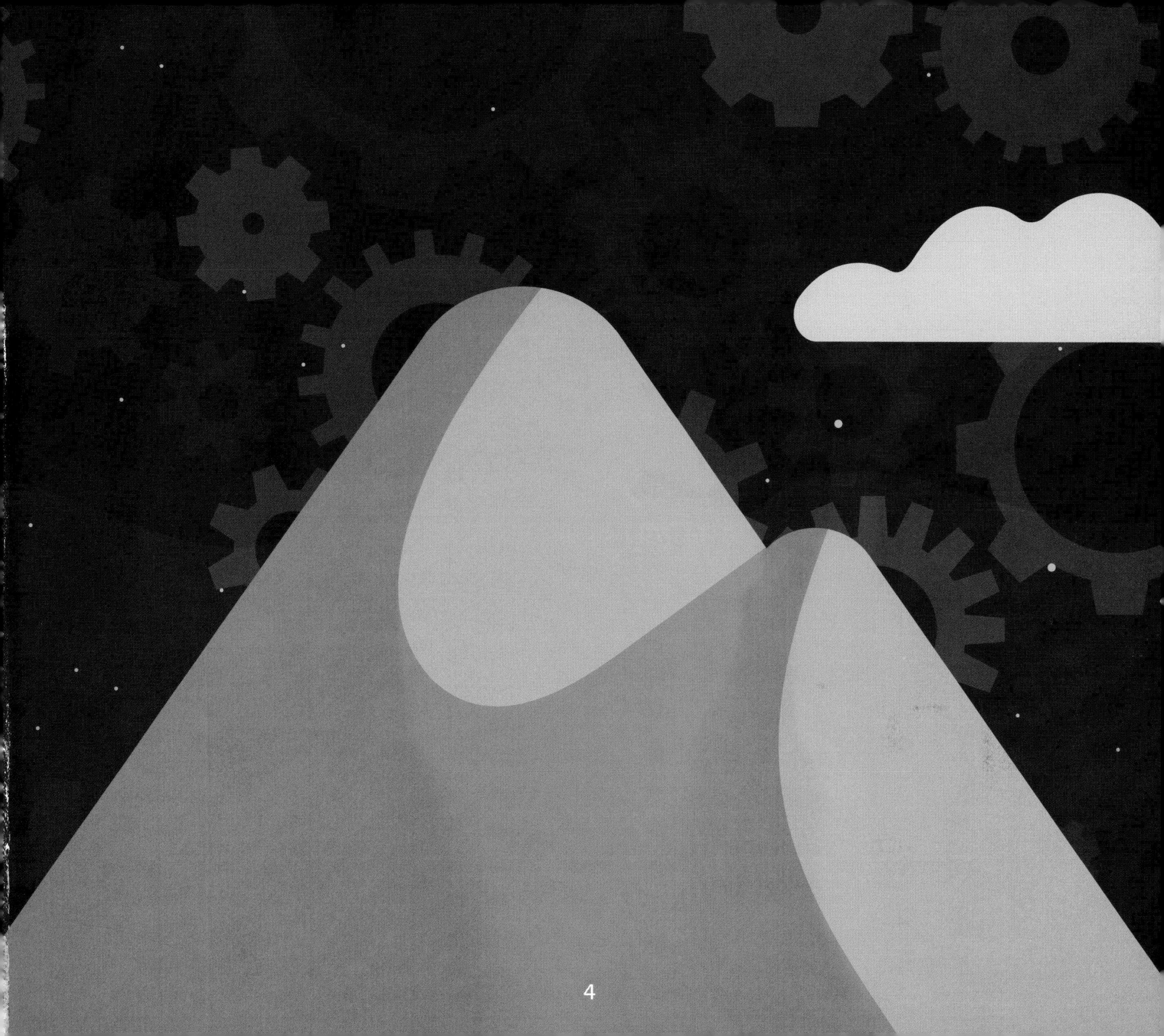

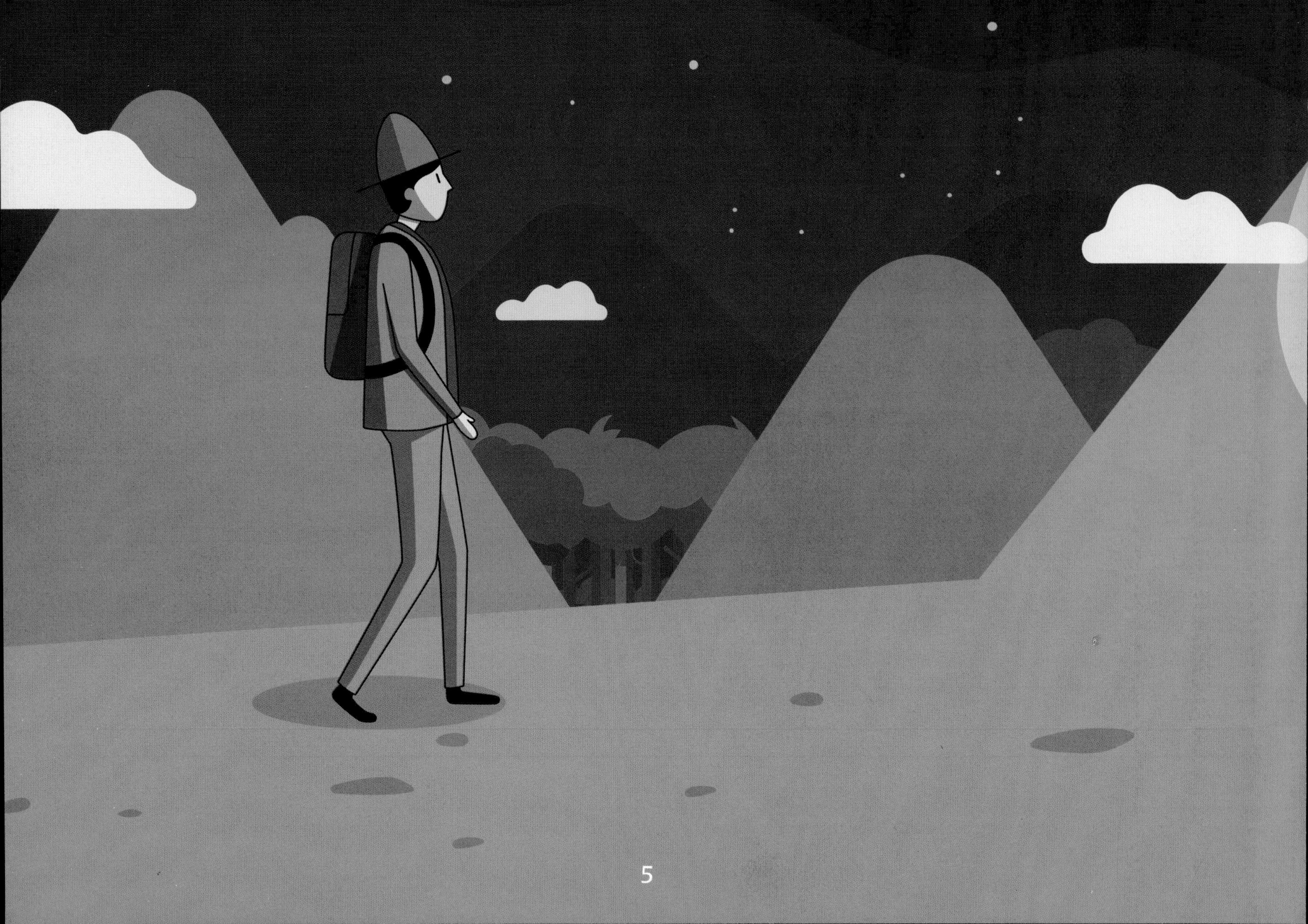

In going through my journey I accumulated hundreds of principles, which I'm passing along in various books.

They, more than me, are responsible for whatever success I've had, and they have helped millions of people, so I believe they can probably help you.

In this brief book I am sharing my most essential principles for success so that you can assess them for yourself and discover the ones that work best for you.

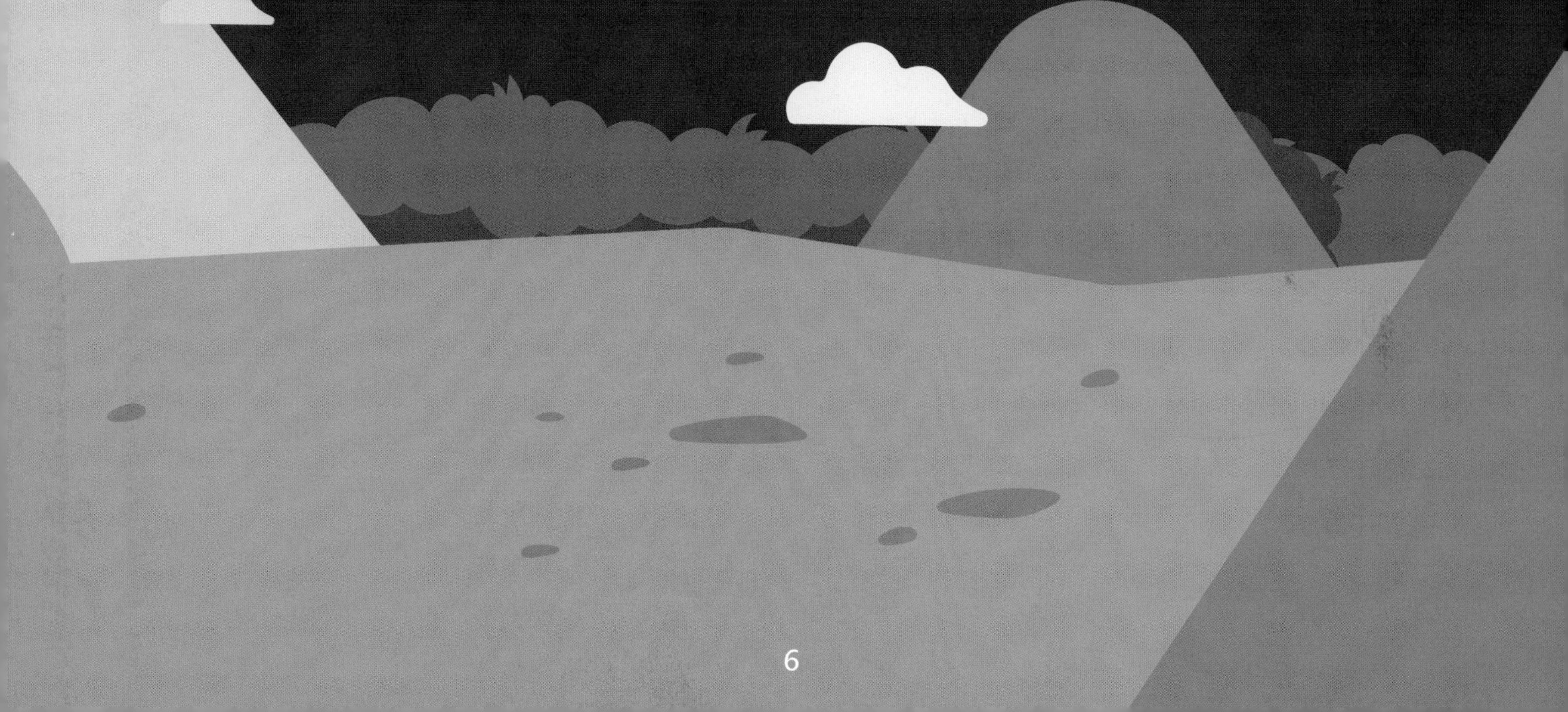

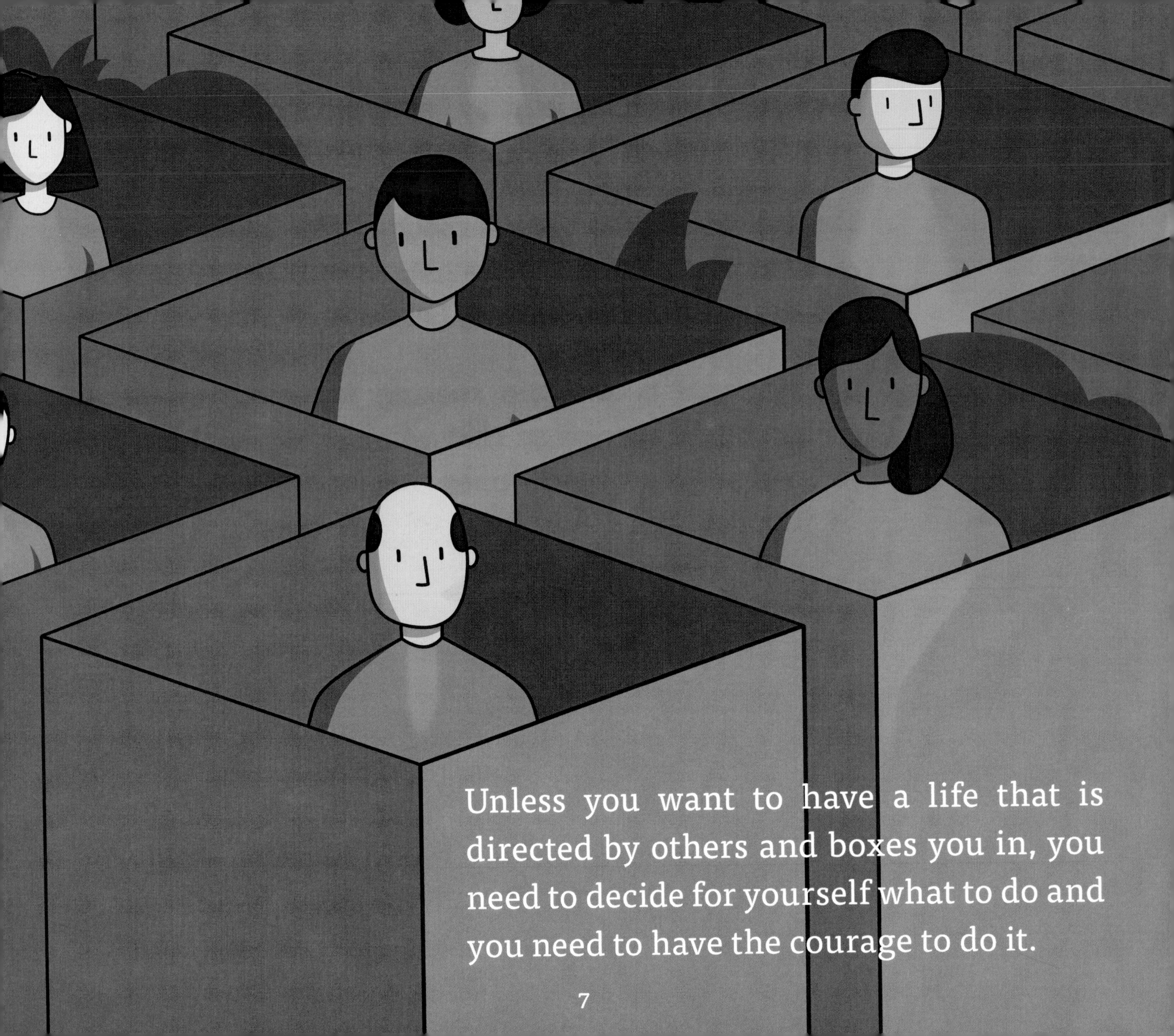

Unless you want to have a life that is directed by others and boxes you in, you need to decide for yourself what to do and you need to have the courage to do it.

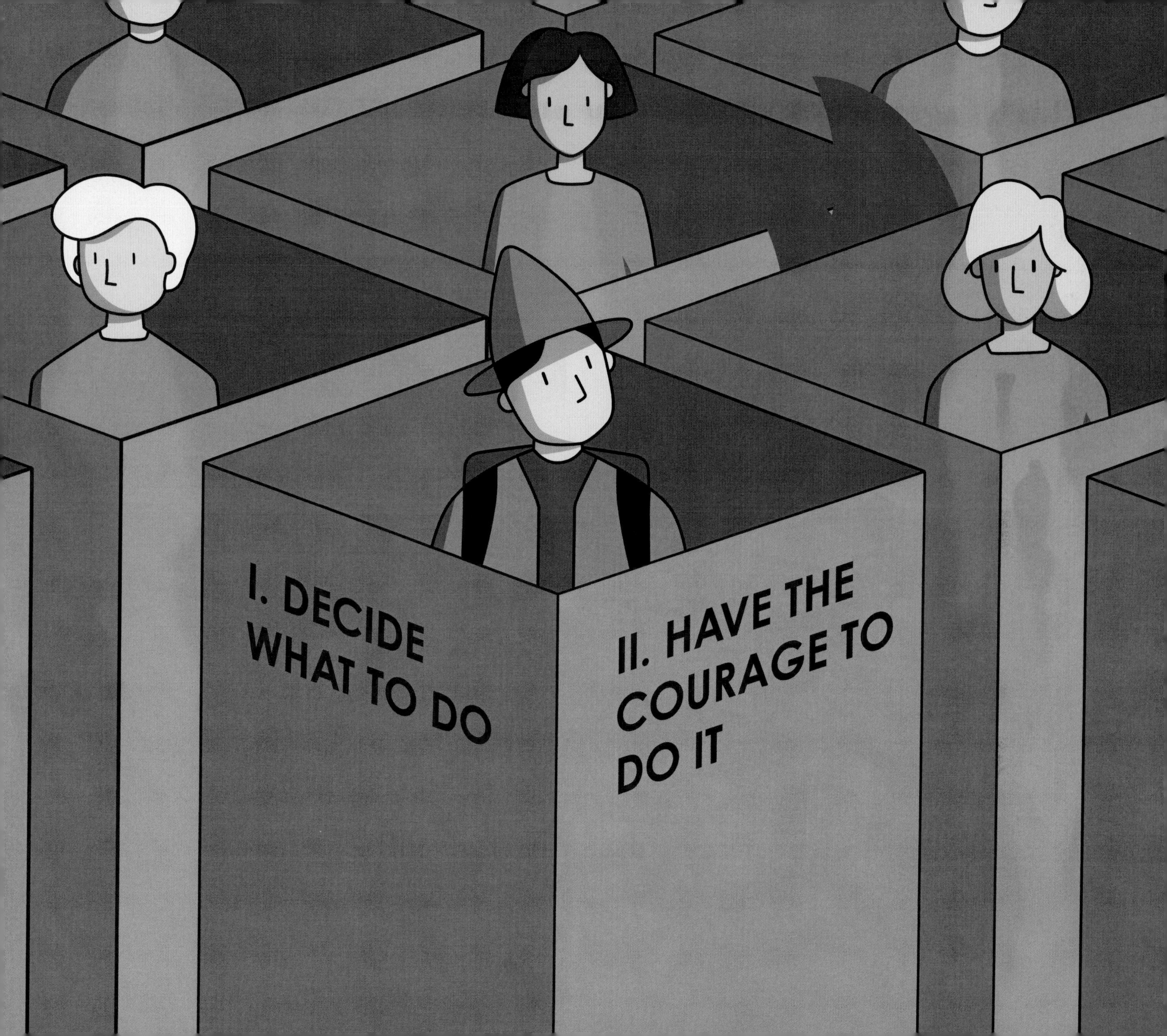
I. DECIDE WHAT TO DO
II. HAVE THE COURAGE TO DO IT

This brings me to my first and most important principle:

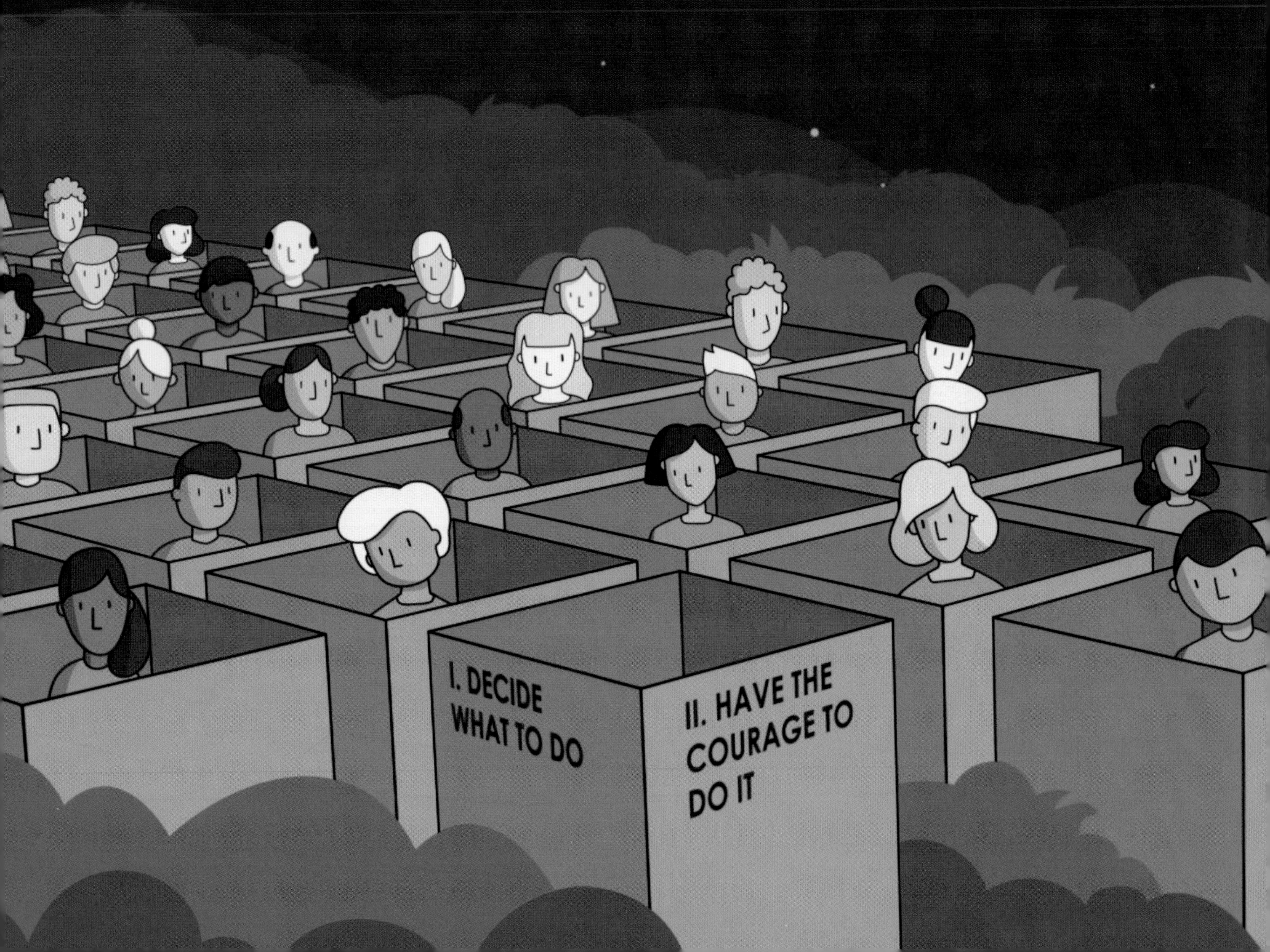
I. DECIDE WHAT TO DO
II. HAVE THE COURAGE TO DO IT

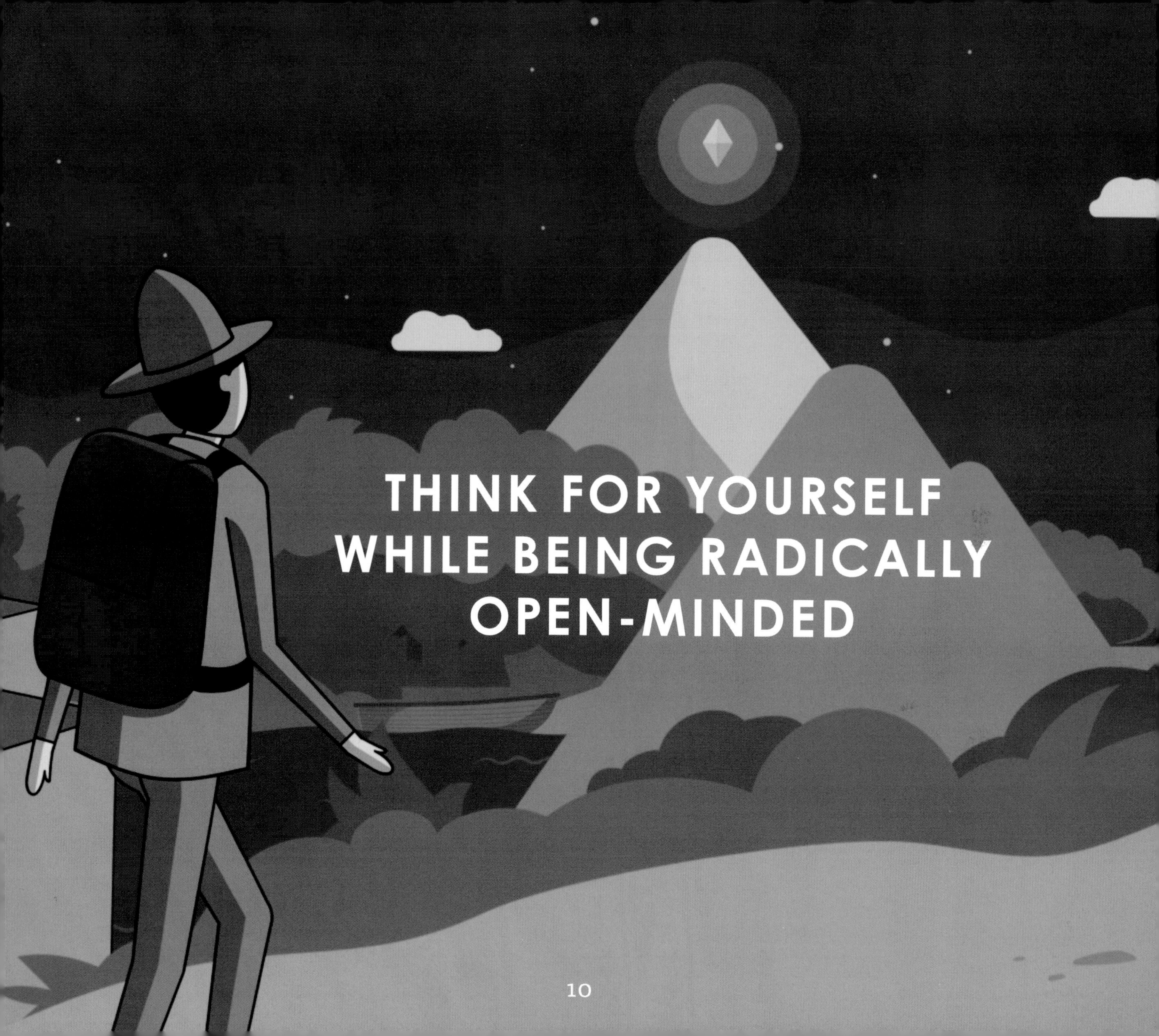

THINK FOR YOURSELF WHILE BEING RADICALLY OPEN-MINDED

Looking back on my own journey, I can now see that time is like a river that carries us forward into our encounters with reality that require us to make decisions.

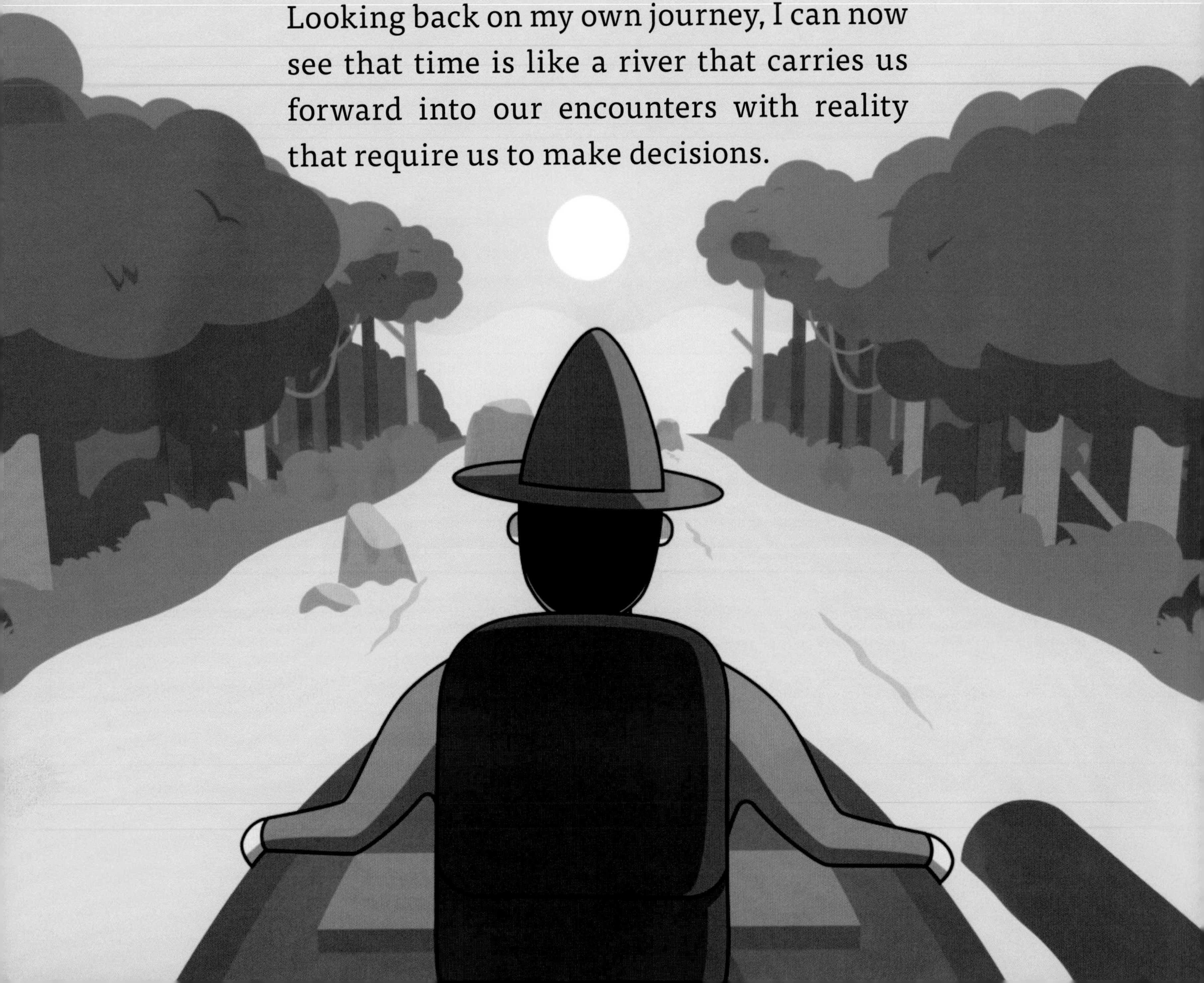

We can't stop the movement down this river
and we can't avoid the encounters.

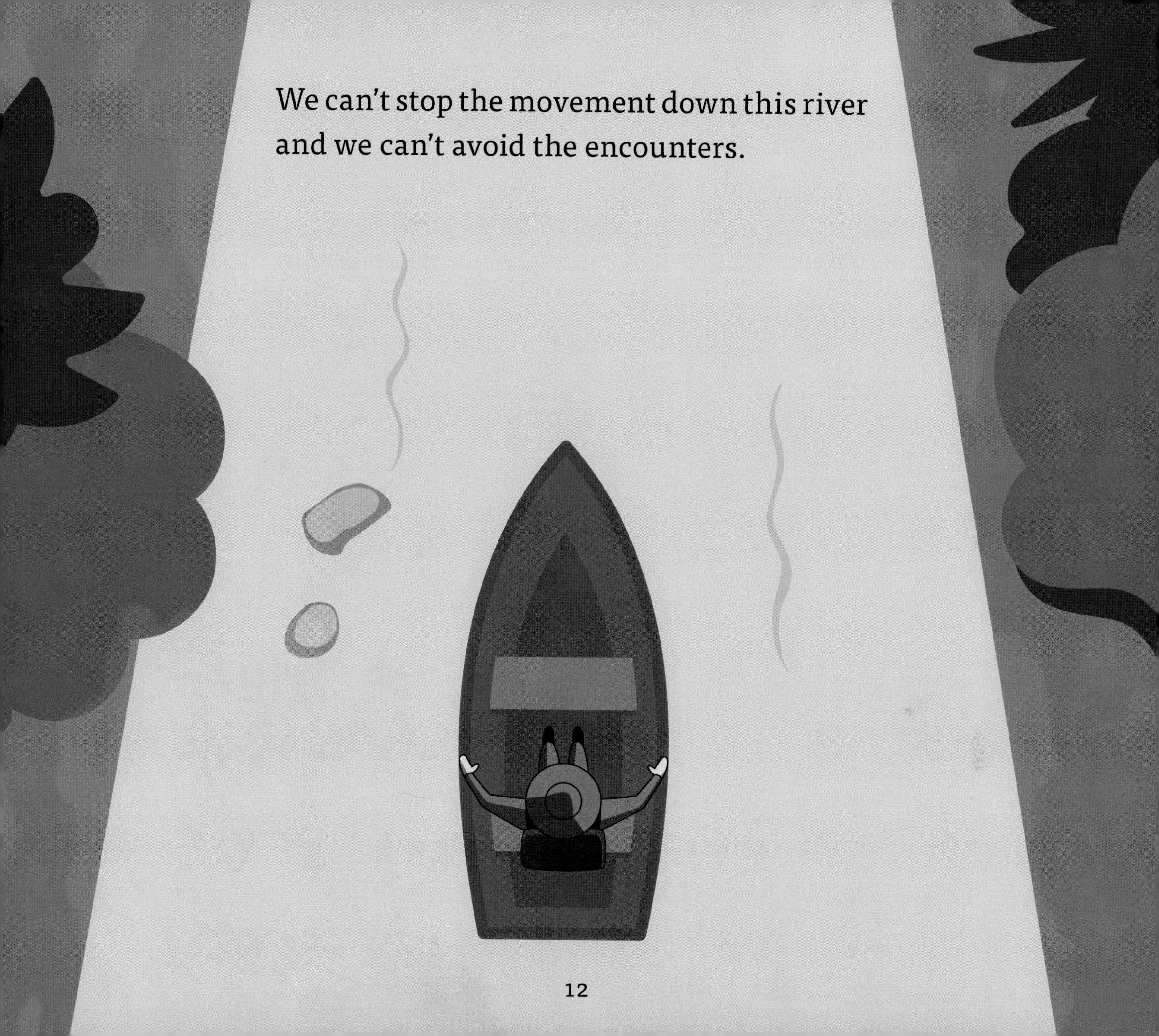

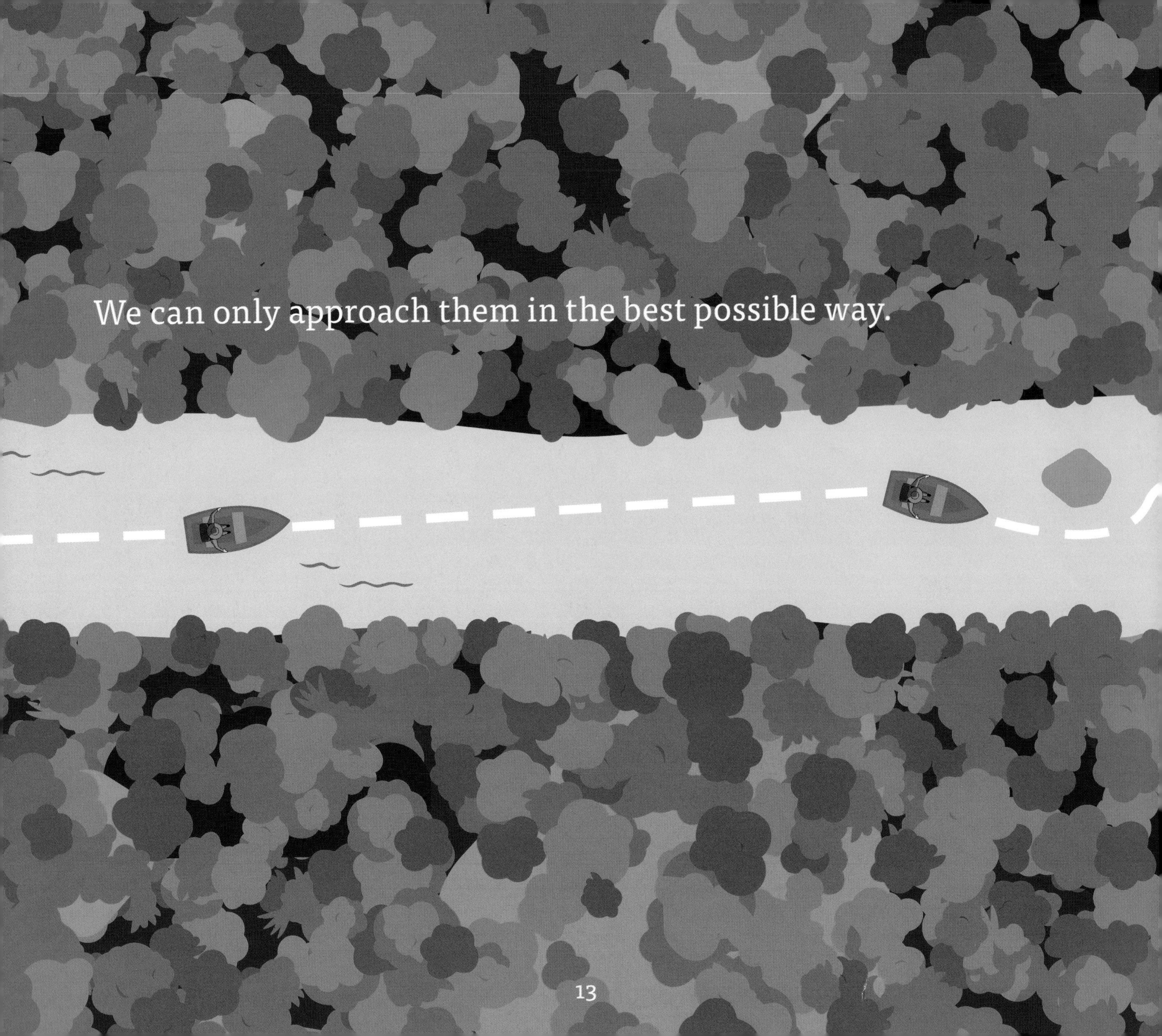

We can only approach them in the best possible way.

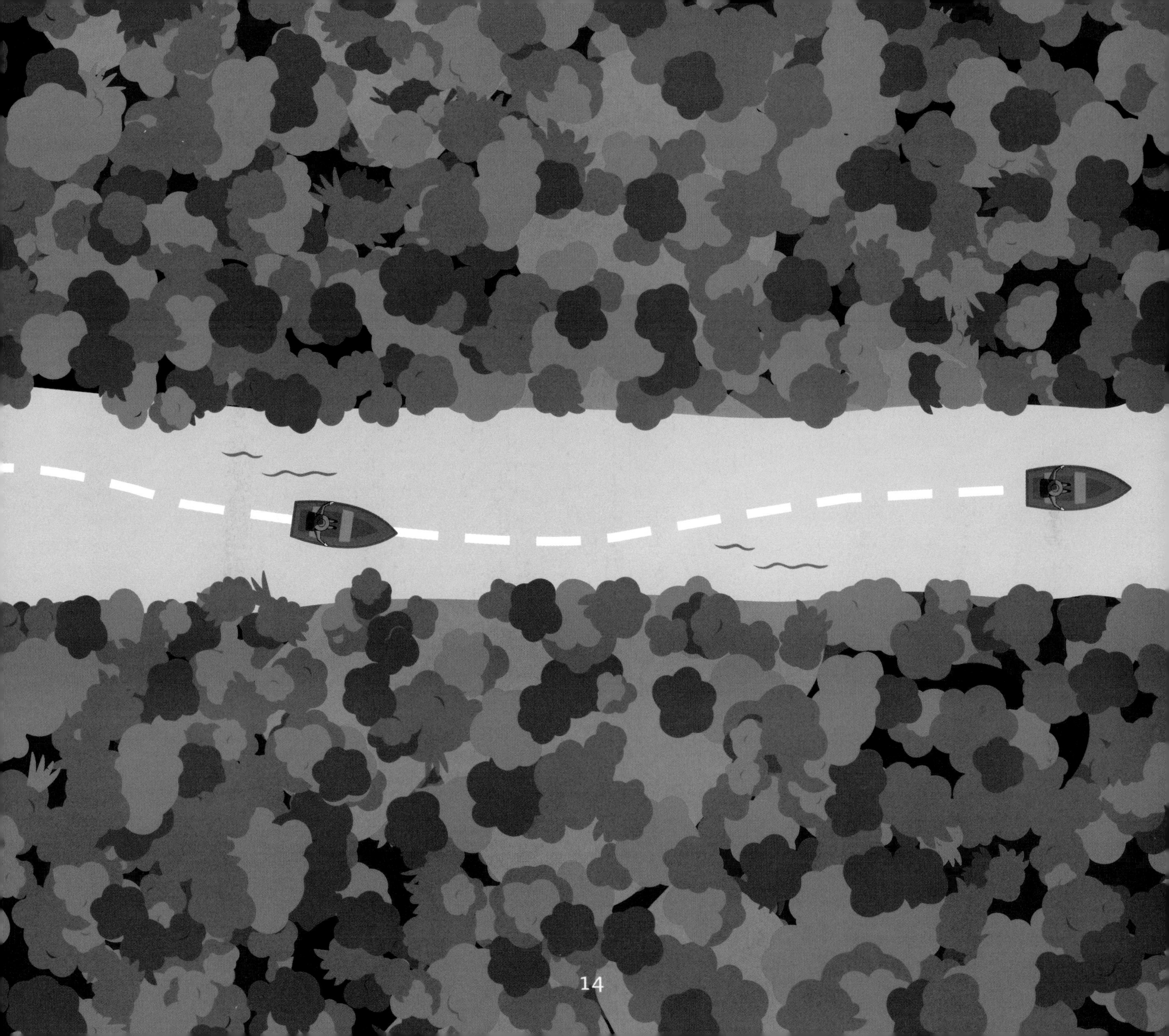

In your lifetime you will have millions of encounters that will require you to make millions of decisions. The quality of your decision making will determine the quality of your life.

Good decisions will reward you with good outcomes and bad decisions will hurt you.

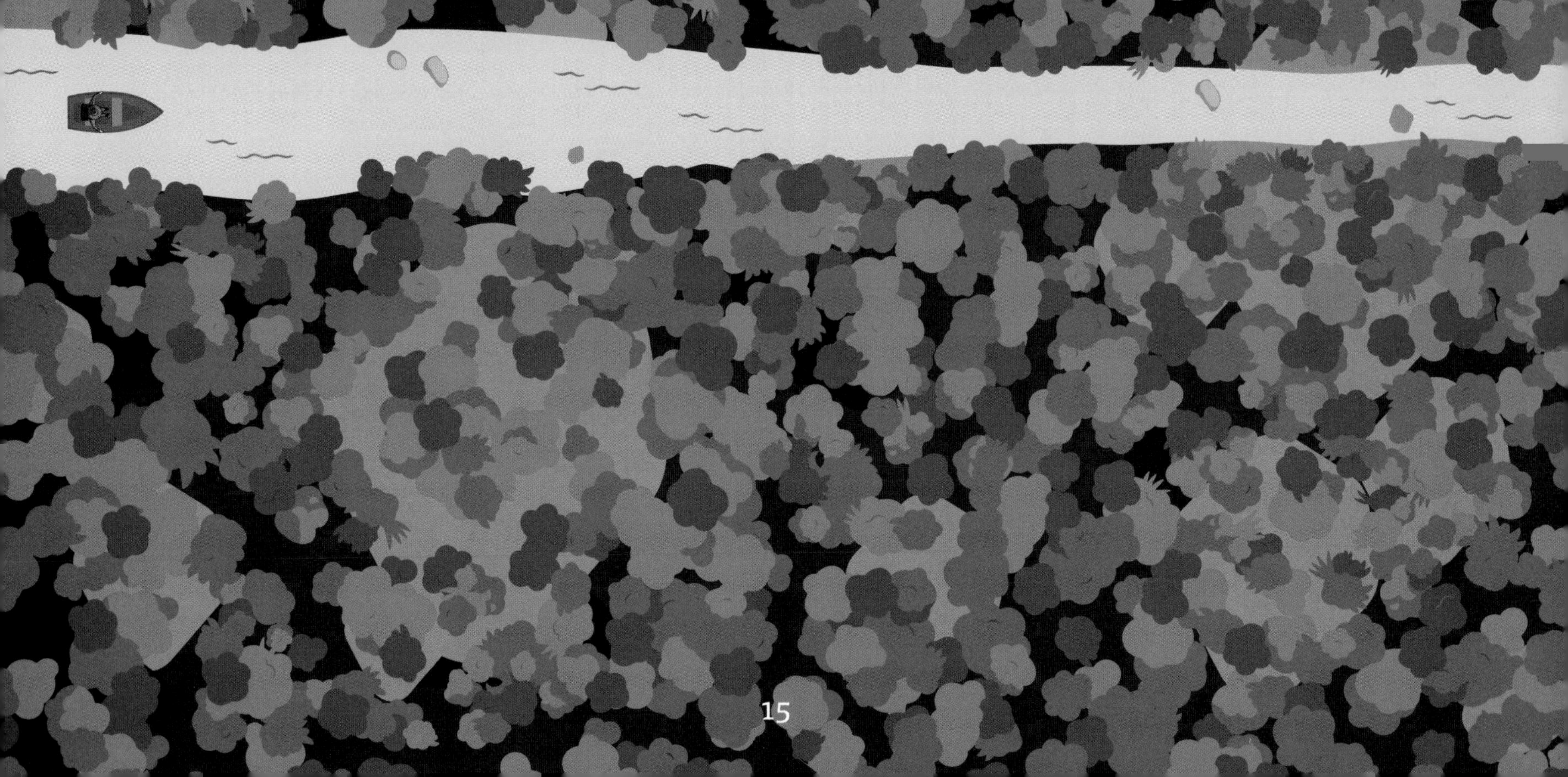

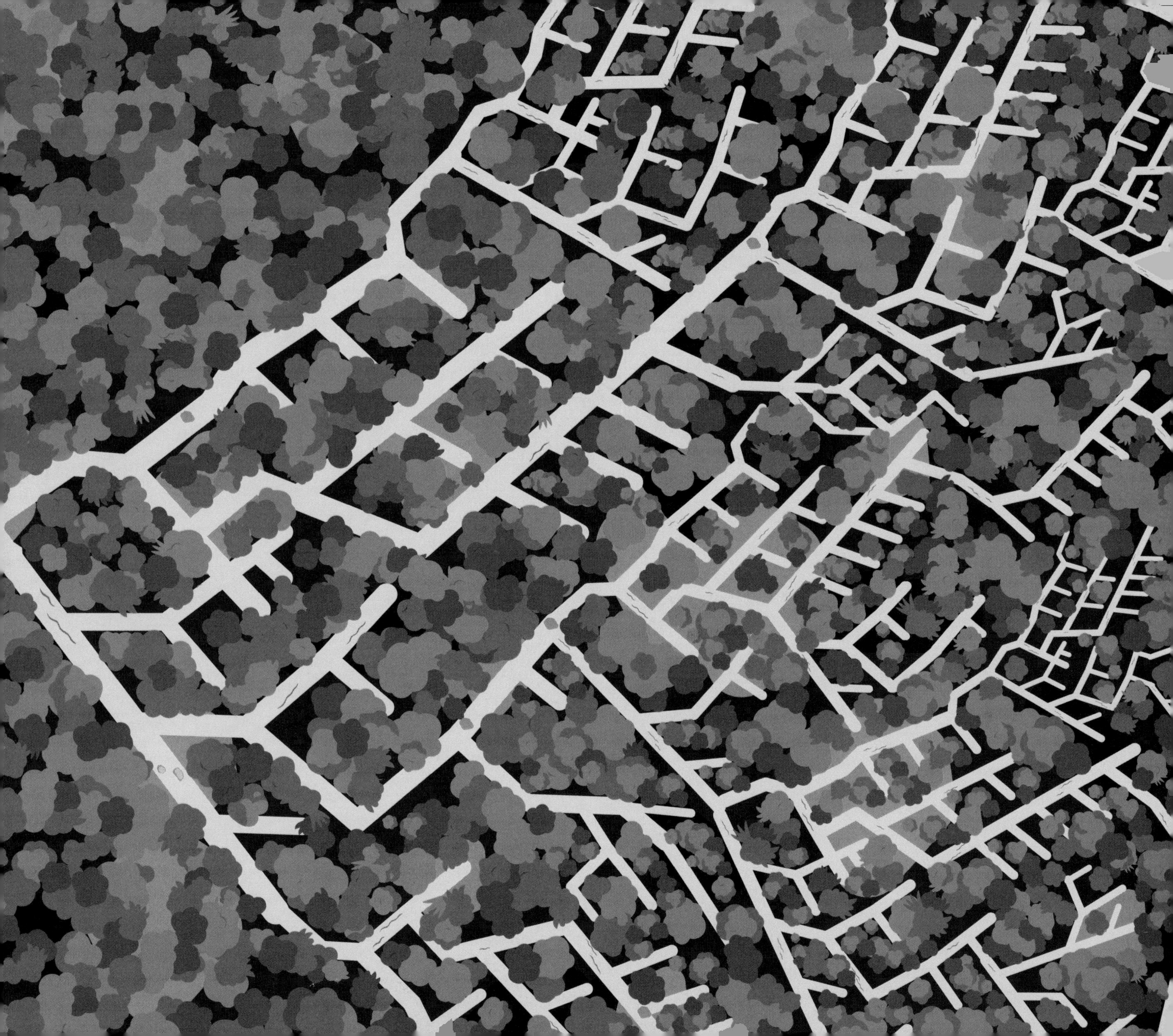

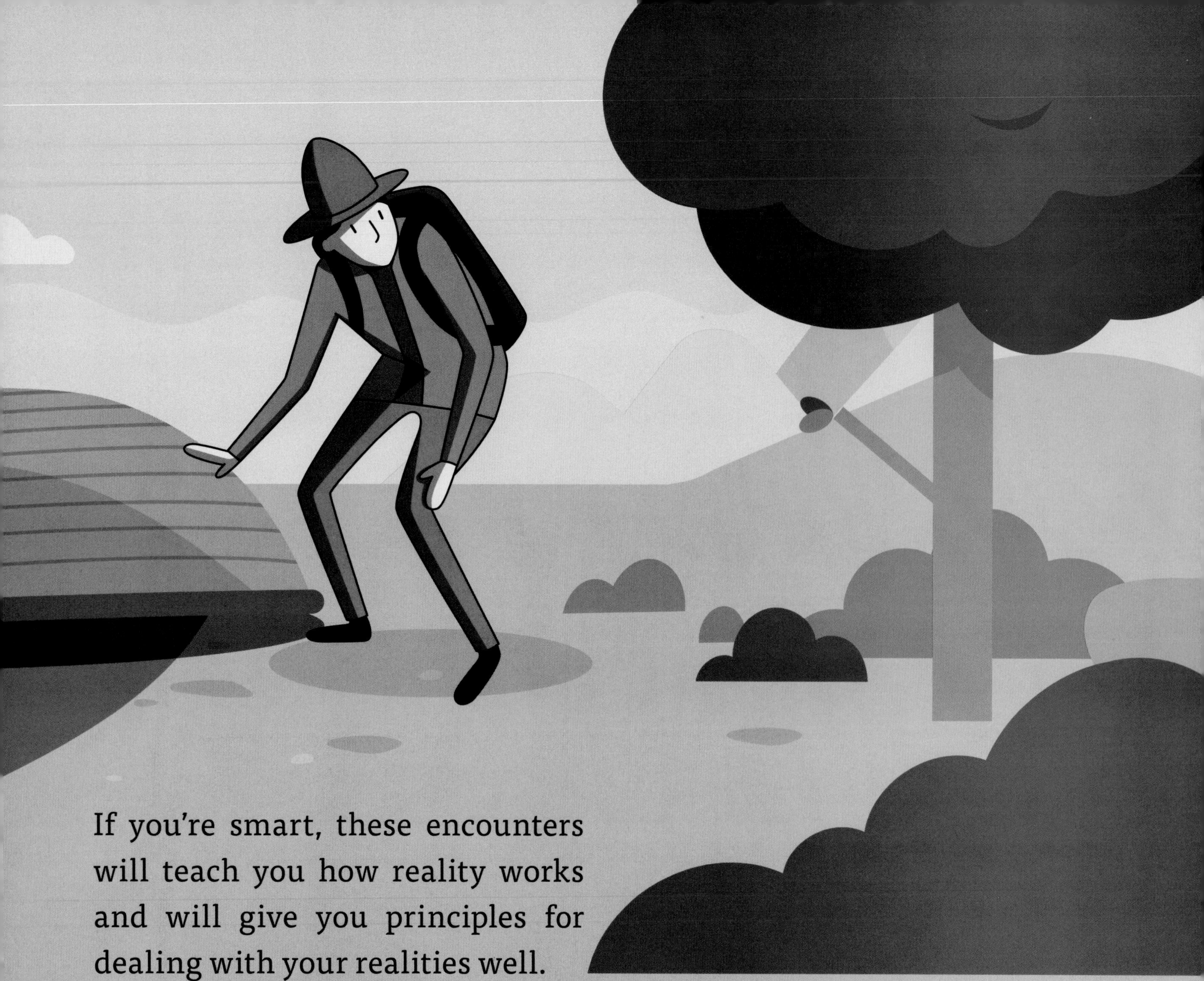

If you're smart, these encounters will teach you how reality works and will give you principles for dealing with your realities well.

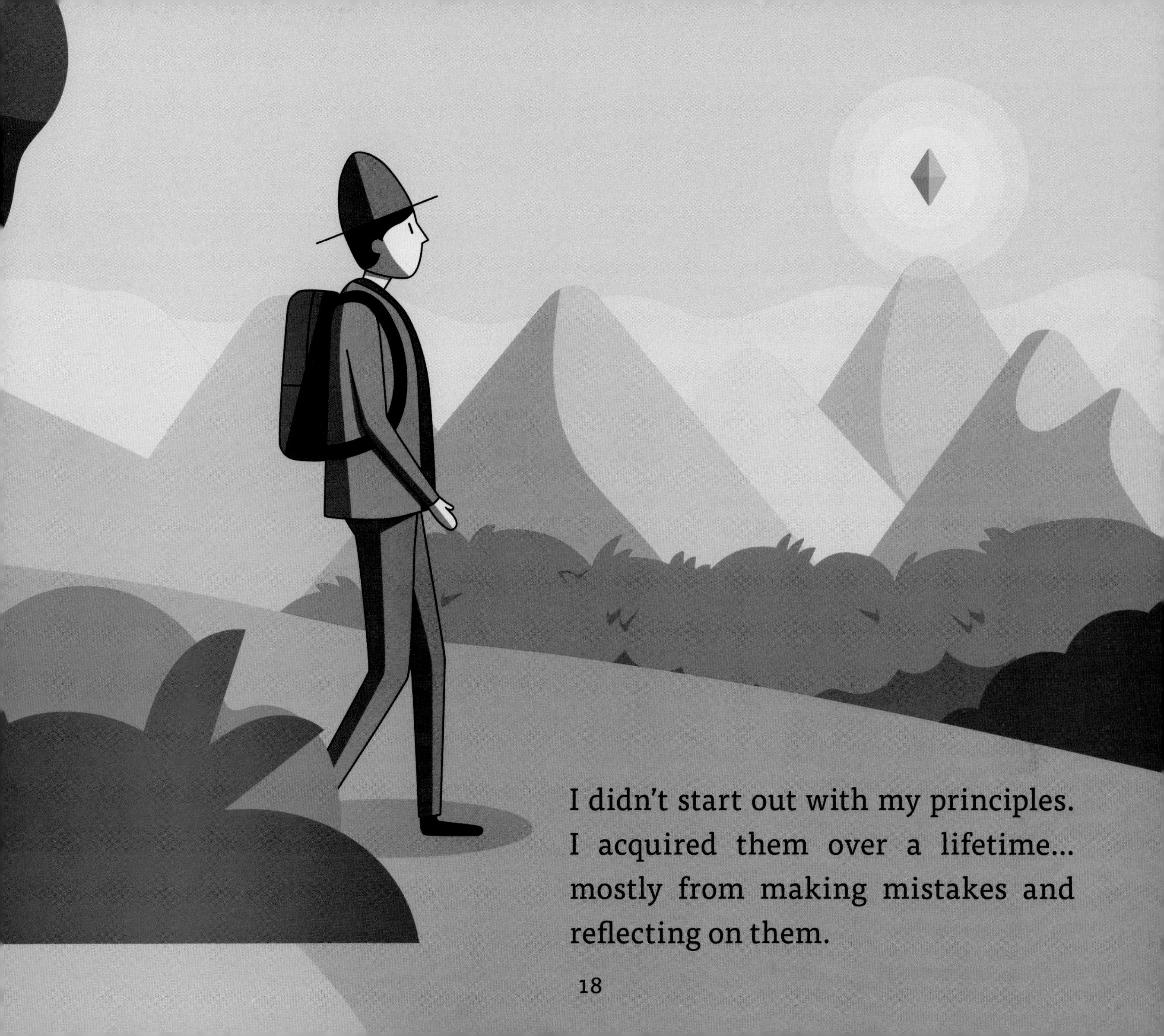

I didn't start out with my principles. I acquired them over a lifetime... mostly from making mistakes and reflecting on them.

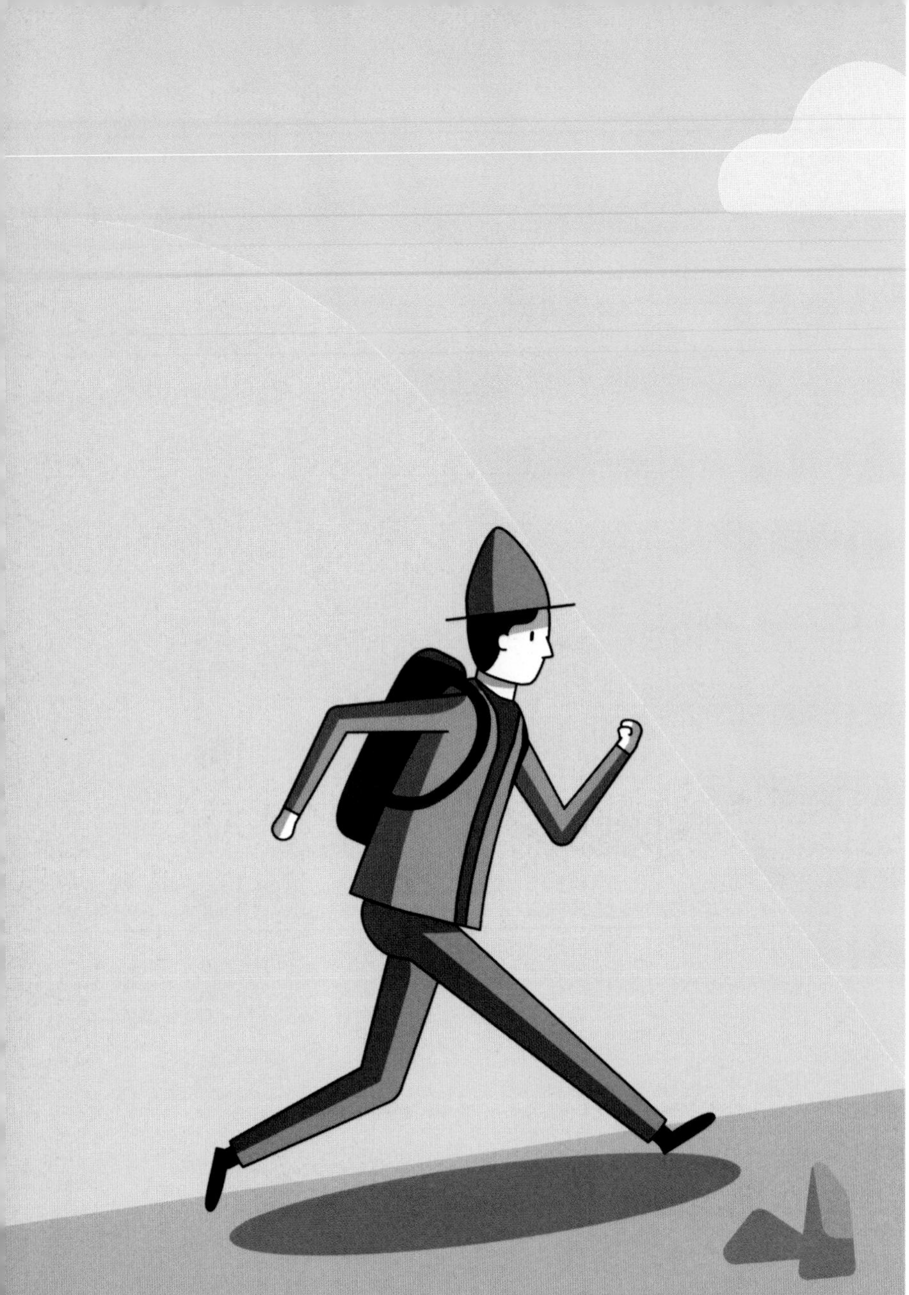

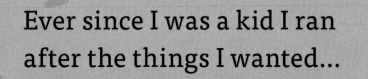

Ever since I was a kid I ran
after the things I wanted...

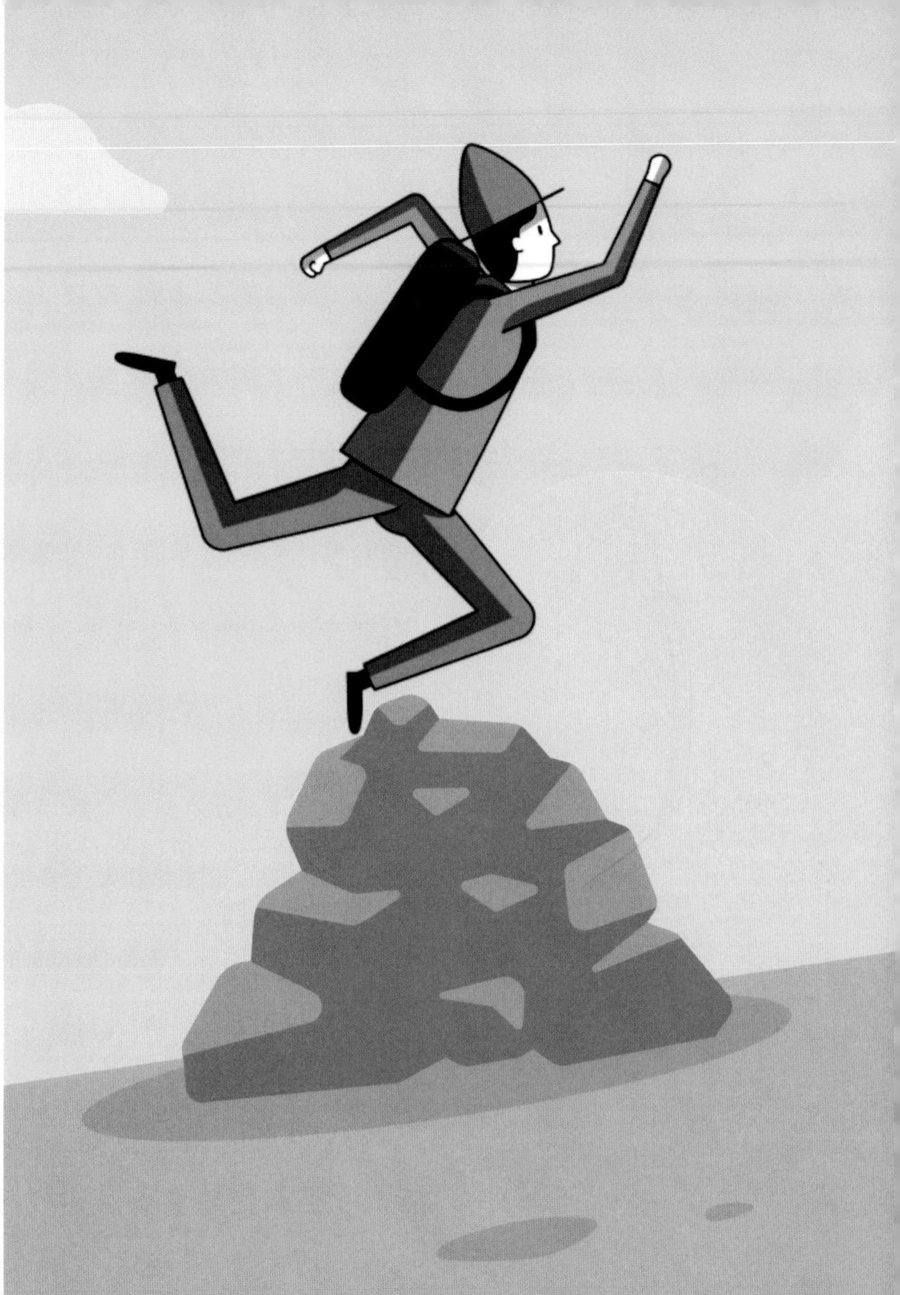

...crashed...

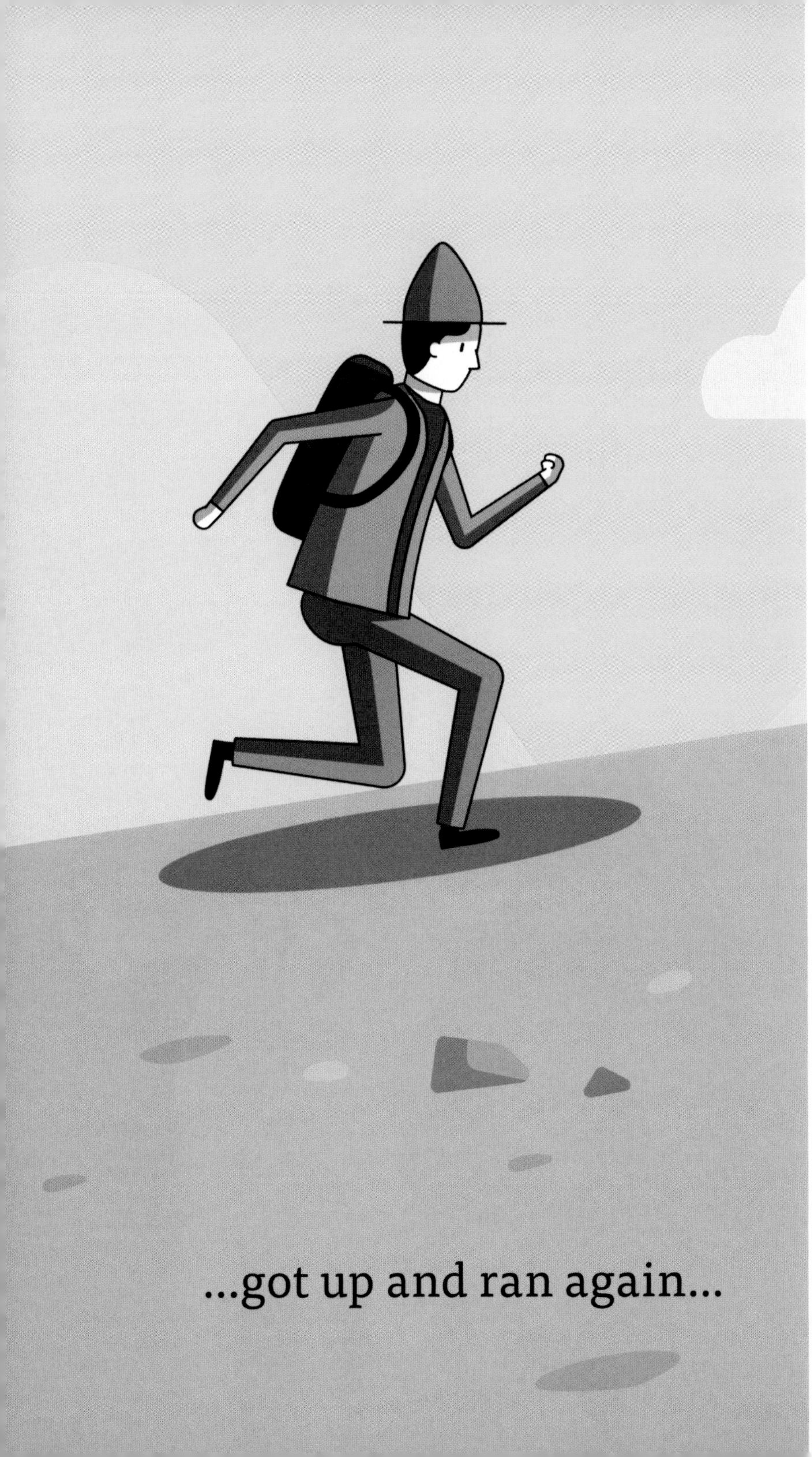

...got up and ran again...

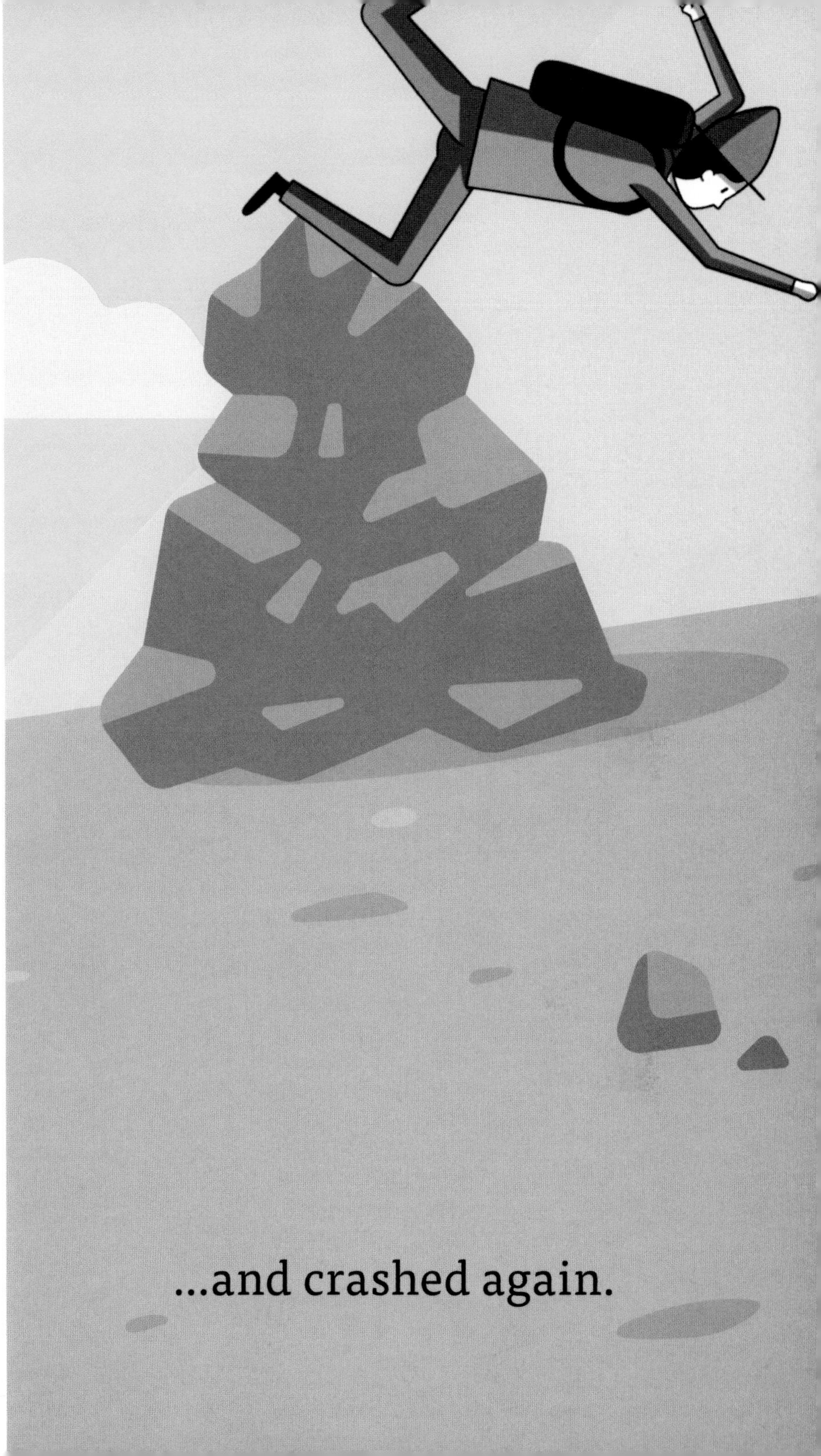

...and crashed again.

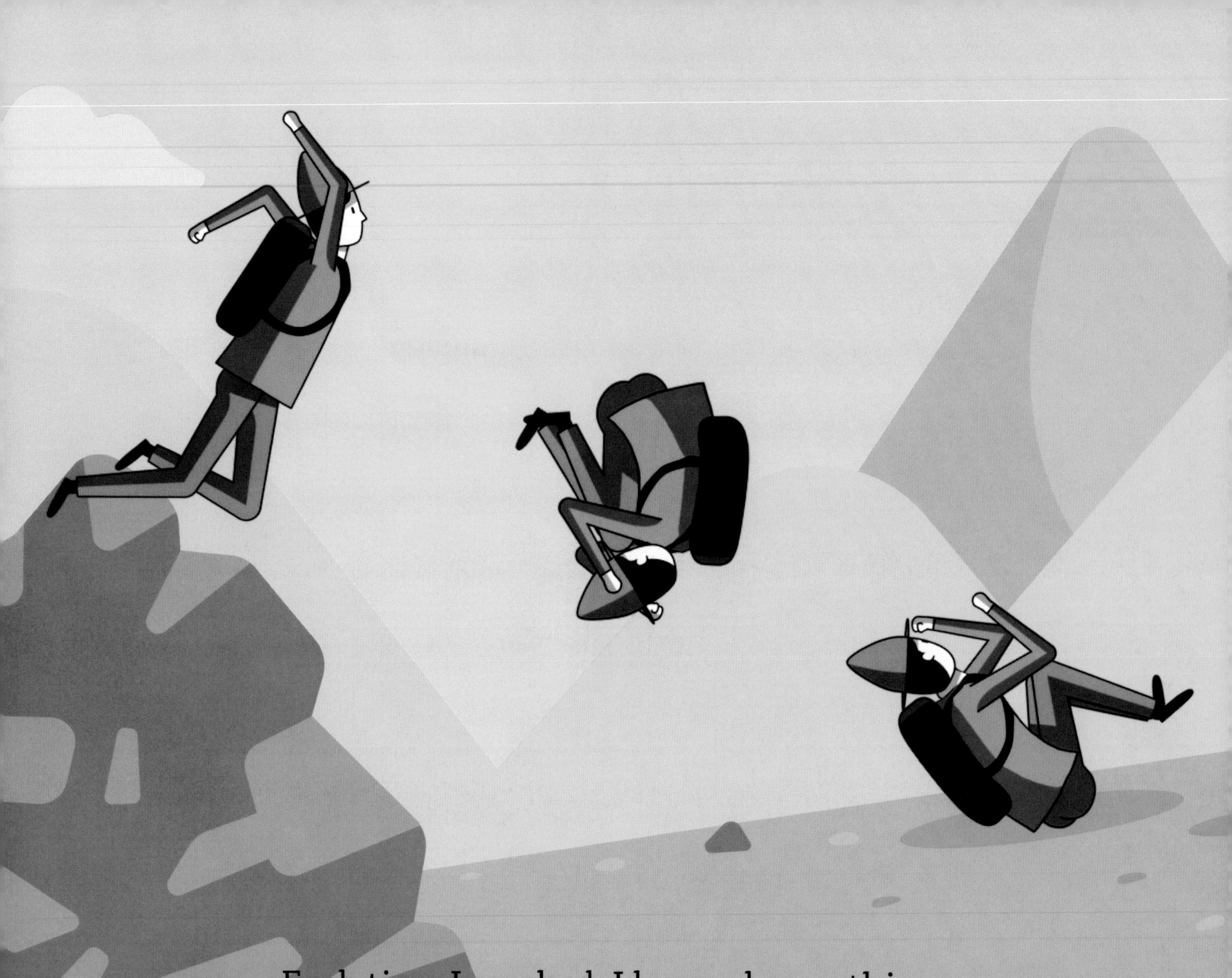

Each time I crashed, I learned something...

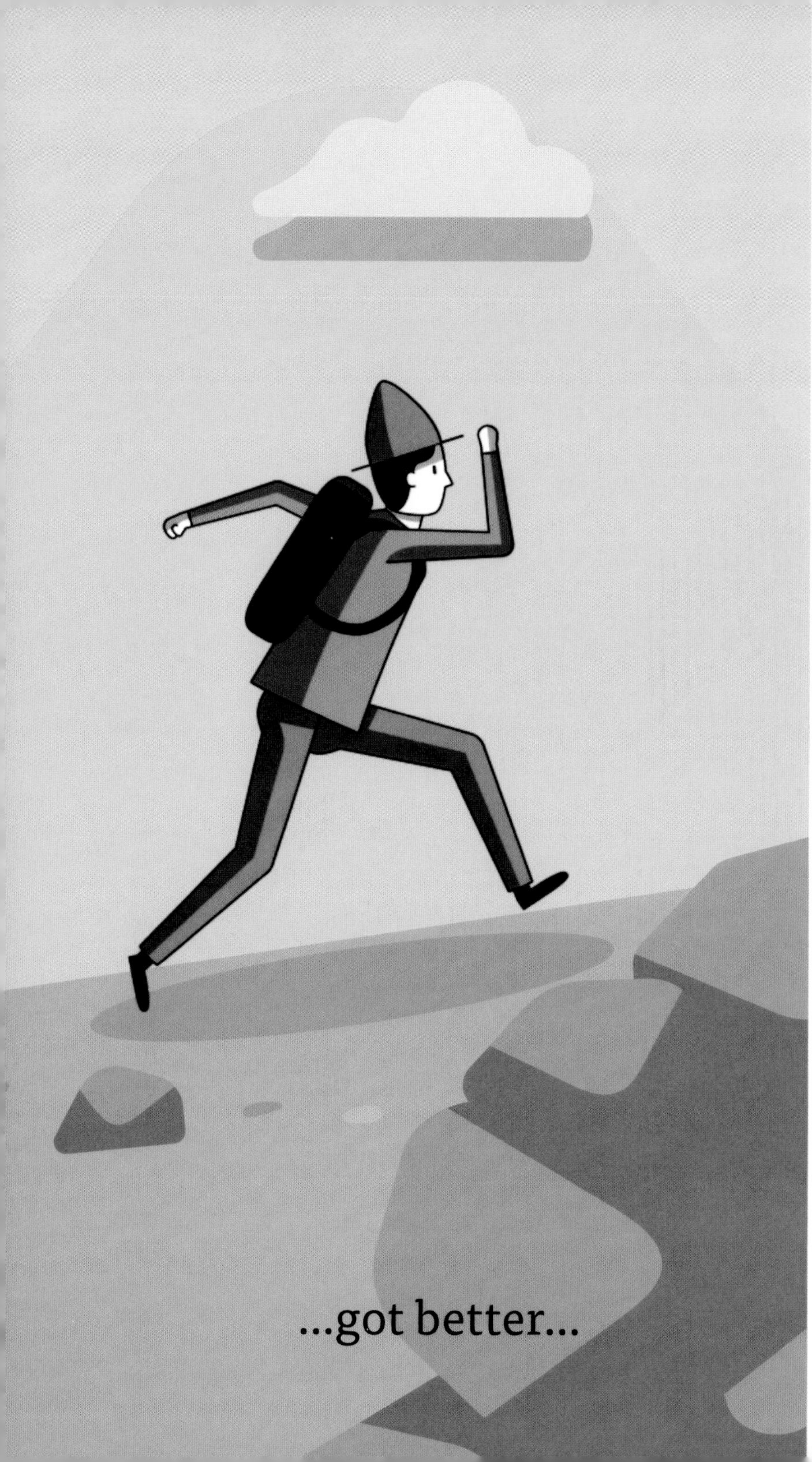

...got better...

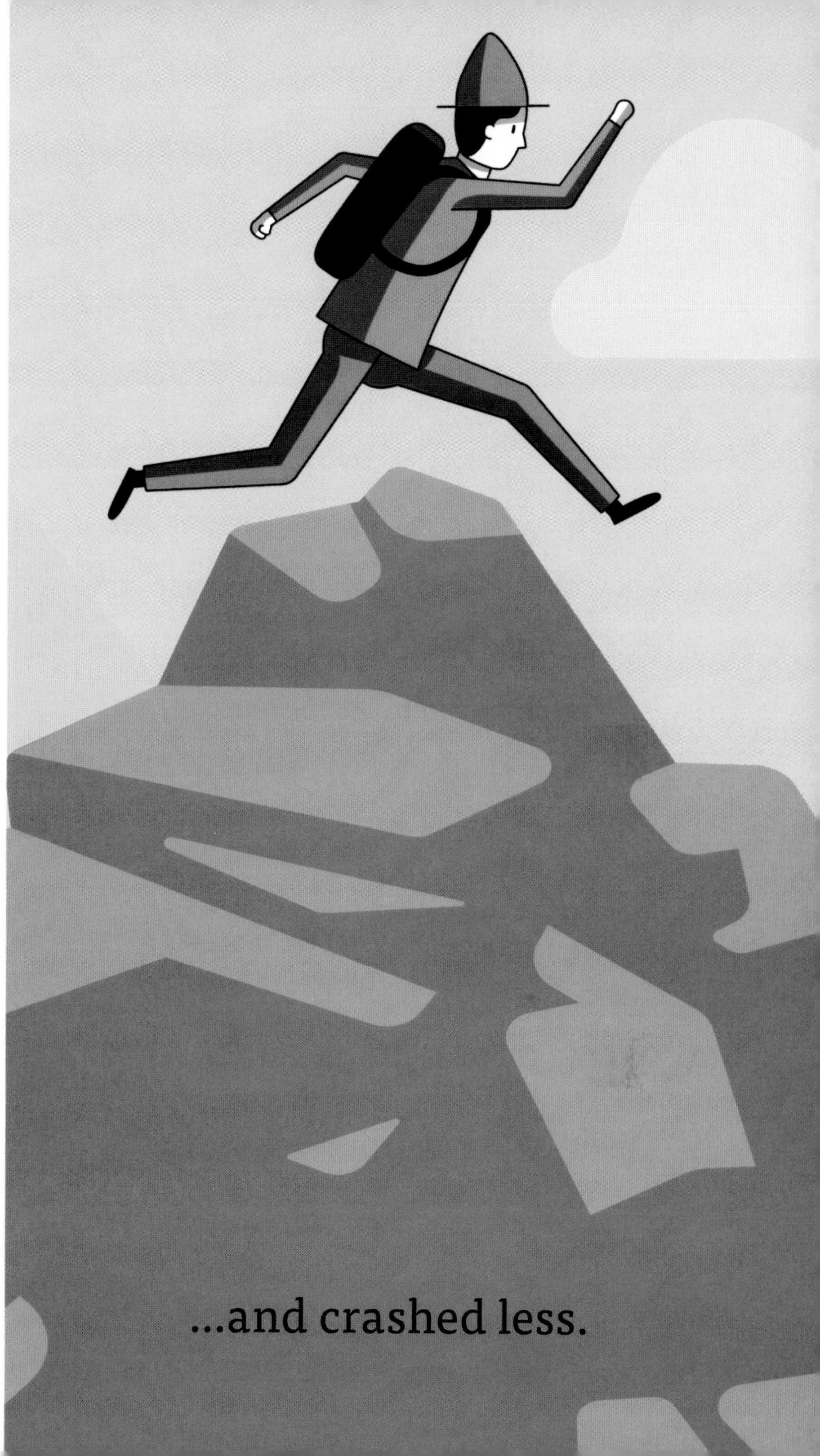

...and crashed less.

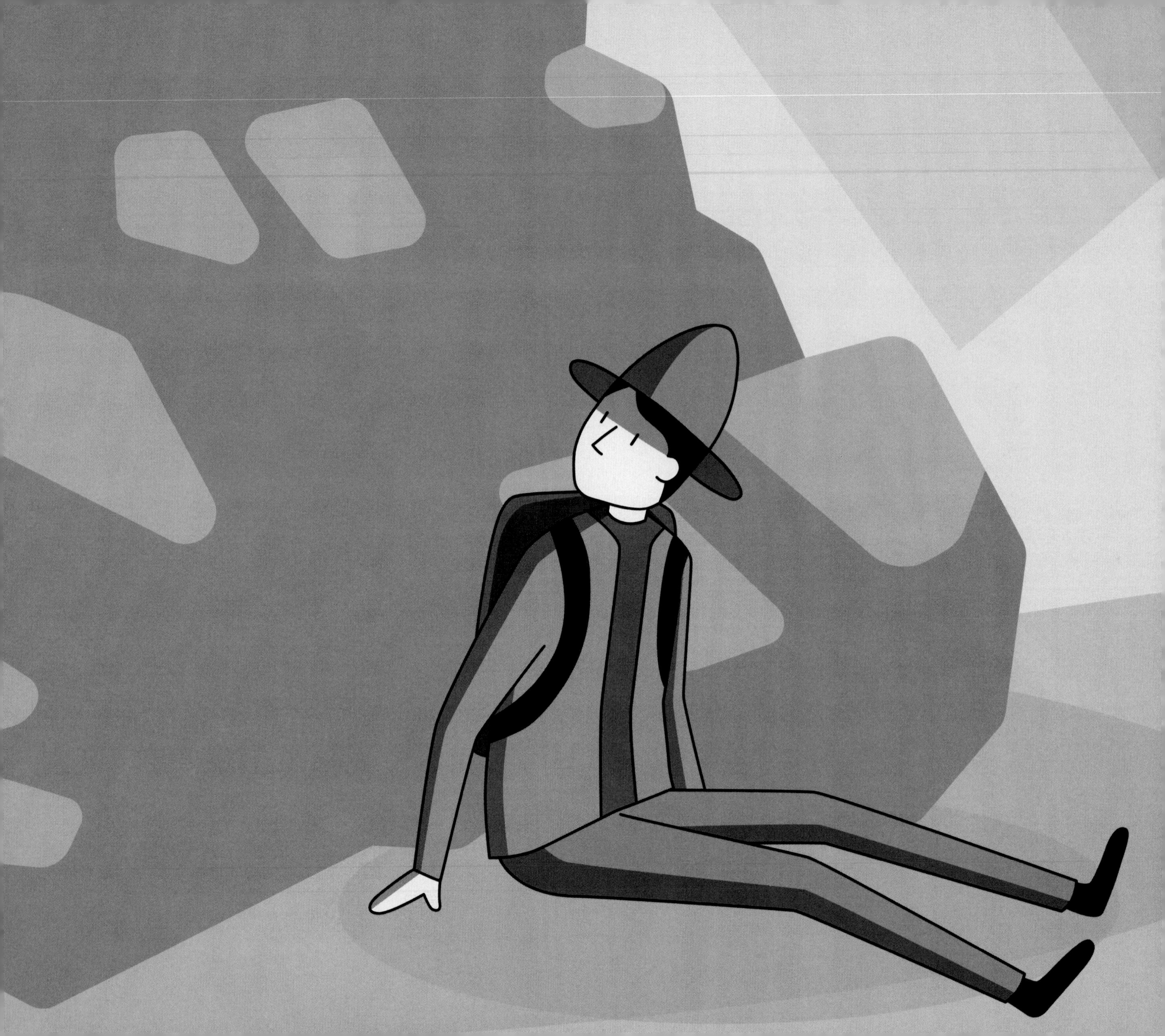

By doing that over and over again I learned to love this process, even the crashing part of it.

I also learned to view problems like puzzles that would give me gems if I could solve them.

The puzzle was "what should I do in this situation next time?" and the gem I would get by solving it was a principle that would help me in the future.

That is how I got my principles. I wrote them down and modified them over time.

I recommend that you do that, too.

This process taught me one of my most fundamental principles, which is that...

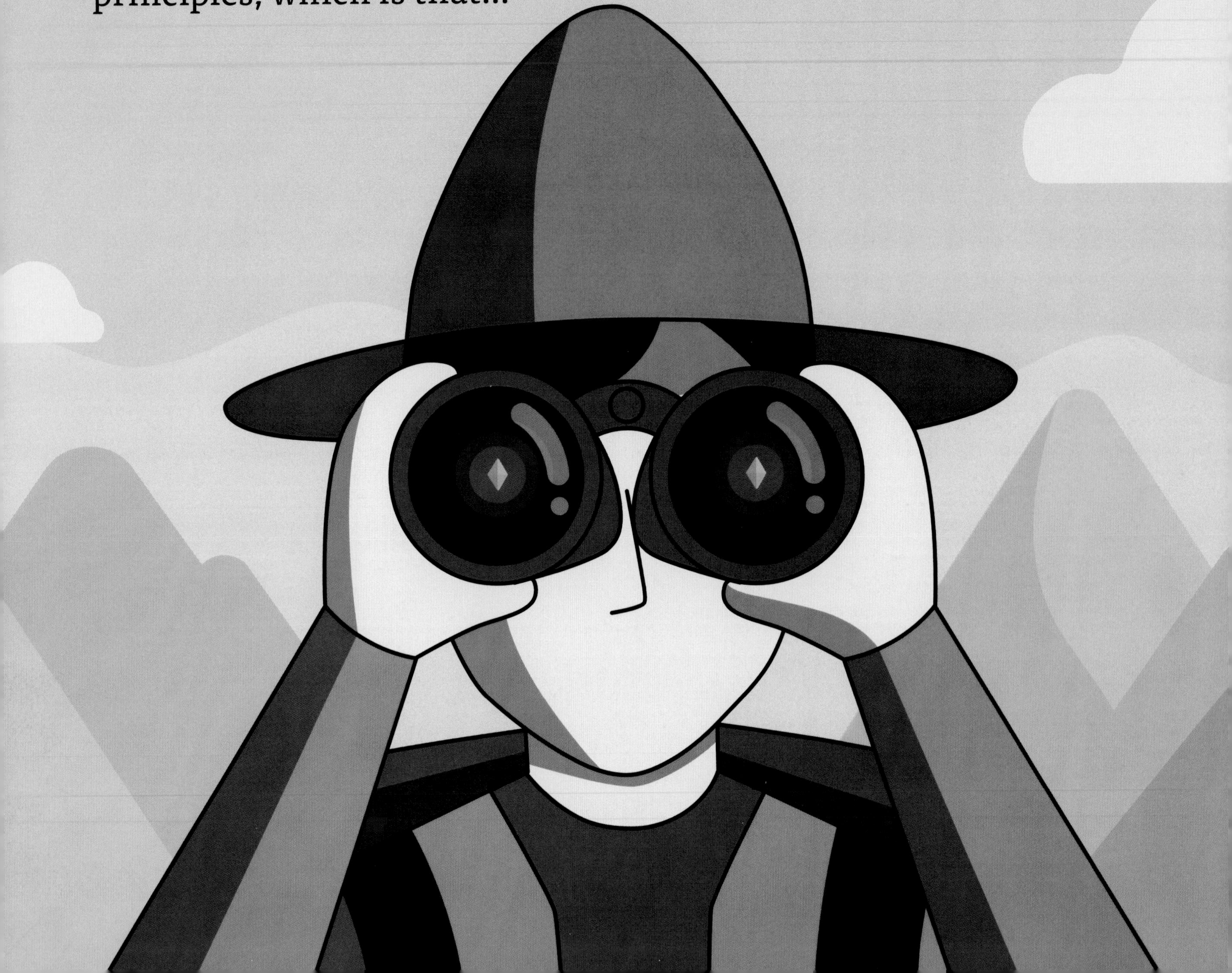

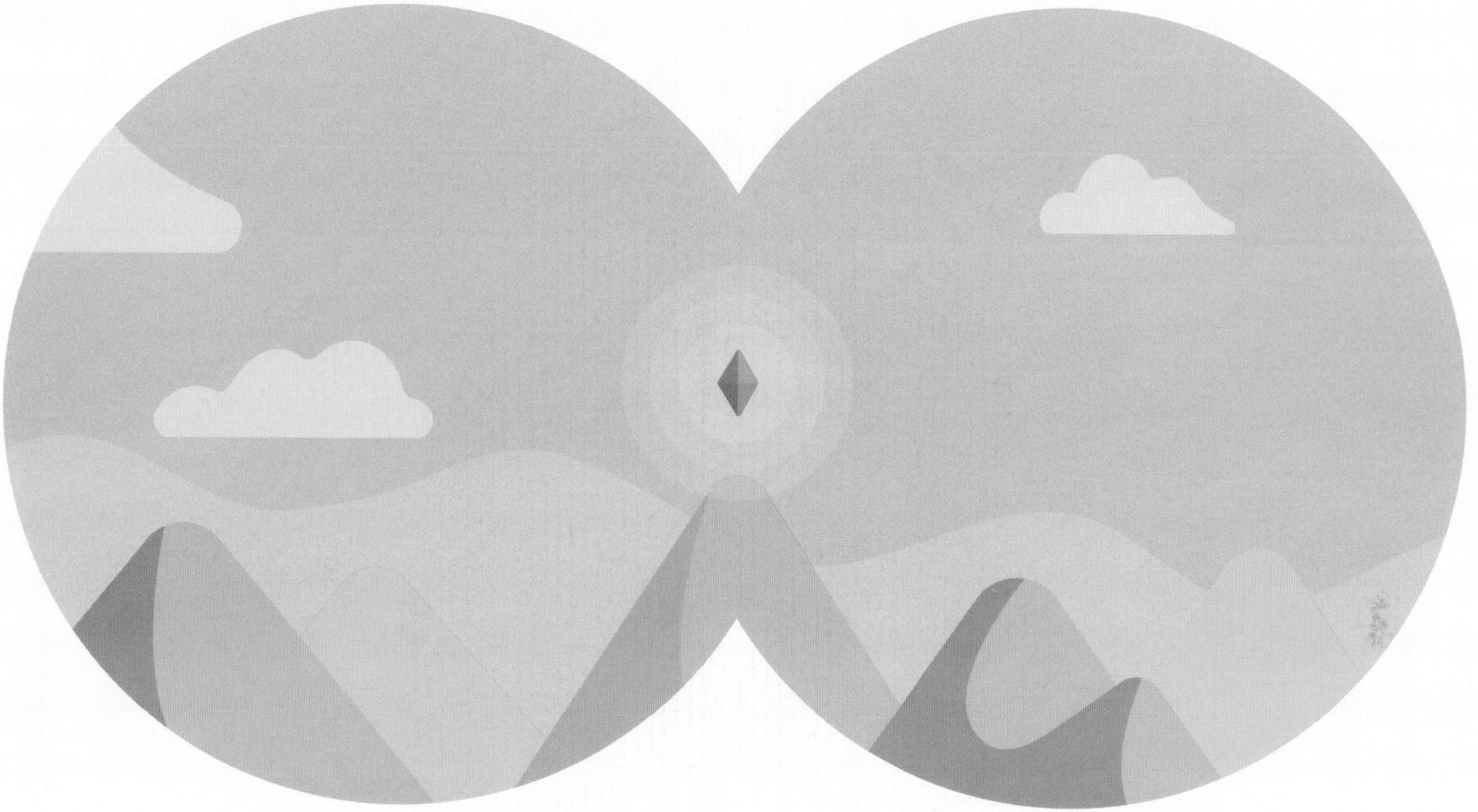

KNOWING WHAT IS TRUE IS ESSENTIAL FOR MAKING GOOD DECISIONS

By knowing what is true, I mean knowing how reality works. People didn't create the laws of nature that we have to live by in order to be successful, but if we can understand these laws we can use them to achieve our goals.

This makes me a hyperrealist: someone who embraces reality and works with it well as it is—not someone who wishes it were different and complains that it is not to their liking.

That brings me to my third principle:

DREAMS + REALITY + DETERMINATION

= A SUCCESSFUL LIFE

In other words, if you keep focused on achieving your dreams, take responsibility for understanding the realities that affect you and how to deal with them well, and do that with determination, you will learn principles that will give you a successful life.

So what is a successful life?

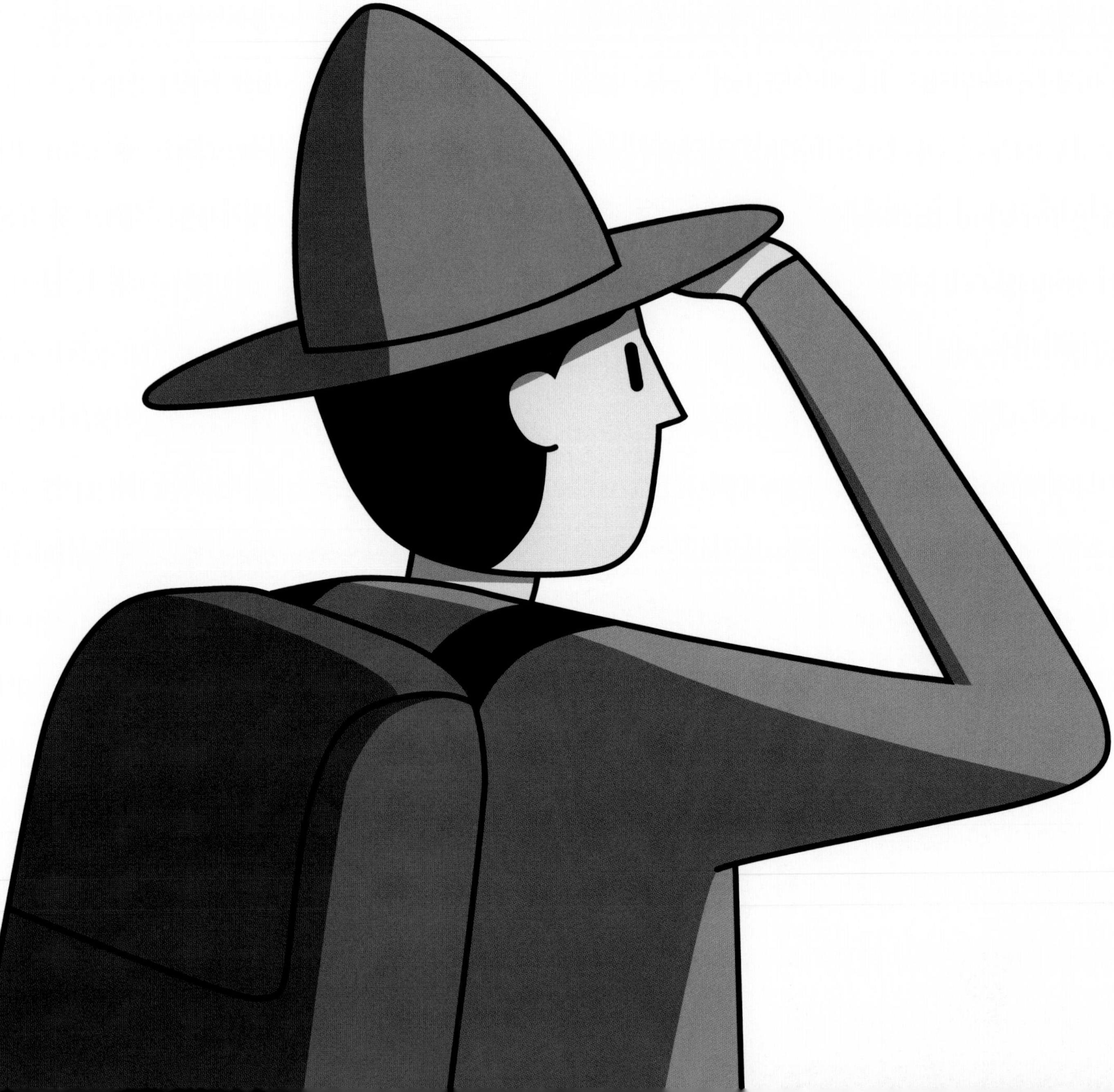

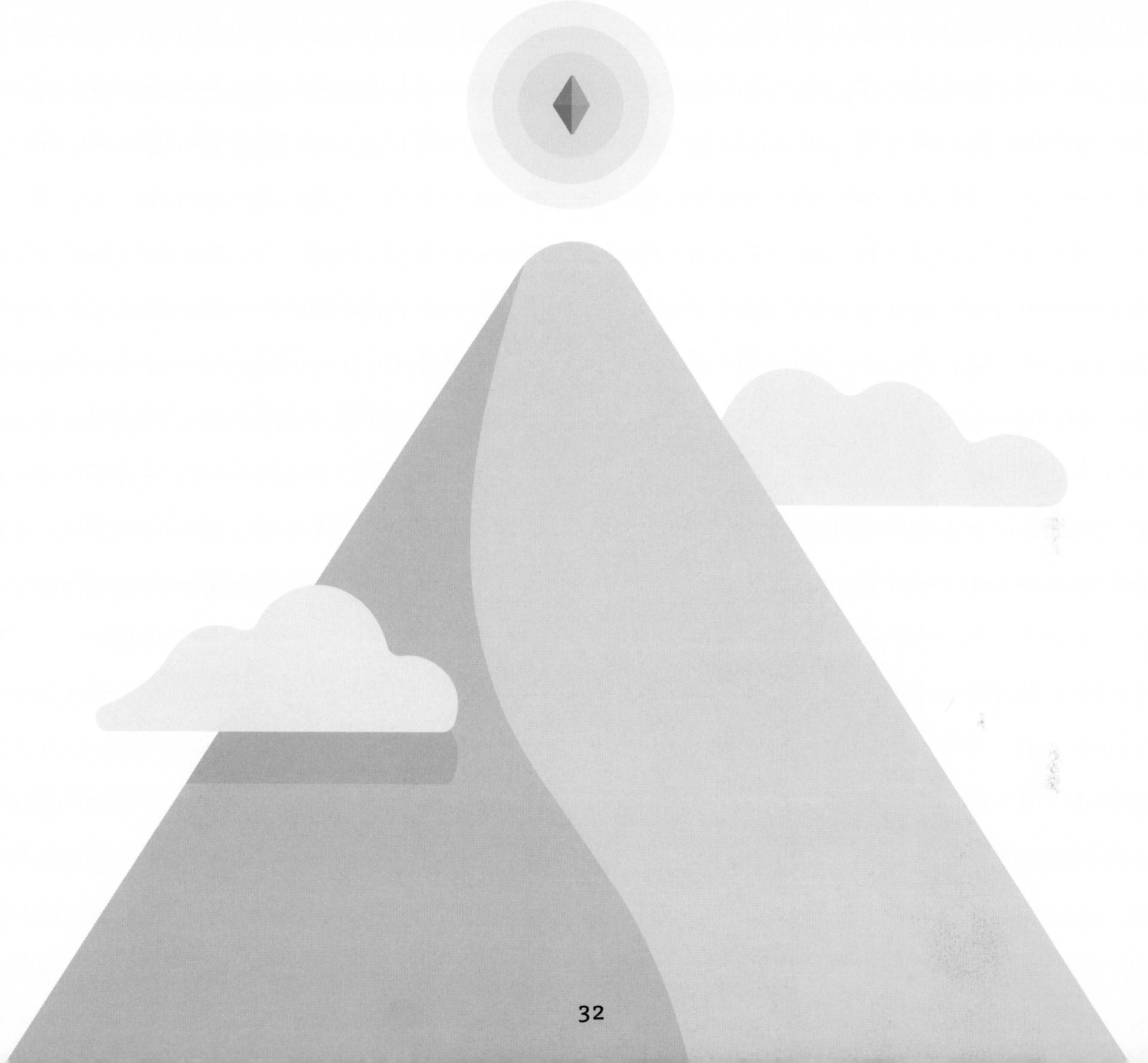

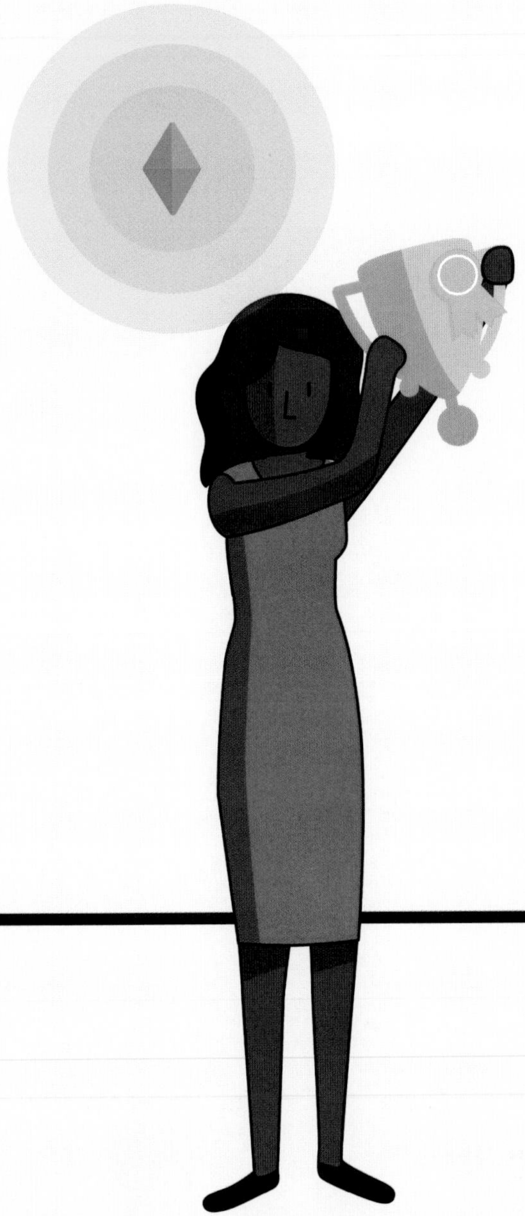

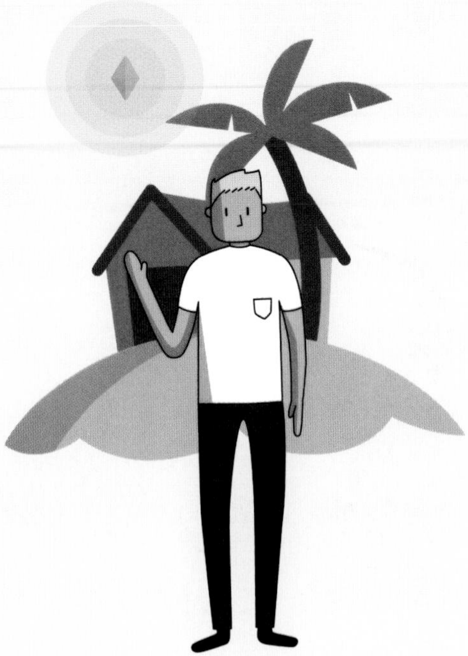

We each have to decide for ourselves what it is. I don't care whether you want to be a "Master of the Universe"...or to live under a palm tree...or anything else. I really don't.

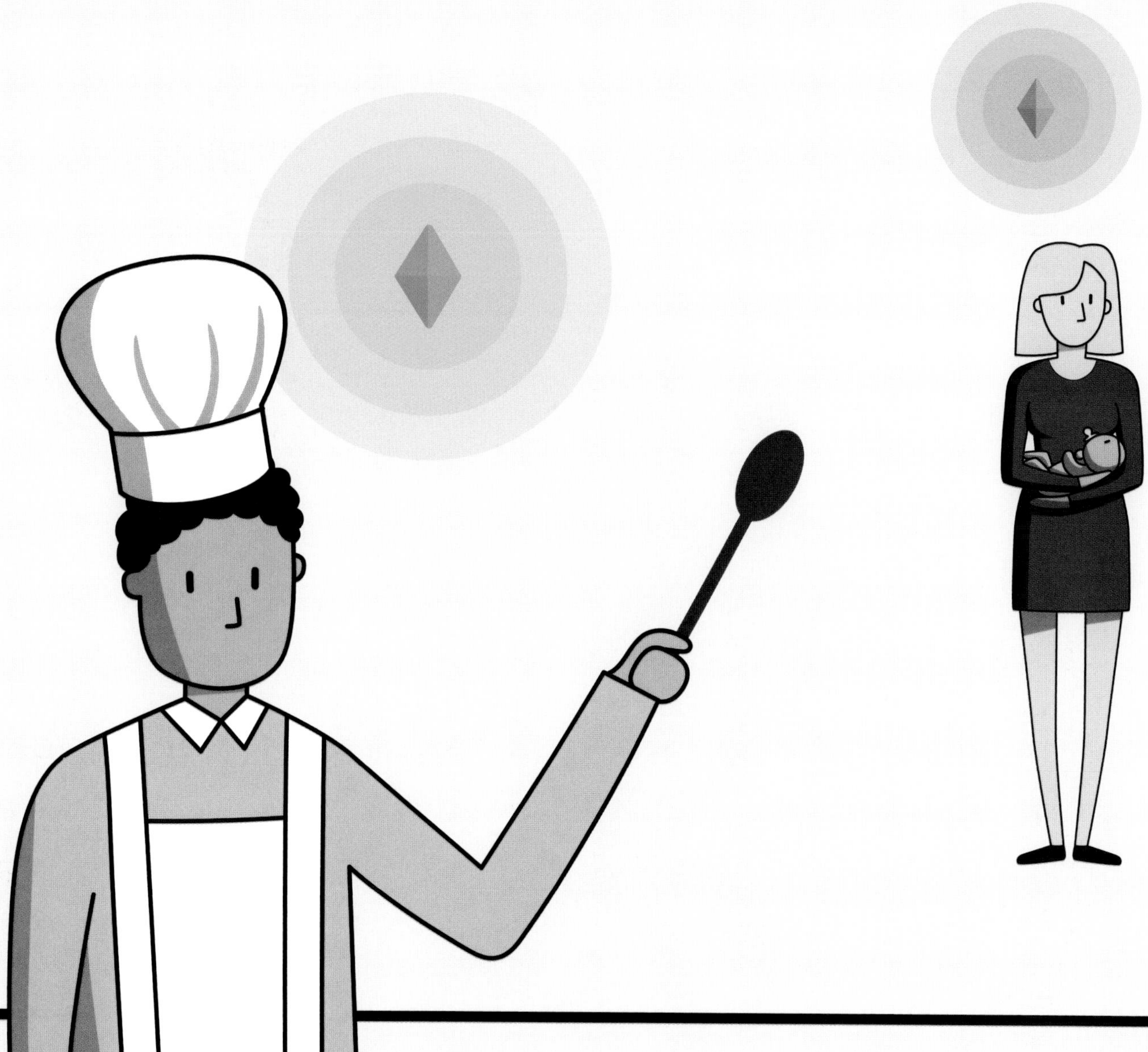

What you want is up to you. I just want you to be happy and healthy, having your own great evolution while contributing to evolution.

However, whatever path you choose, you must embrace your realities...

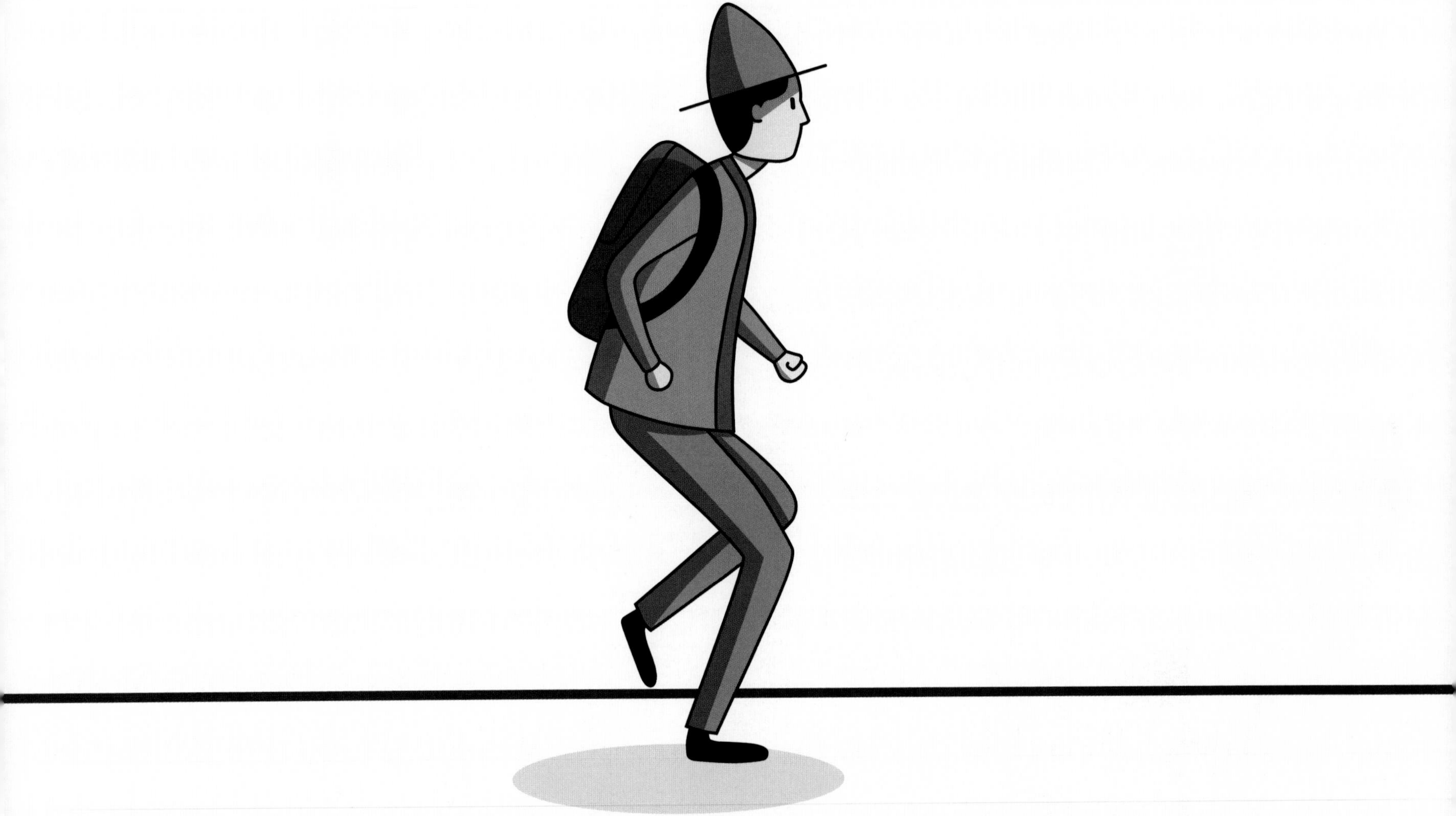

...especially the ones you wish weren't true.

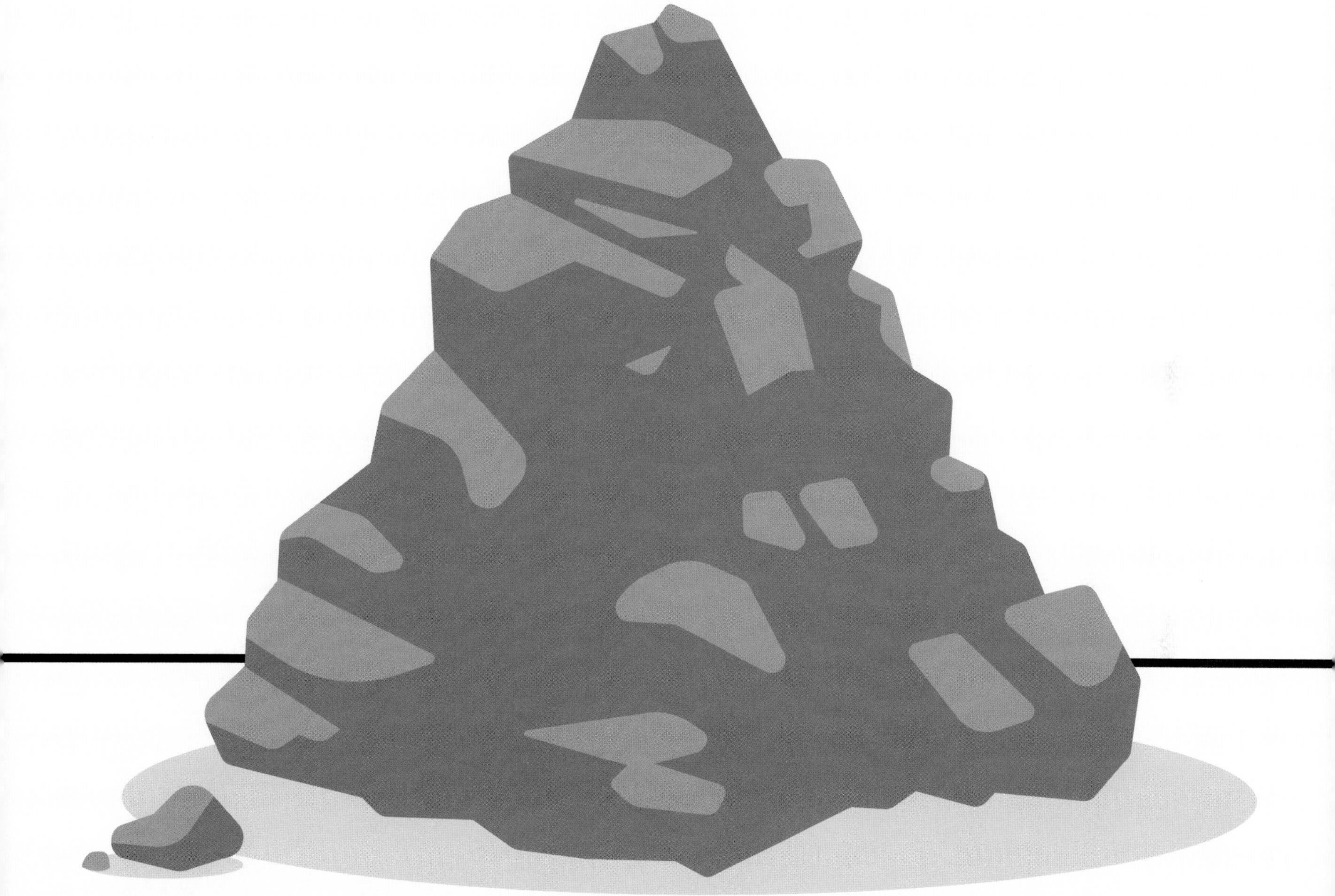

At first, my problems, mistakes, and weaknesses caused me a lot of pain, mostly because I was stuck wishing I didn't have them.

After a while, I learned that these pains were messages that were signaling that I needed to reflect on my realities and how to best deal with them.

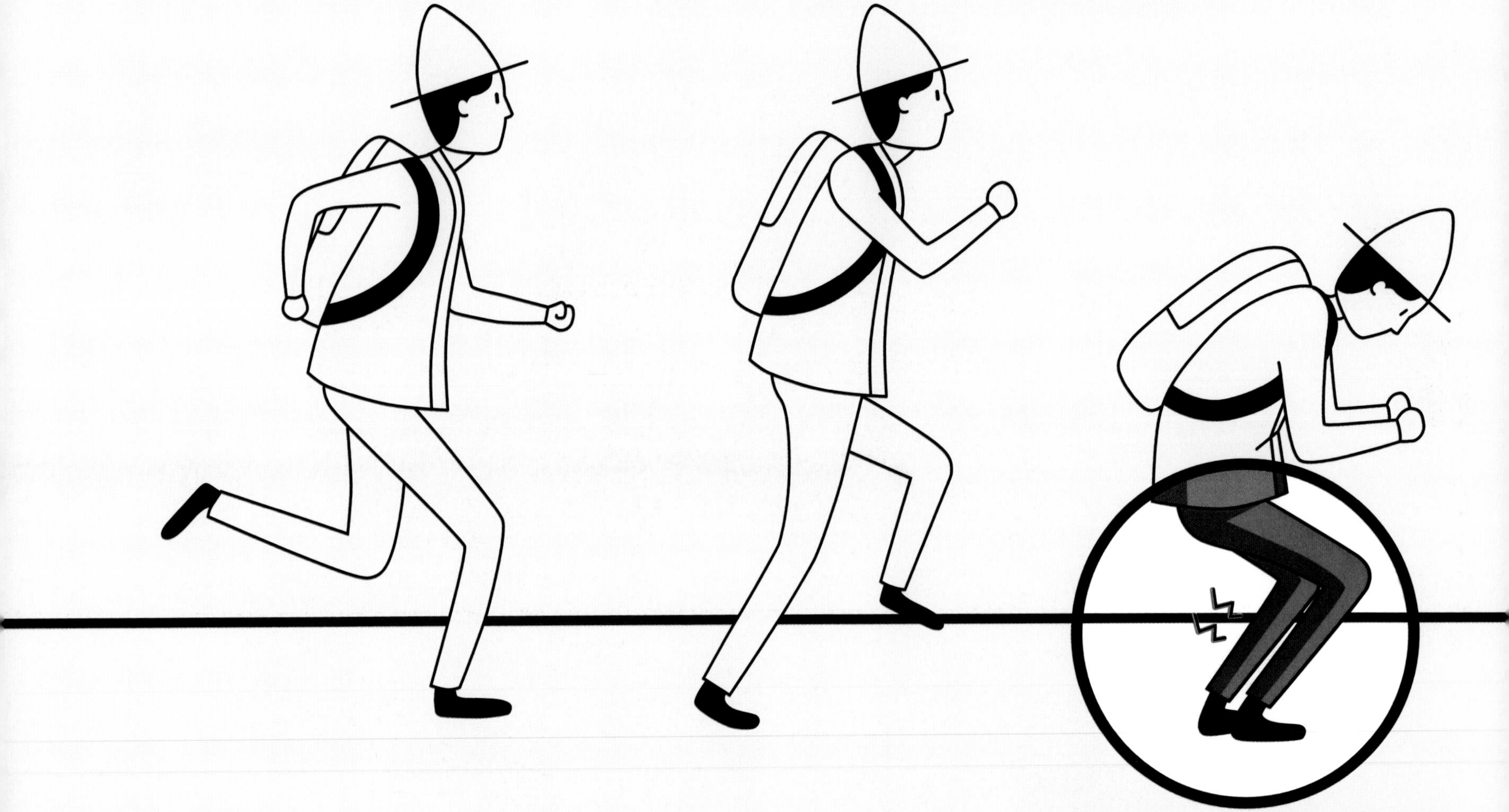

WEAKNESSES

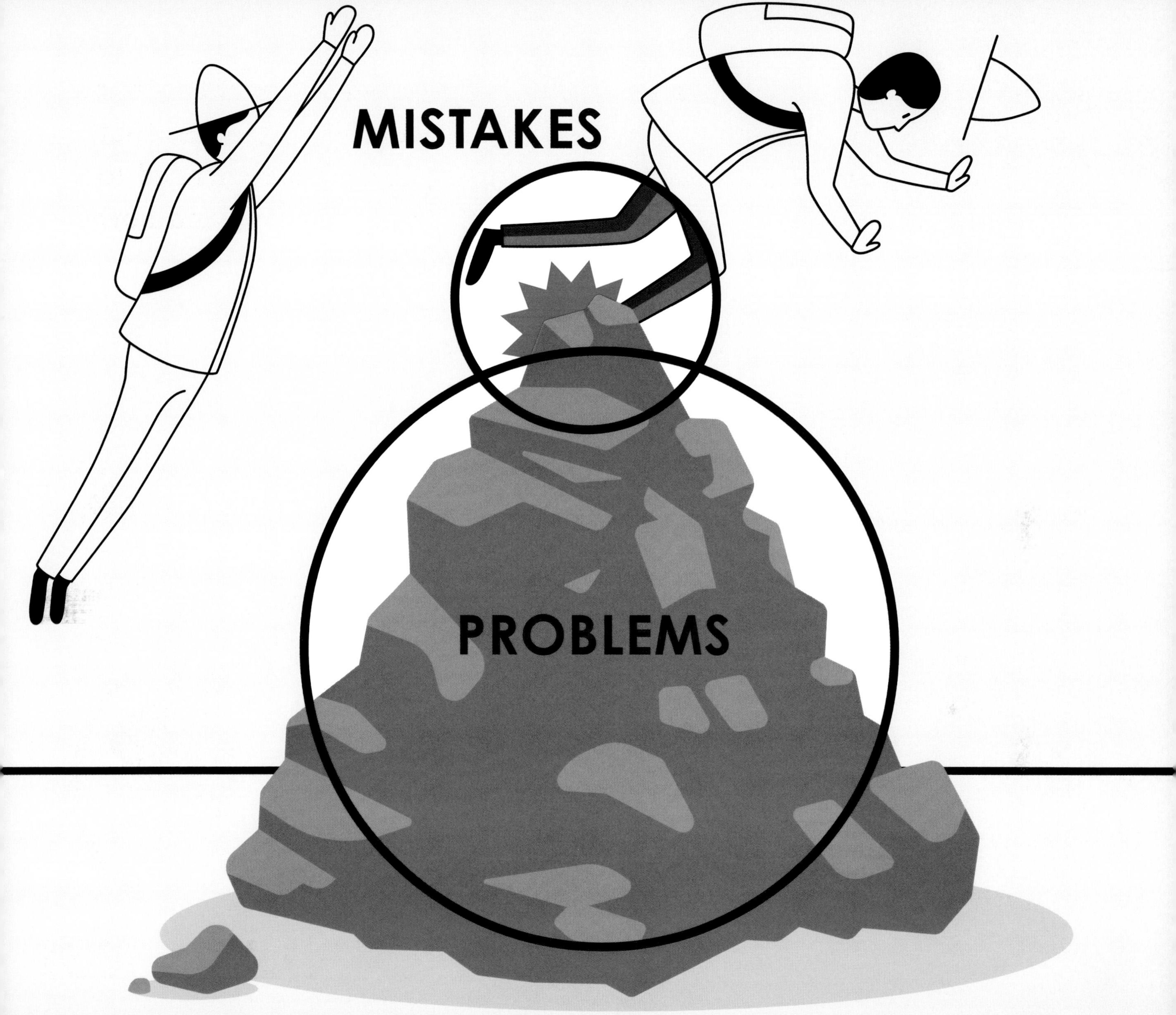
MISTAKES
PROBLEMS

That's when I learned that:

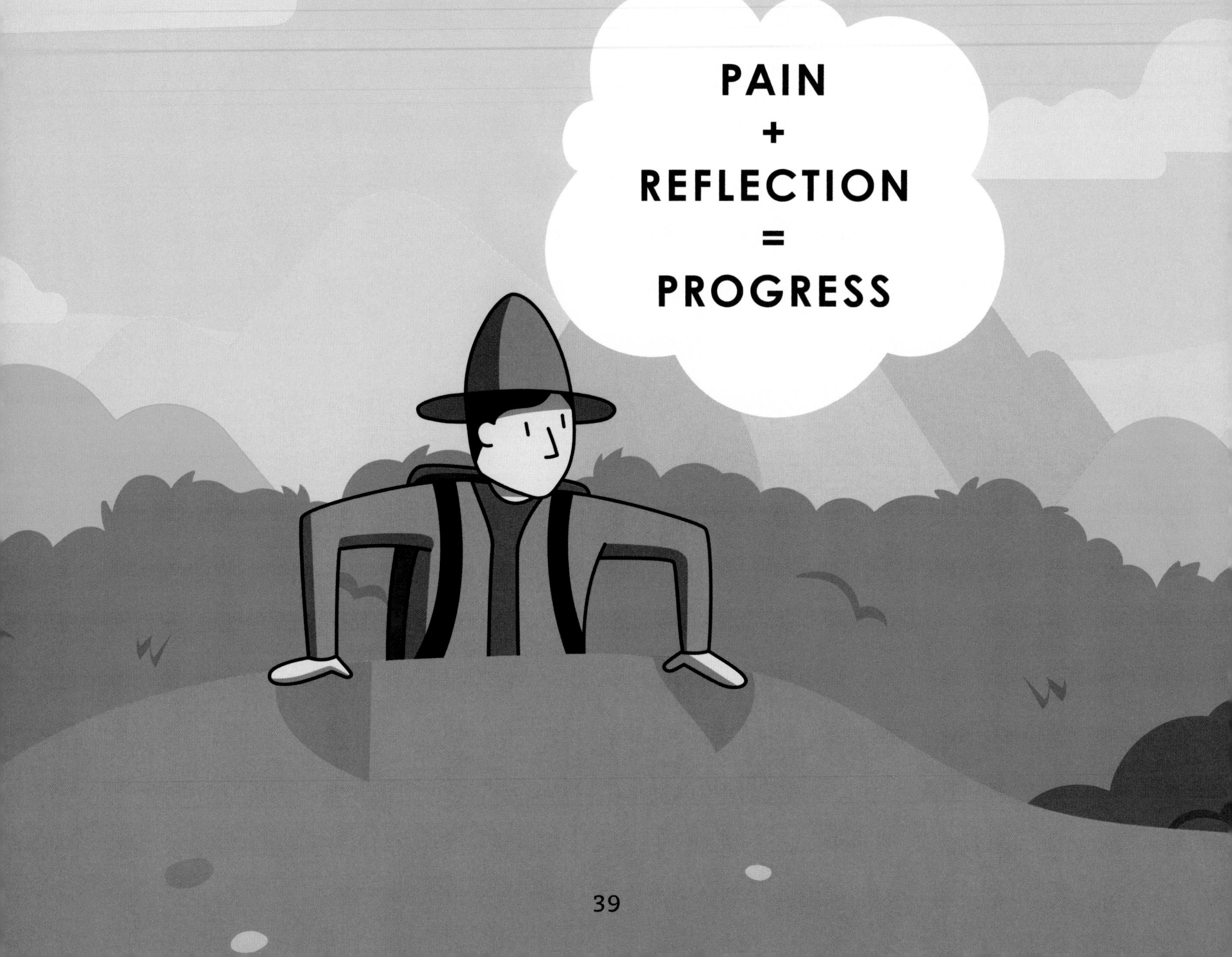
PAIN
+
REFLECTION
=
PROGRESS

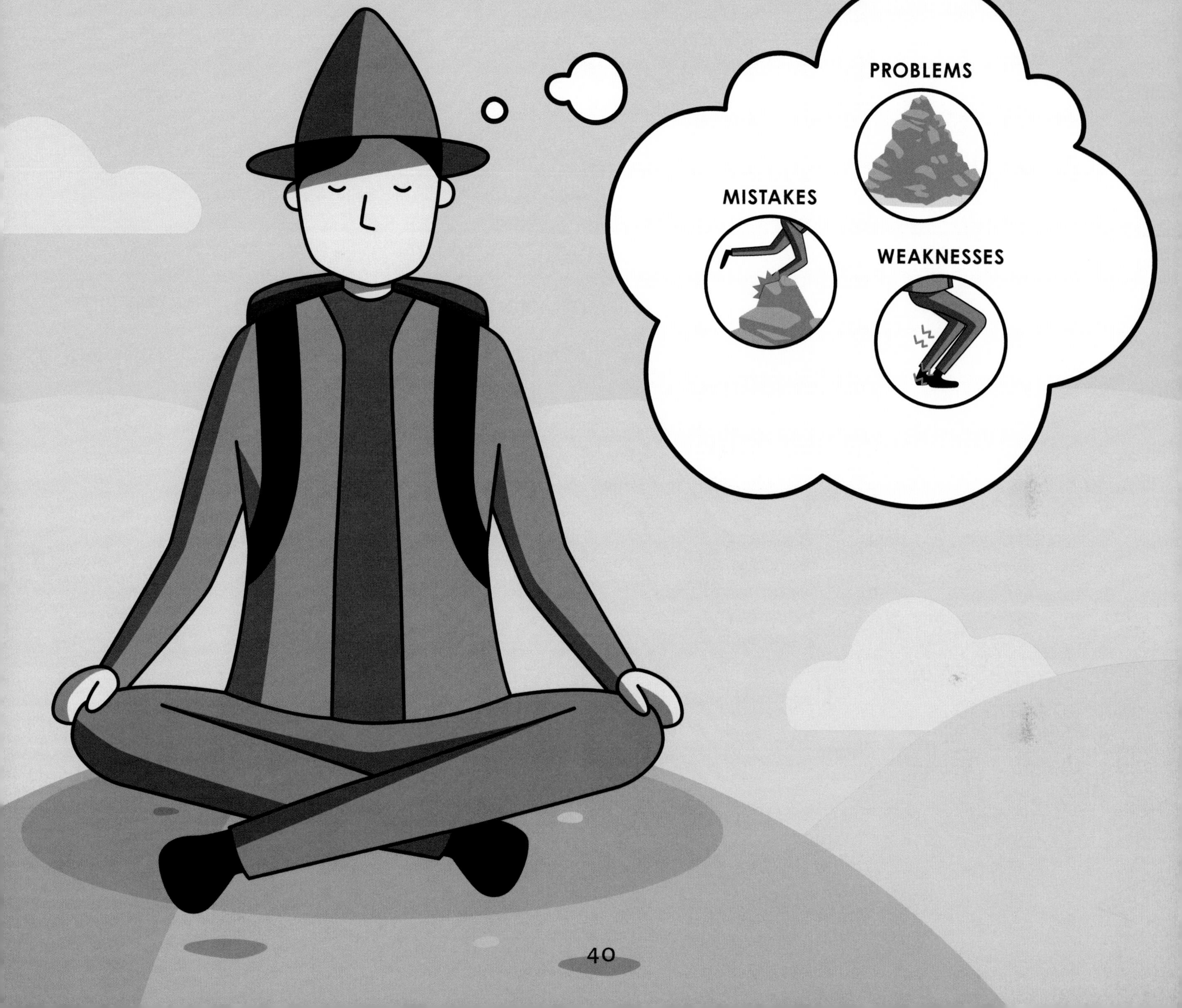
PROBLEMS
MISTAKES
WEAKNESSES

Discovering these things made me see that being successful is just a matter of following the 5-Step Process.

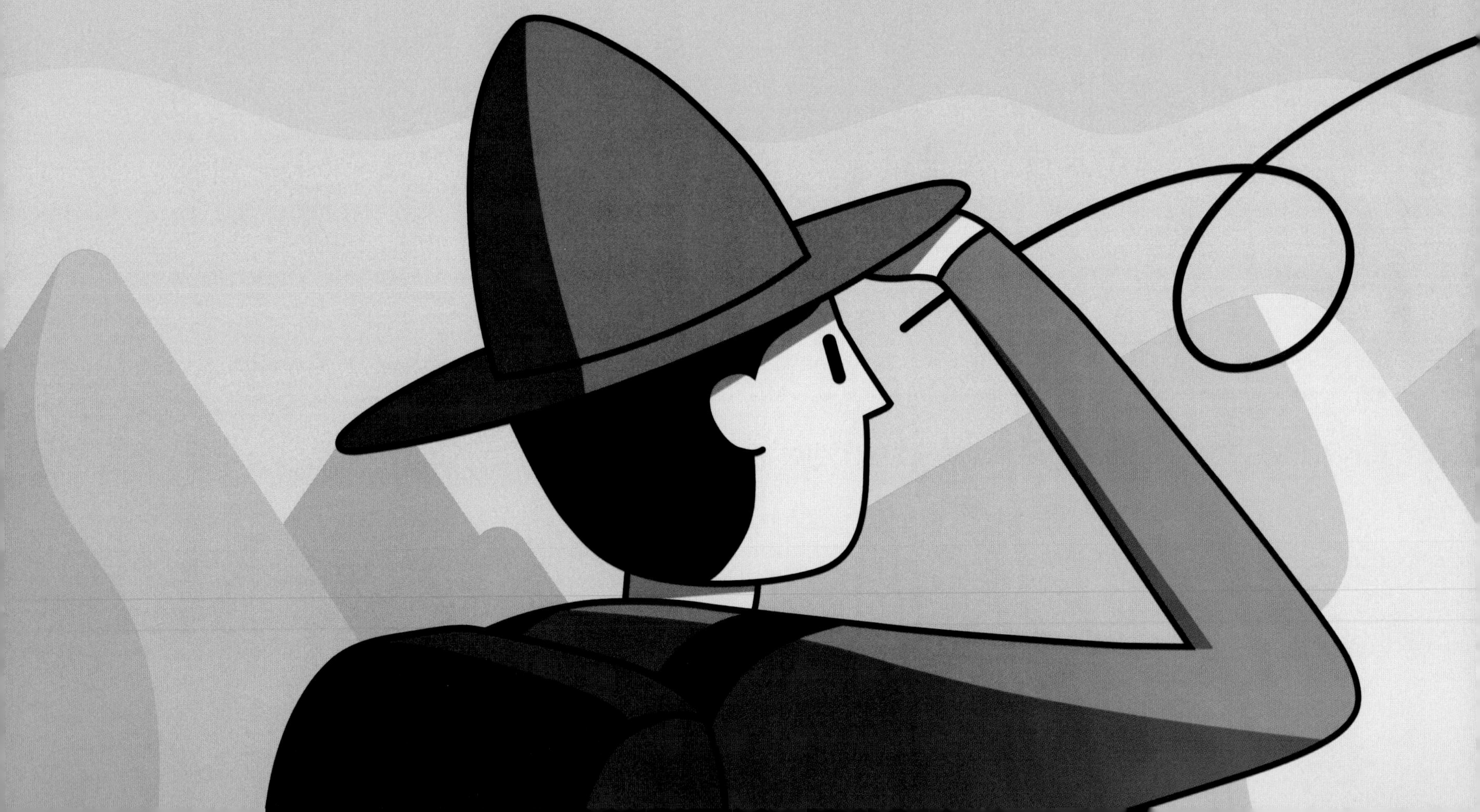

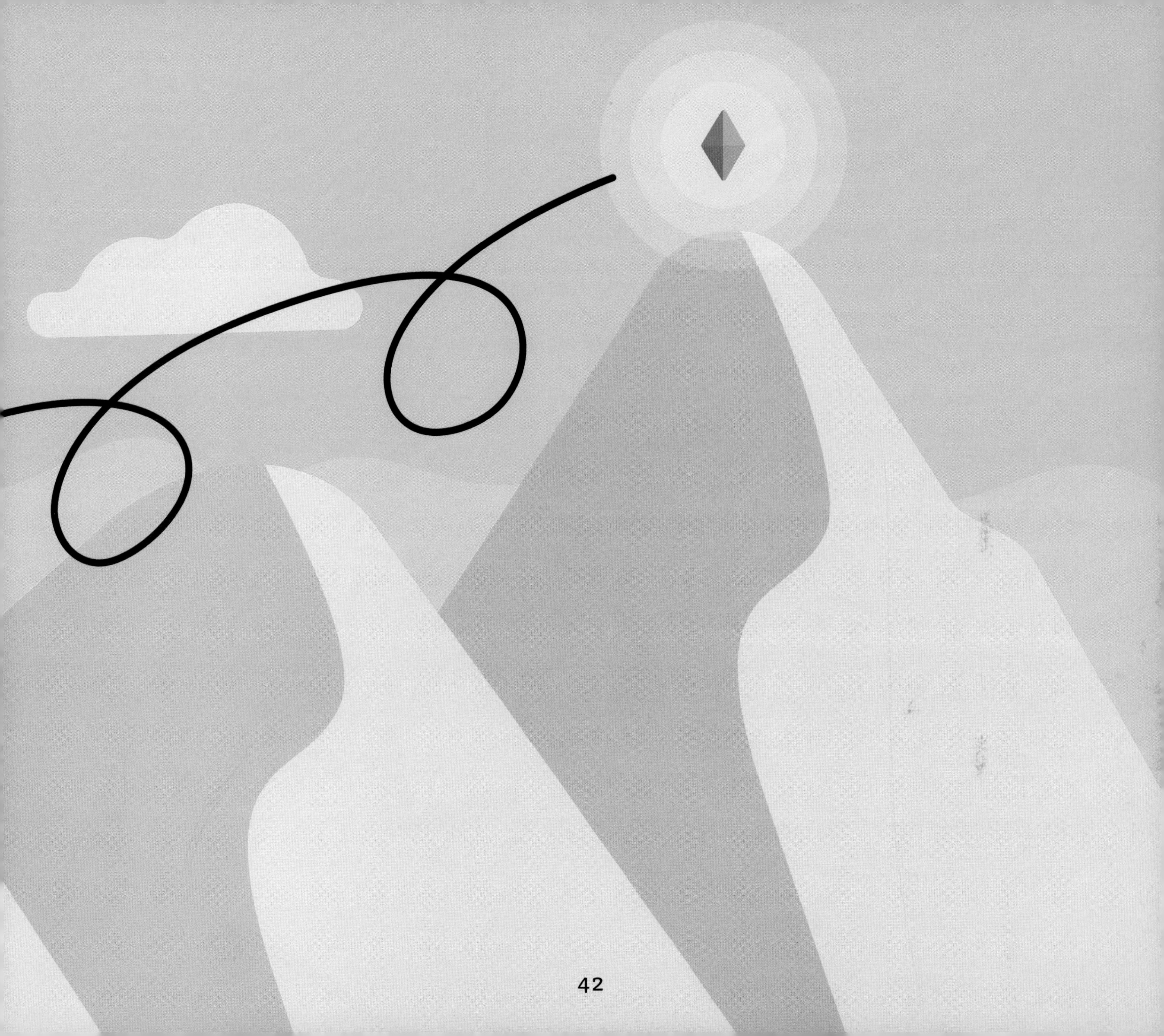

STEP 1

GOALS

Step One is to know your goals and run after them. While you can have most anything you want, you can't have everything you want, so you will need to make some decisions about your priorities. What is best for you depends on your passions, your strengths, and your weaknesses, so you need to really understand yourself and how to match your goals with what you're like to determine your path in life. There are always wonderful paths for you. You just have to find them by reflecting well, learning through trial and error, and showing determination to push toward your goals.

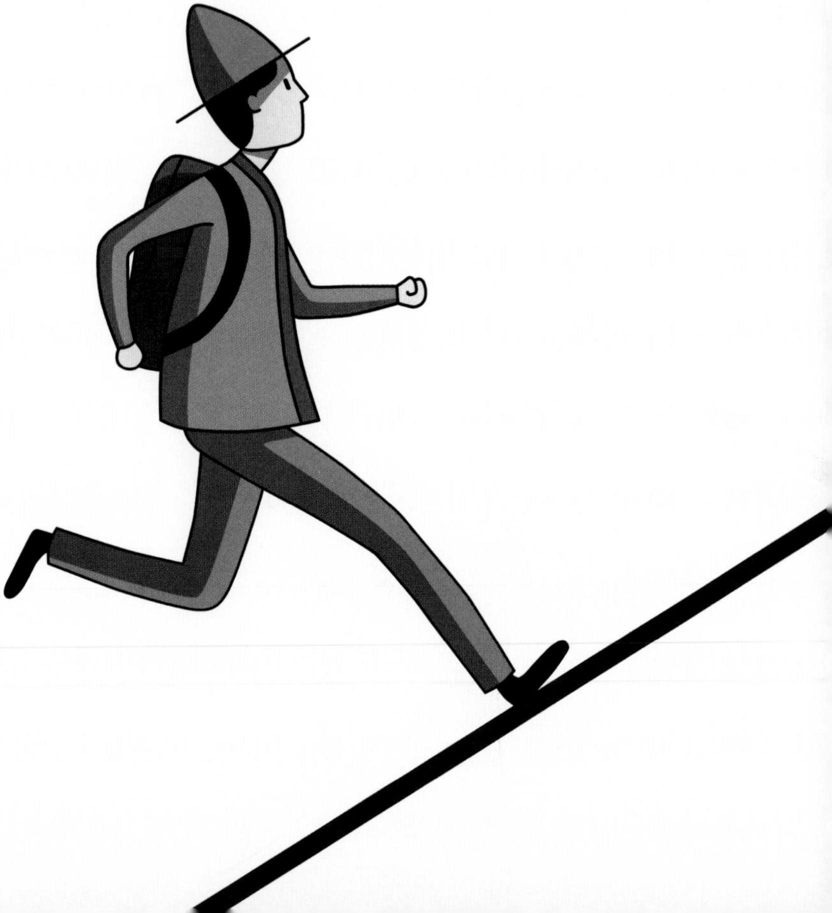

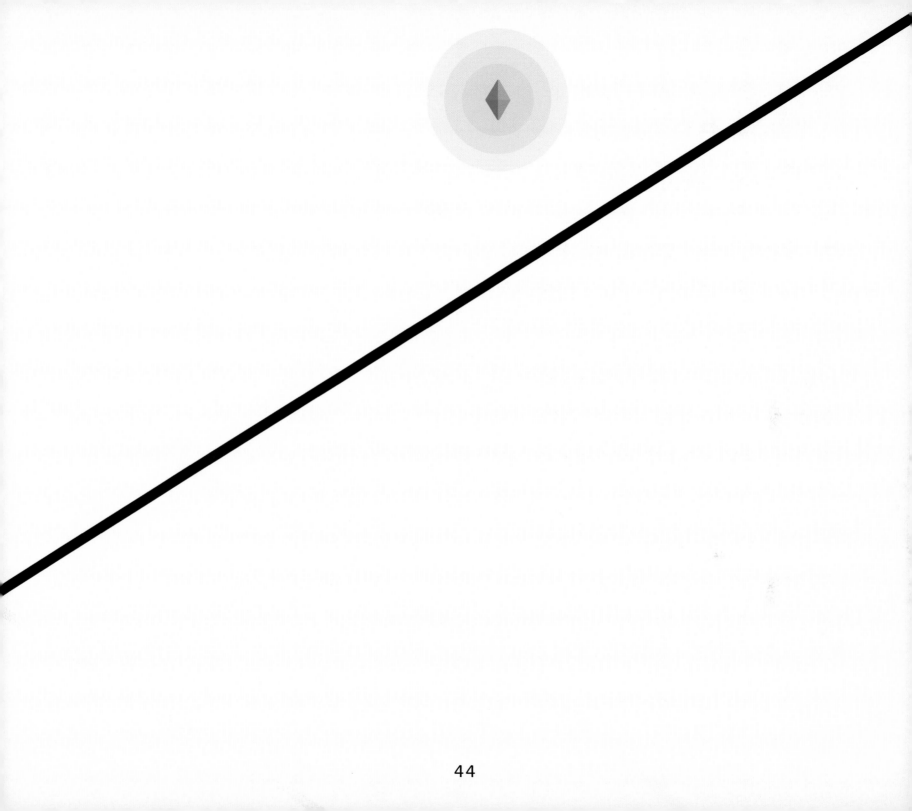

STEP 2

PROBLEMS

Step Two is to encounter the problems that stand in the way of you achieving your goals. There are always problems, which are typically painful. To evolve, you need to identify them and not tolerate them.

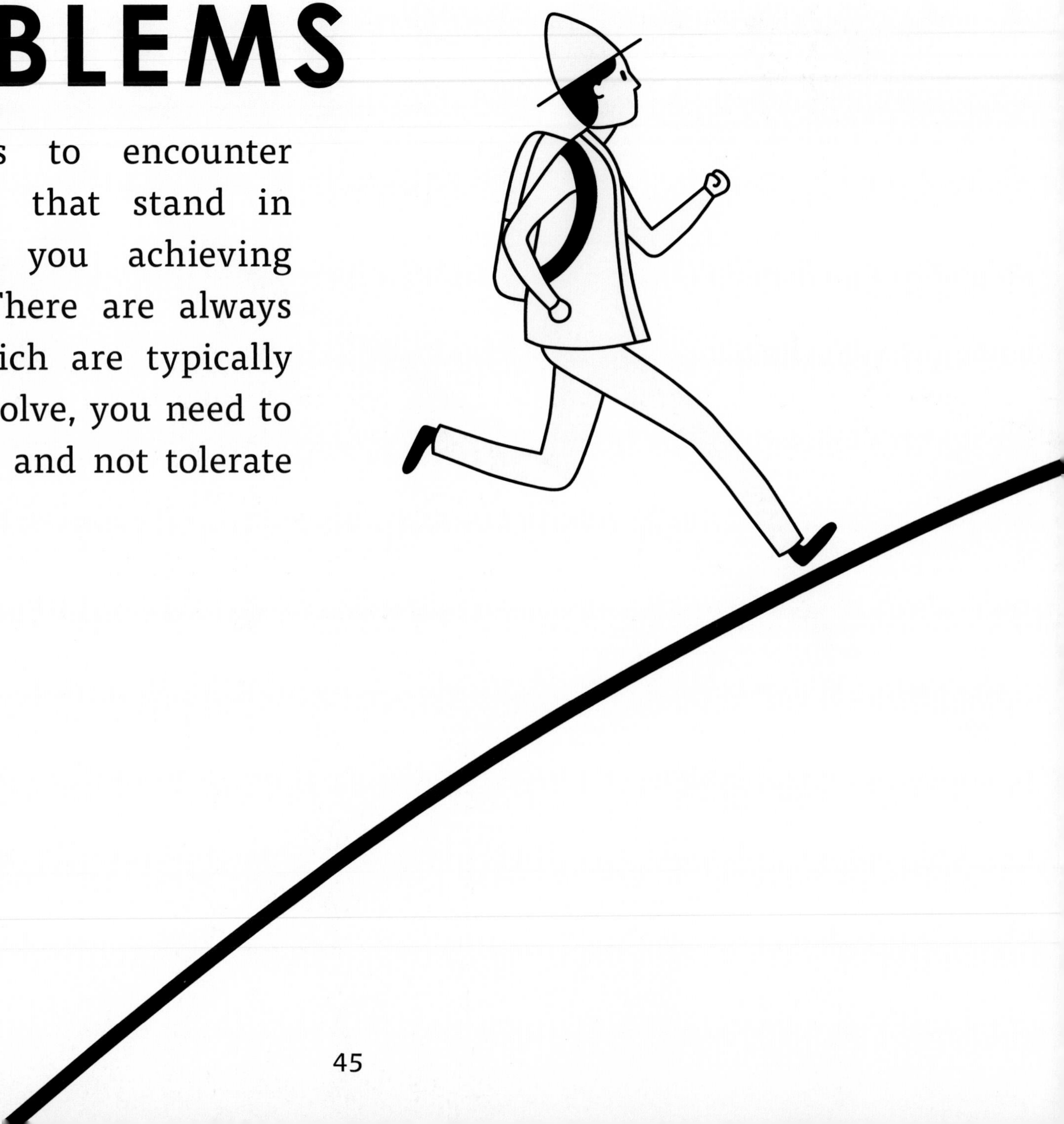

STEP 3

DIAGNOSIS

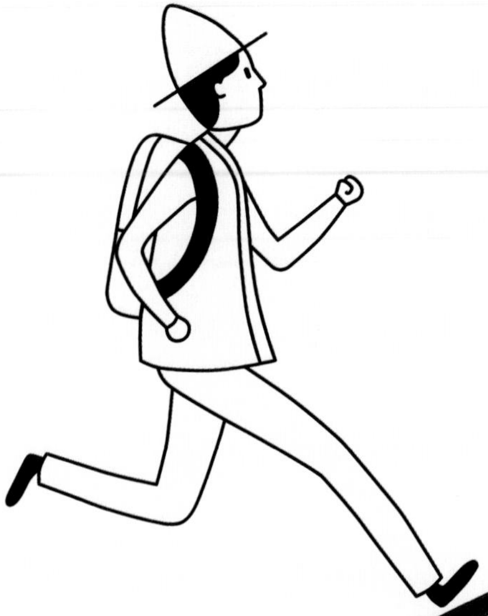

Step Three is to diagnose these problems to get at their root causes. Sometimes a weakness of yours or others' is the cause of your problems so you have to consider that possibility. Remember that this evolutionary journey you're on requires you to learn what you're not doing well and to change. Whatever it is, you need to find it out and get around it.

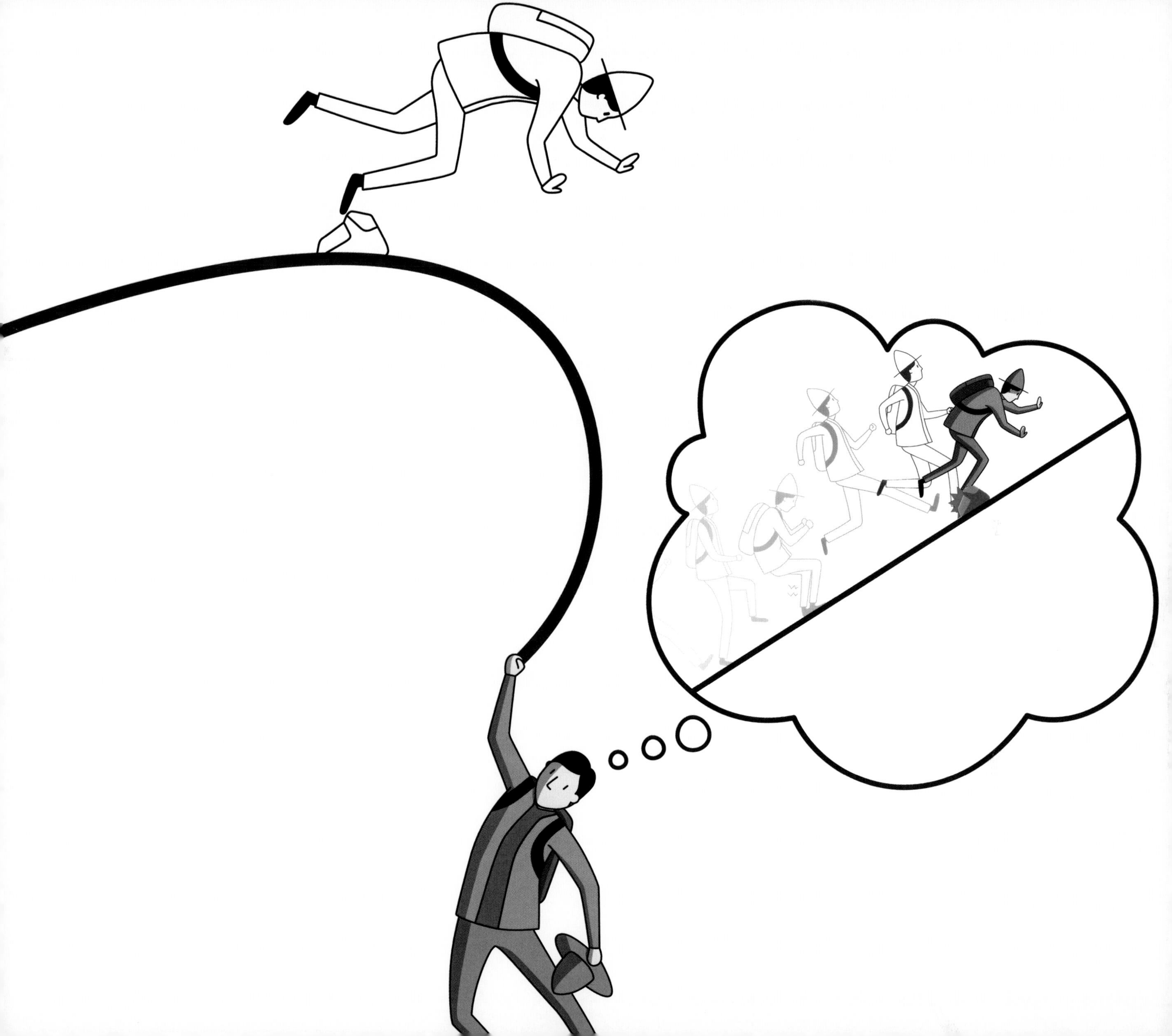

STEP 4

DESIGN

Step Four is to design plans to get around the problem that is standing in the way of your progress.

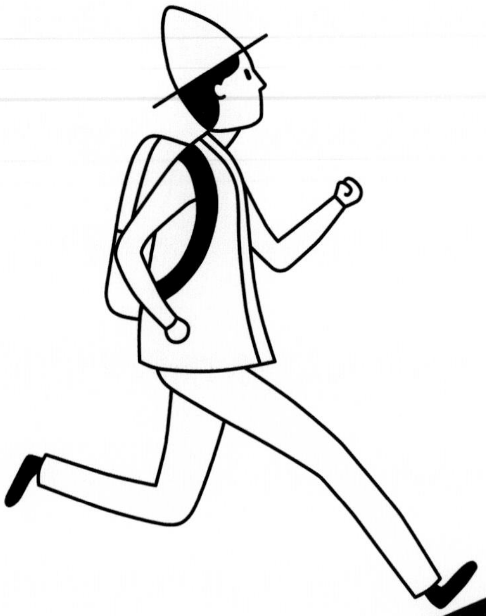

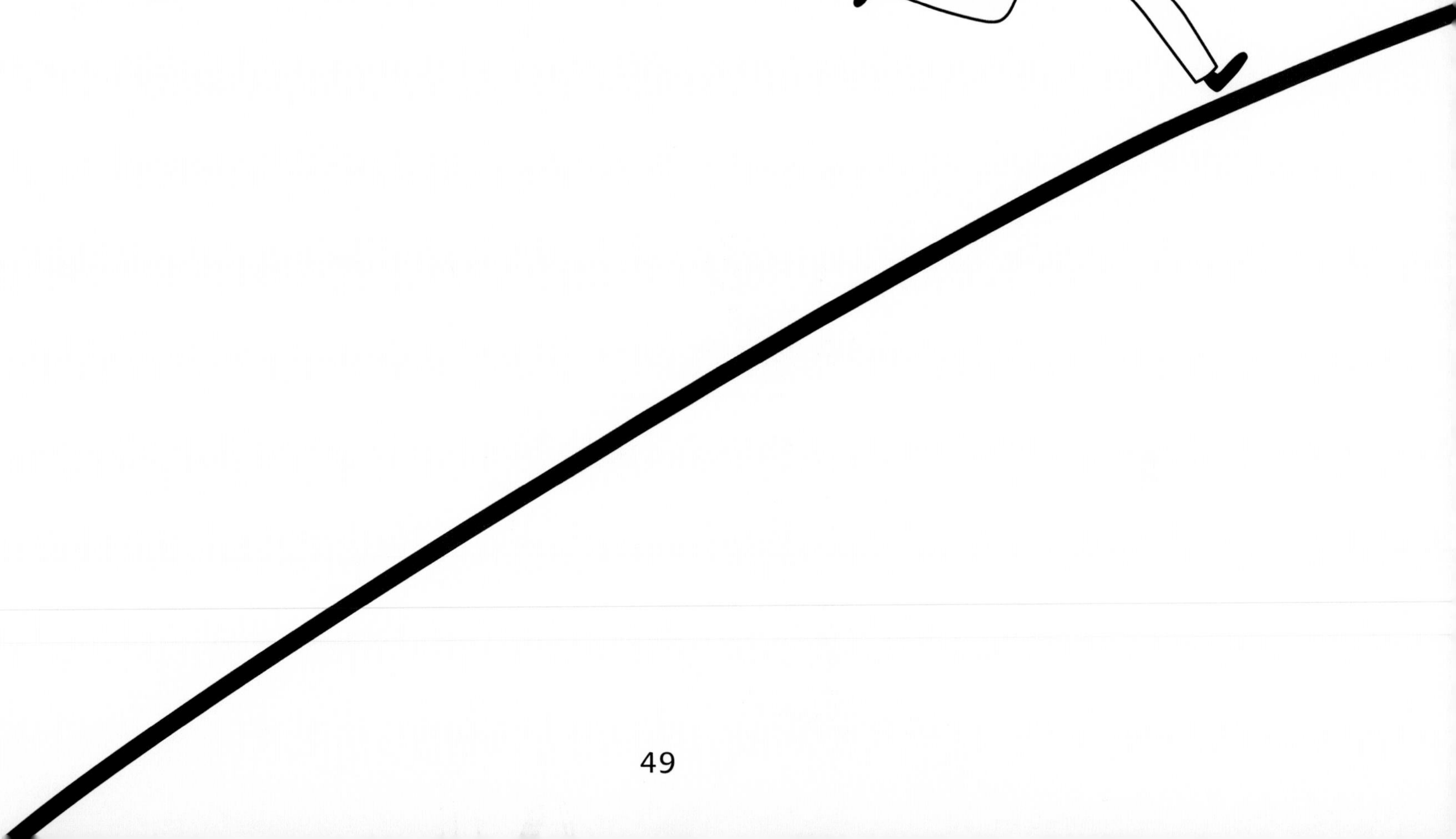

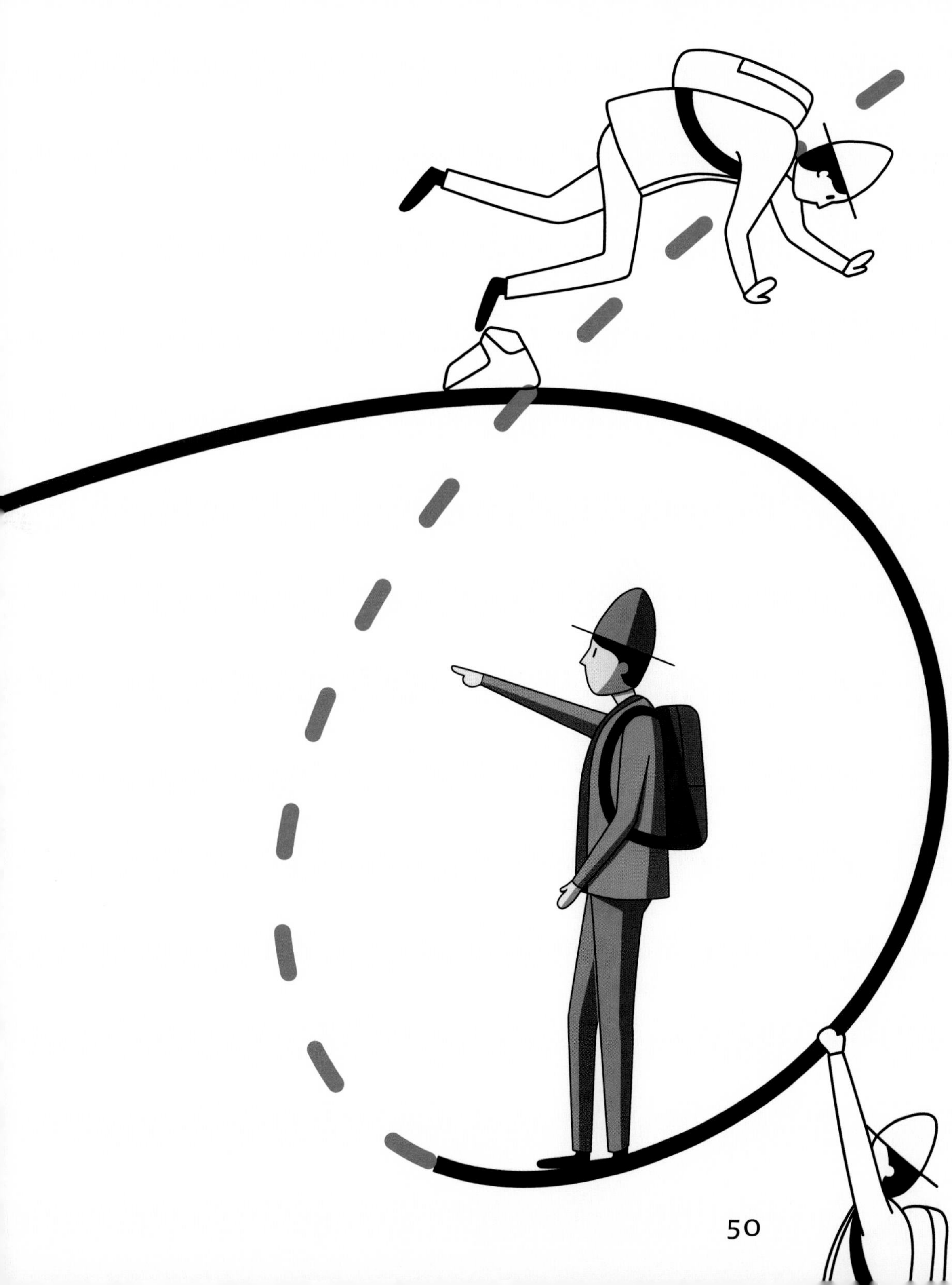

STEP 5

DO IT

Step Five is to execute those designs, pushing yourself to do what's needed.

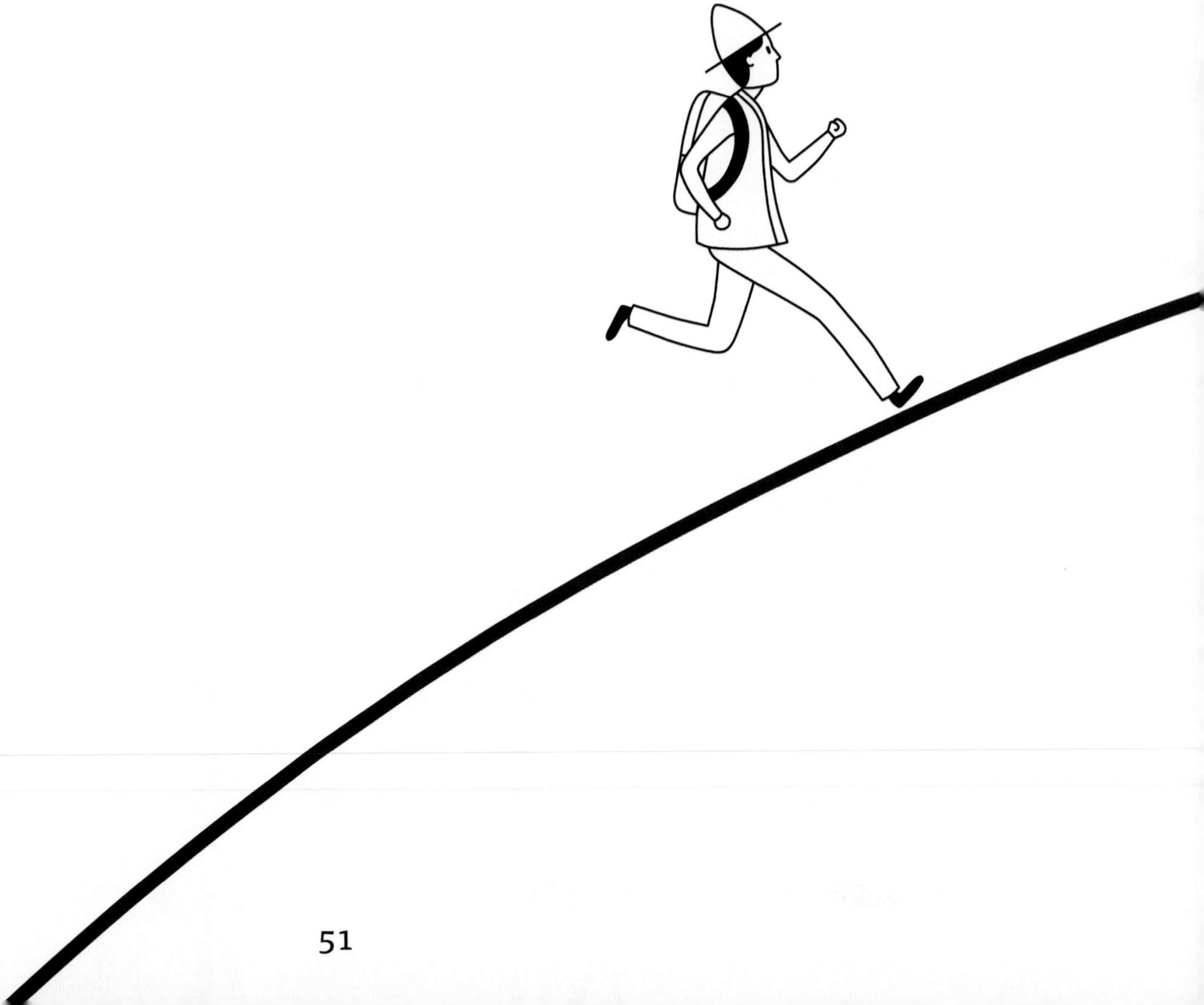

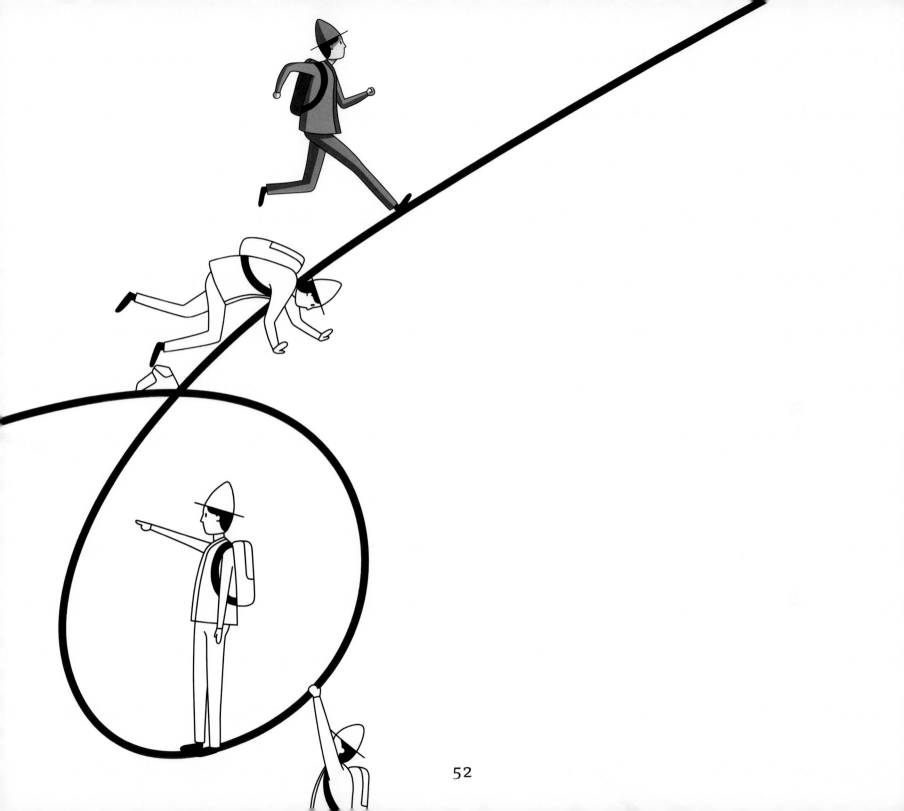

52

A successful life consists of doing these five steps over and over again. Doing them well will naturally create the ups and downs and improvements that lead to your personal evolution to higher levels of success. To me, evolution looks like this:

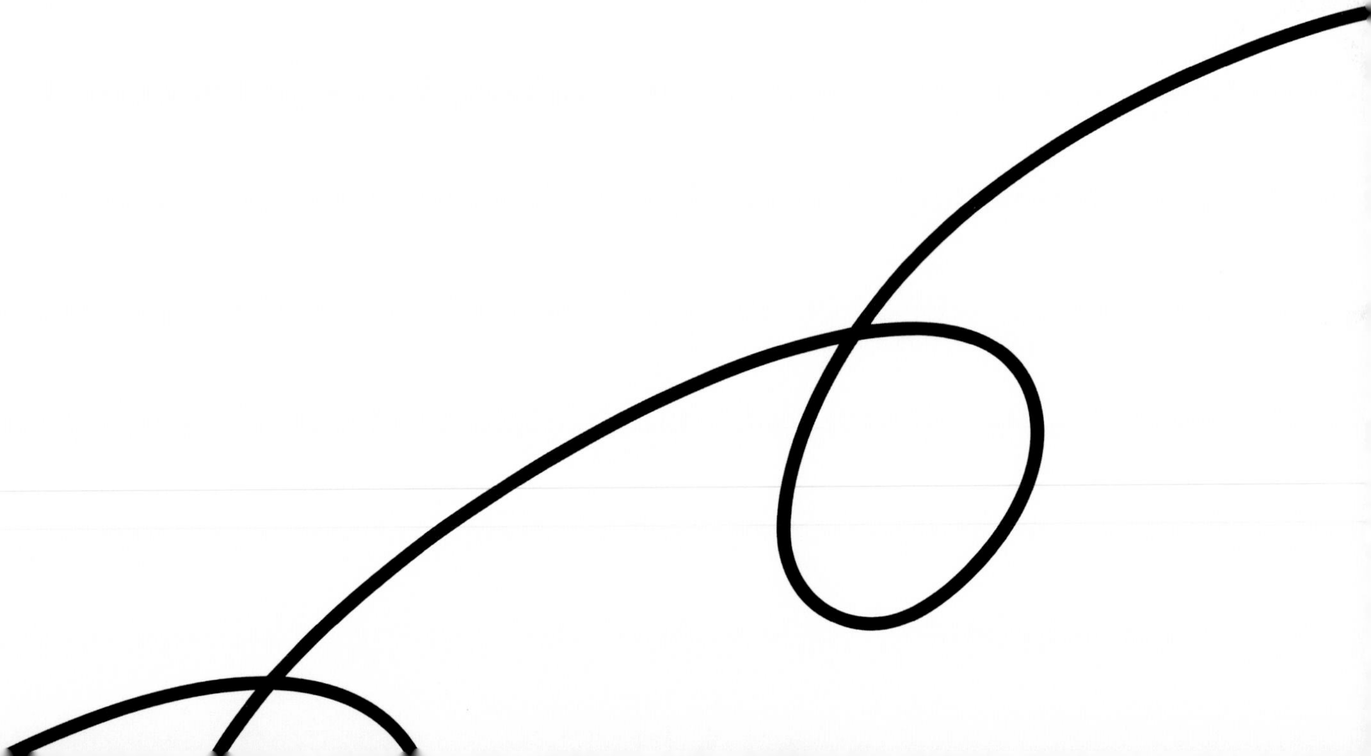

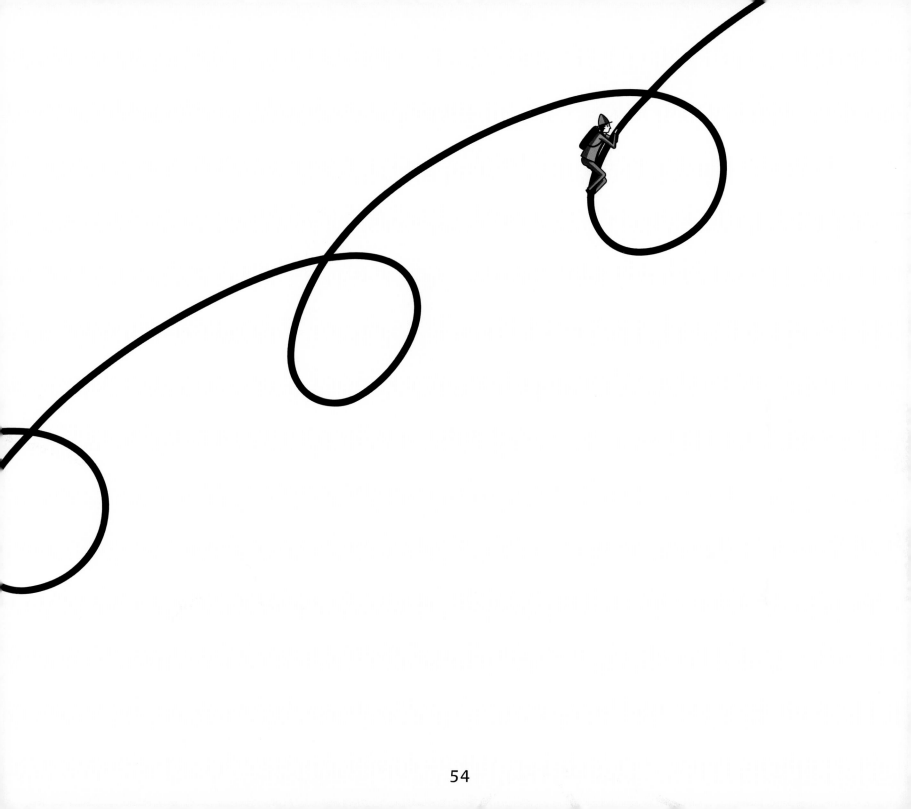

You see this 5-Step Process everywhere: in any product, organization, or person you know.

It is just a law of nature.

Evolution is simply a process of either adapting or dying.

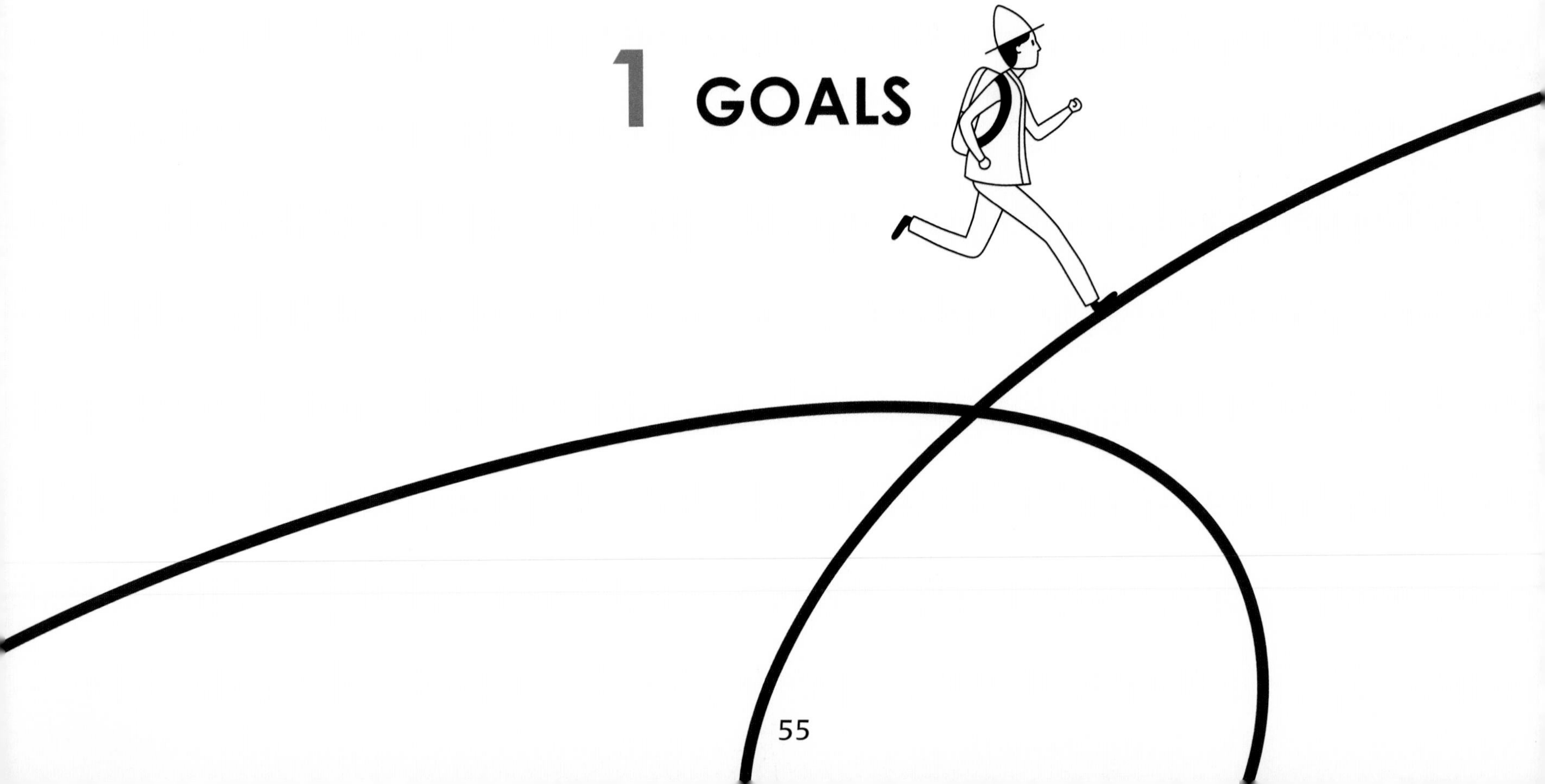
1 GOALS

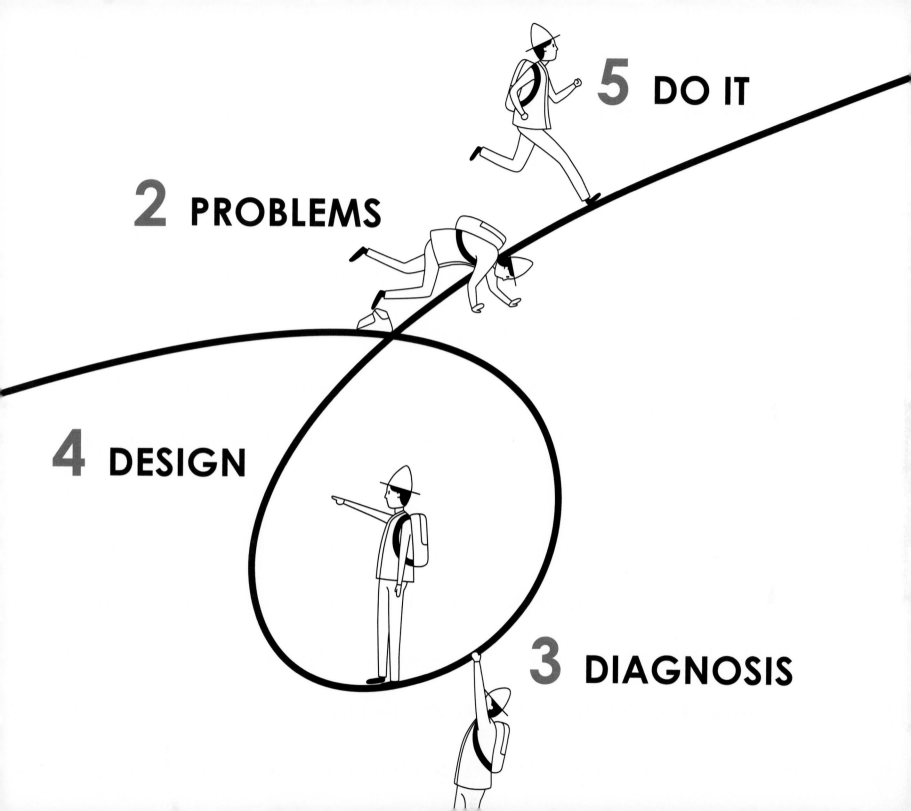

5 DO IT

2 PROBLEMS

4 DESIGN

3 DIAGNOSIS

As you push through this process, you'll ascend to higher levels of success—which also bring greater challenges.

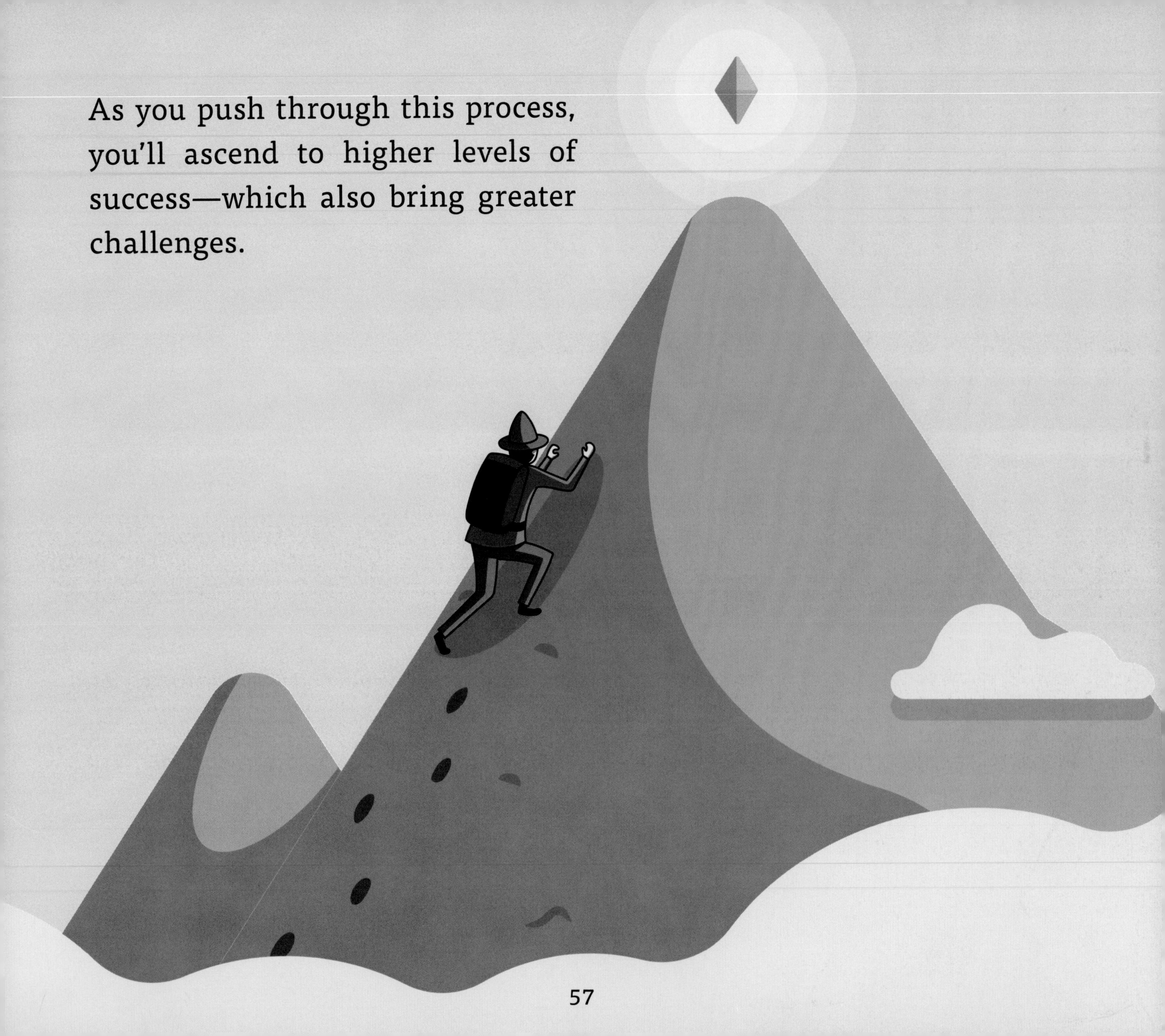

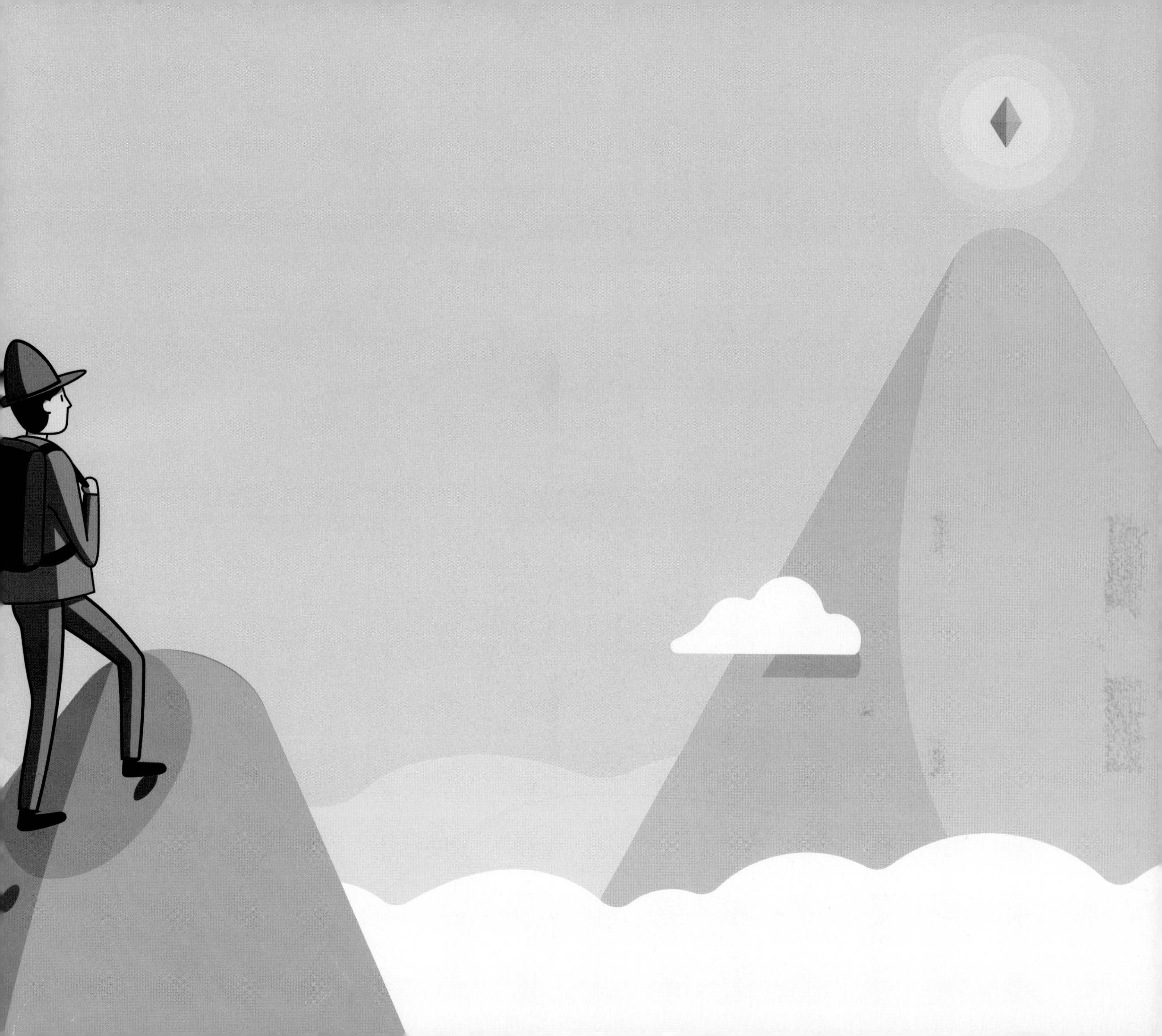

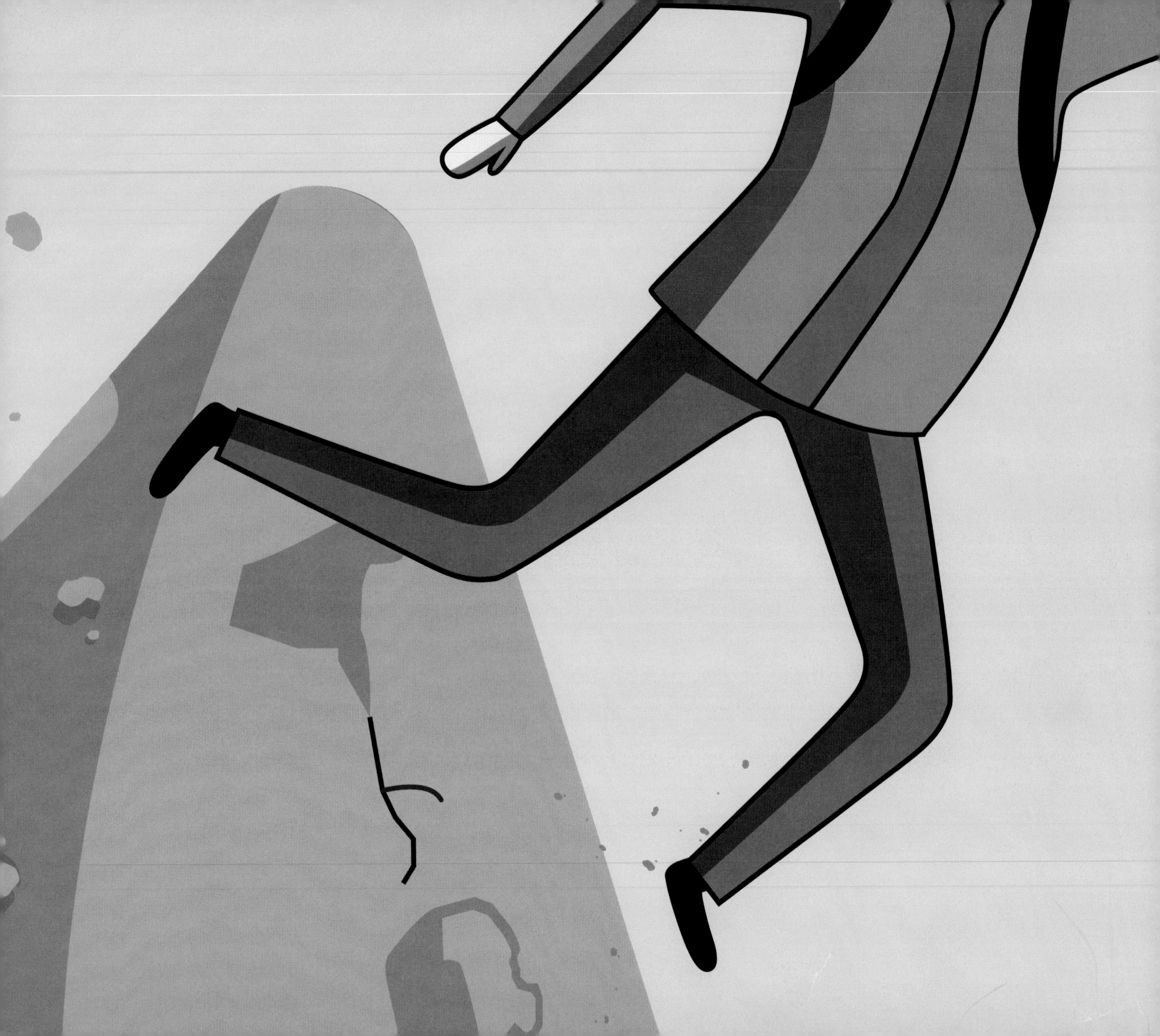

Of course as the heights get greater, the falls get greater, too.

Terrible things happen to all of us. Depending on how we handle them, they can ruin us...or they can profoundly improve us.

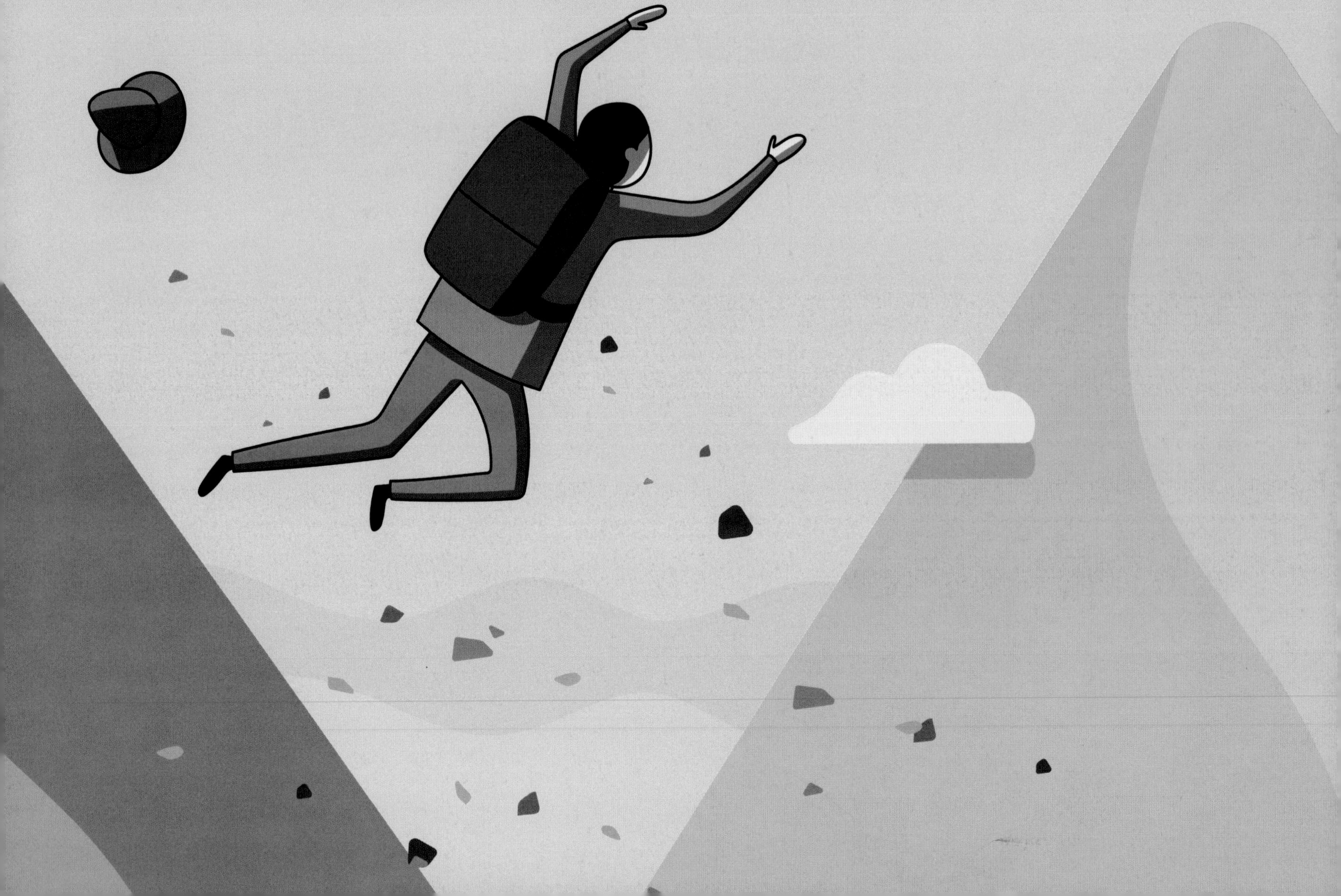

Whether we get through them or spiral downward depends on whether we're willing to face the failure objectively and make the right decisions.

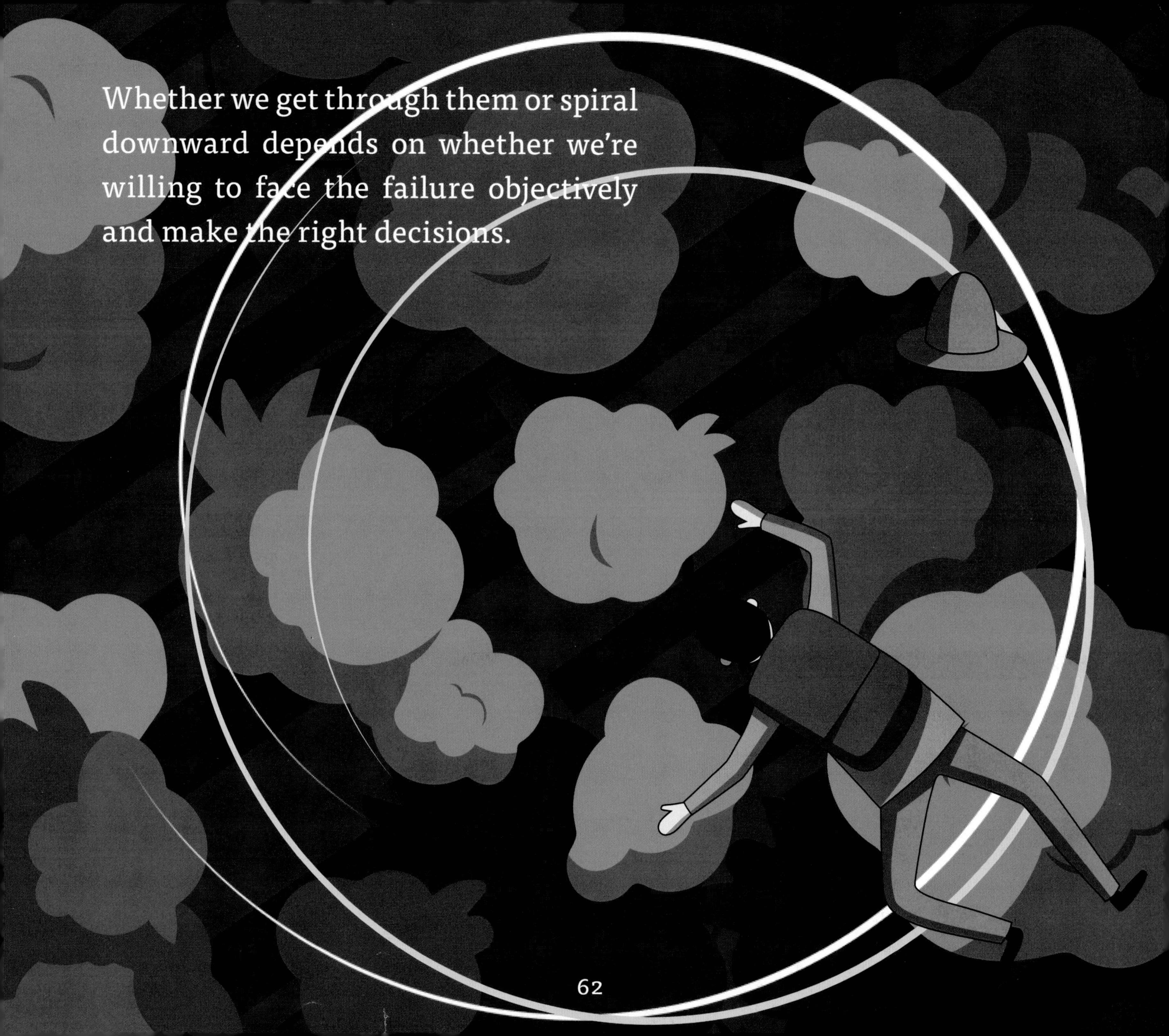

My big failure came in 1982 when I bet everything on a depression that never came.

The markets were very turbulent and I believed the U.S. economy (with the world economy tied to it) was headed into a crisis.

This was an extremely controversial view. I very publicly took a big risk... and was dead wrong. The U.S. economy enjoyed the greatest growth period in its history.

Losing this bet was like a blow to my head with a baseball bat. I had to borrow $4,000 from my dad just to pay my bills...

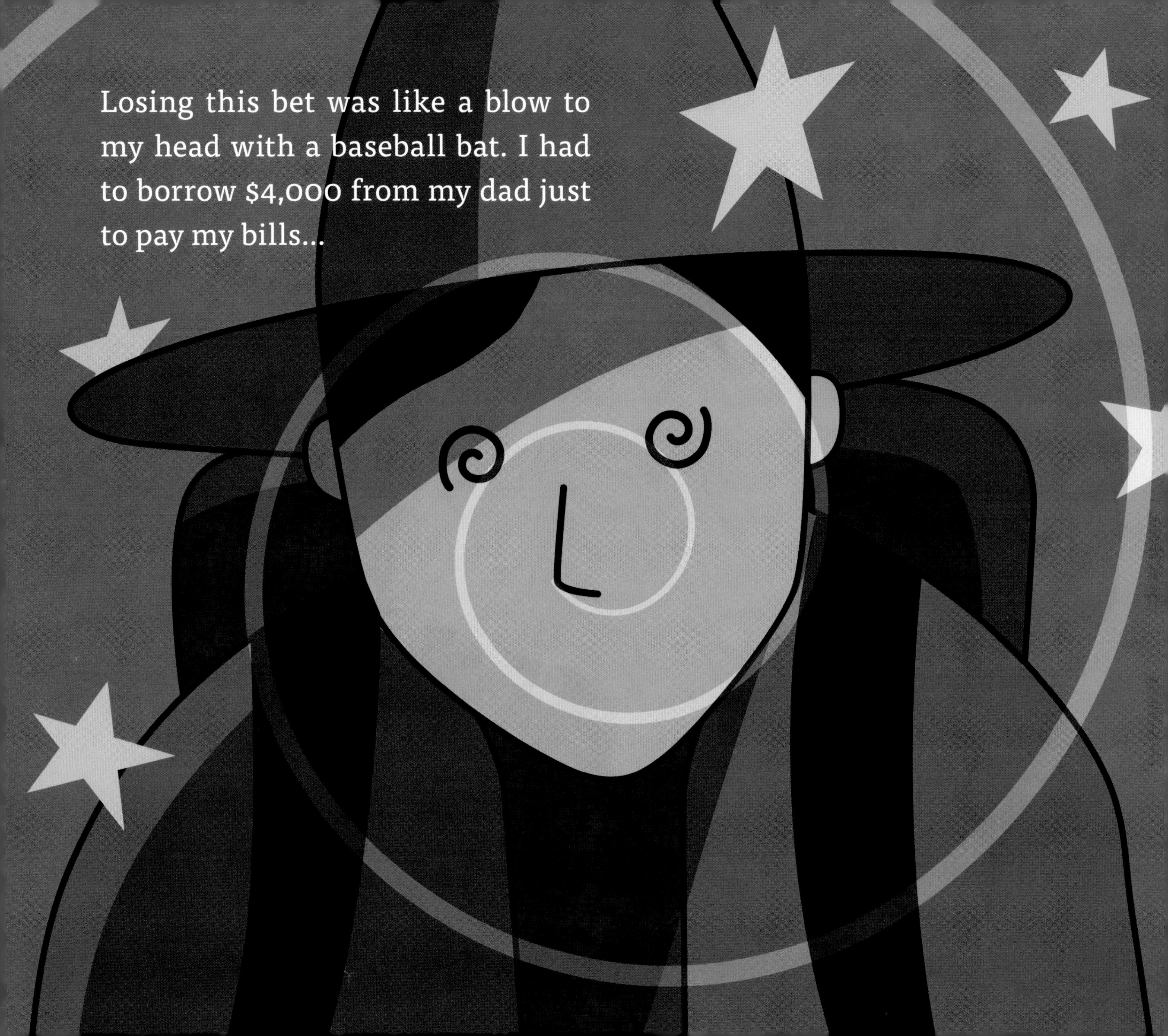

...but even worse, I had to let go people I cared about so that my company was left with one employee: me.

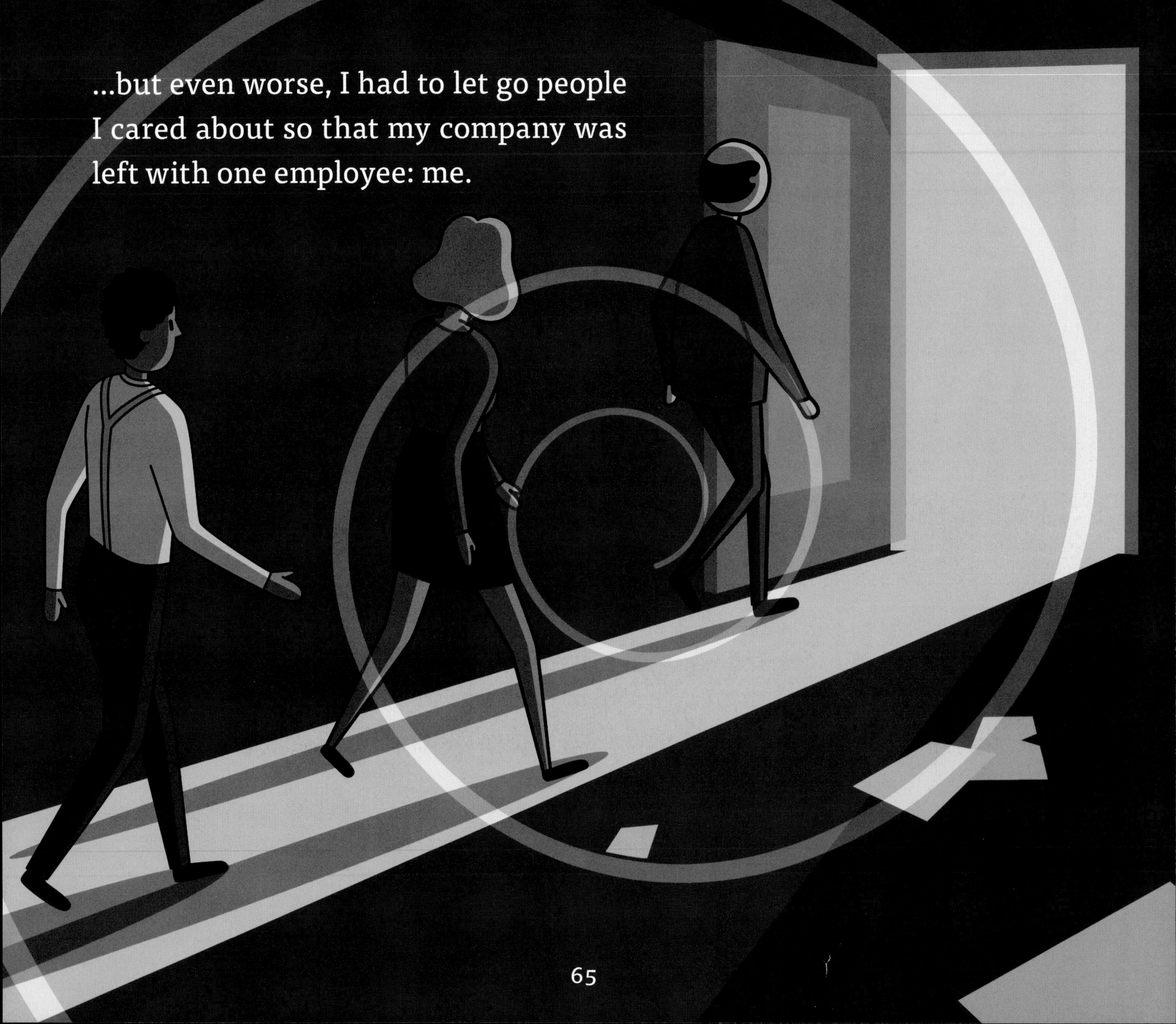

I wondered what to do. Should I put on a tie
and give up my dream of working for myself?

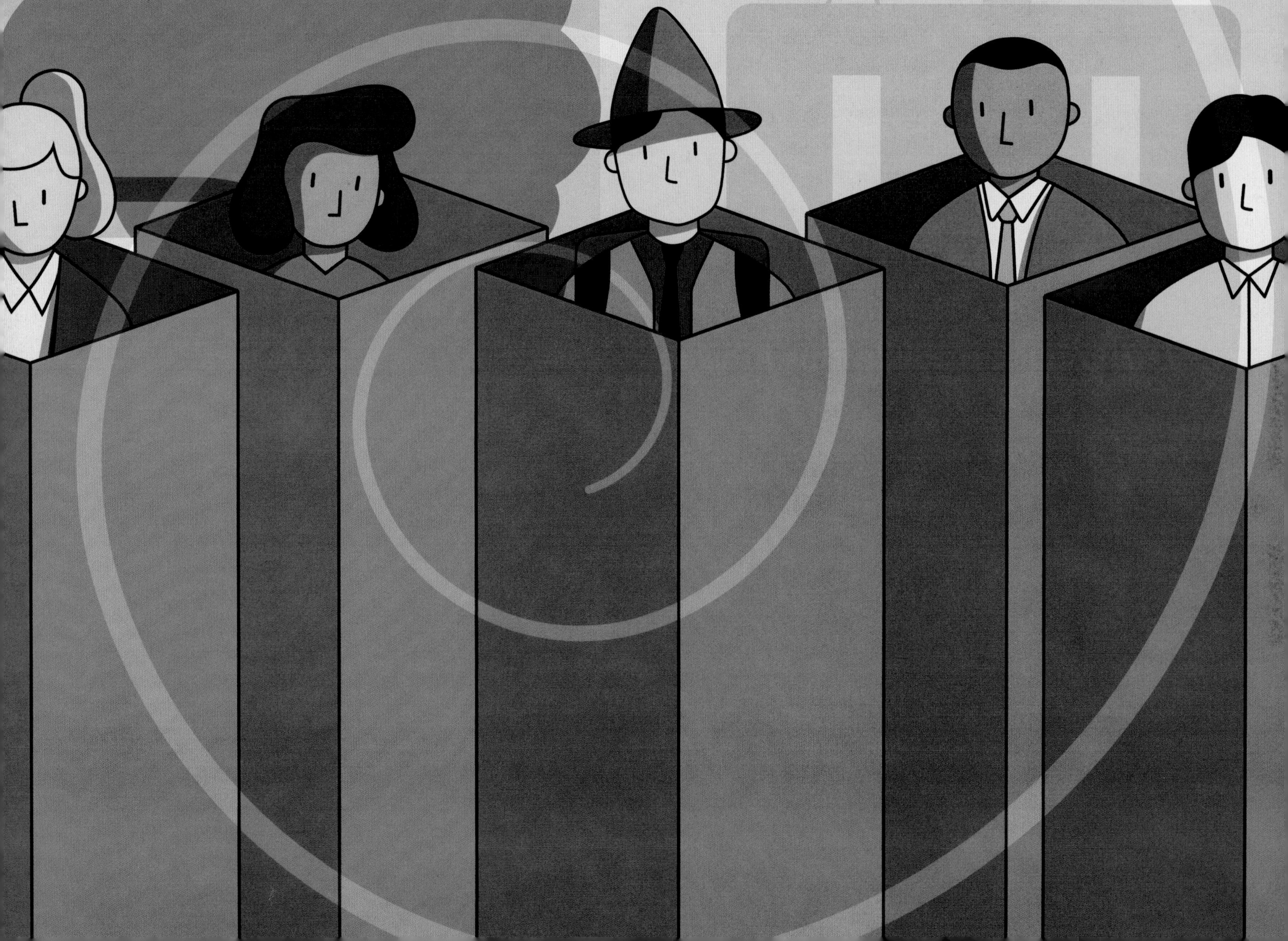

Being so wrong—and so publicly—
was painfully humbling.

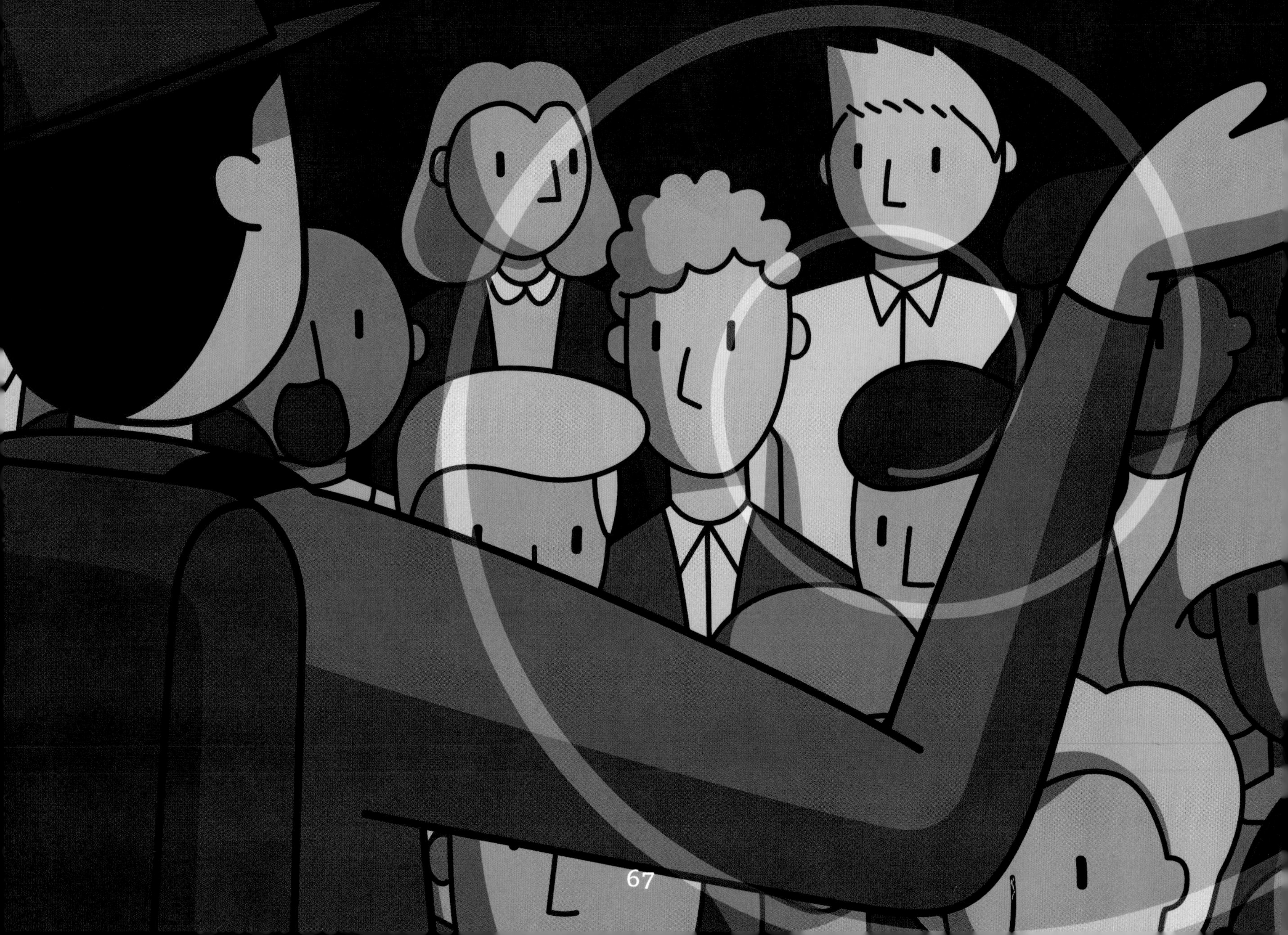

I had let one bad bet erase all my good ones. And I couldn't see a path that would give me the rewards I wanted without unacceptable risk.

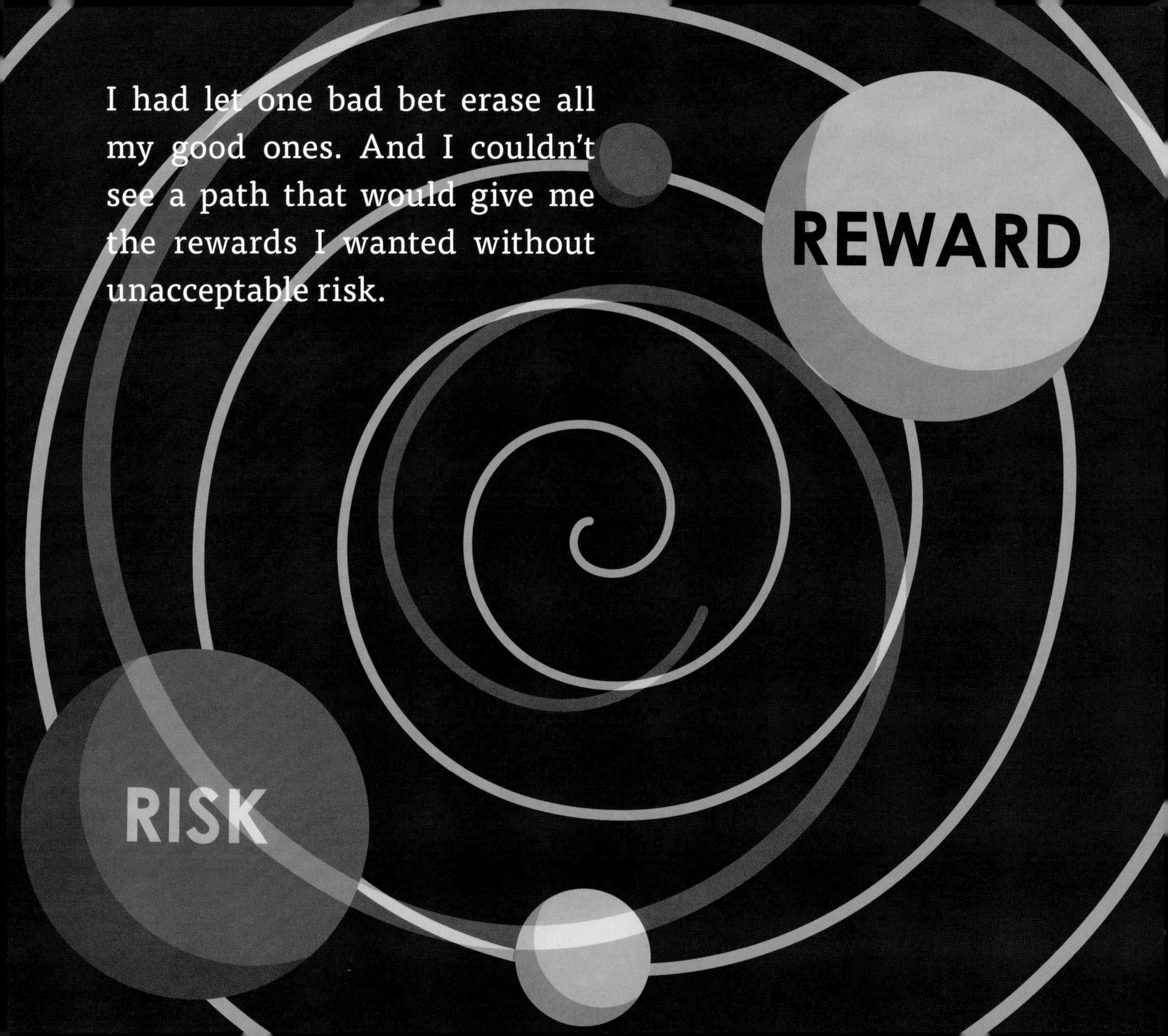
REWARD
RISK

Something like this will happen to you. You will lose something you think you can't live without, or suffer a terrible illness or injury, or your career will fall apart before your eyes.

You might think your life is ruined and there's no way to go forward...

But it will pass...

There is always a best path forward though you might not see it yet.

You just have to calm yourself down and reflect in order to find it...

...and then embrace your reality and deal with it well.

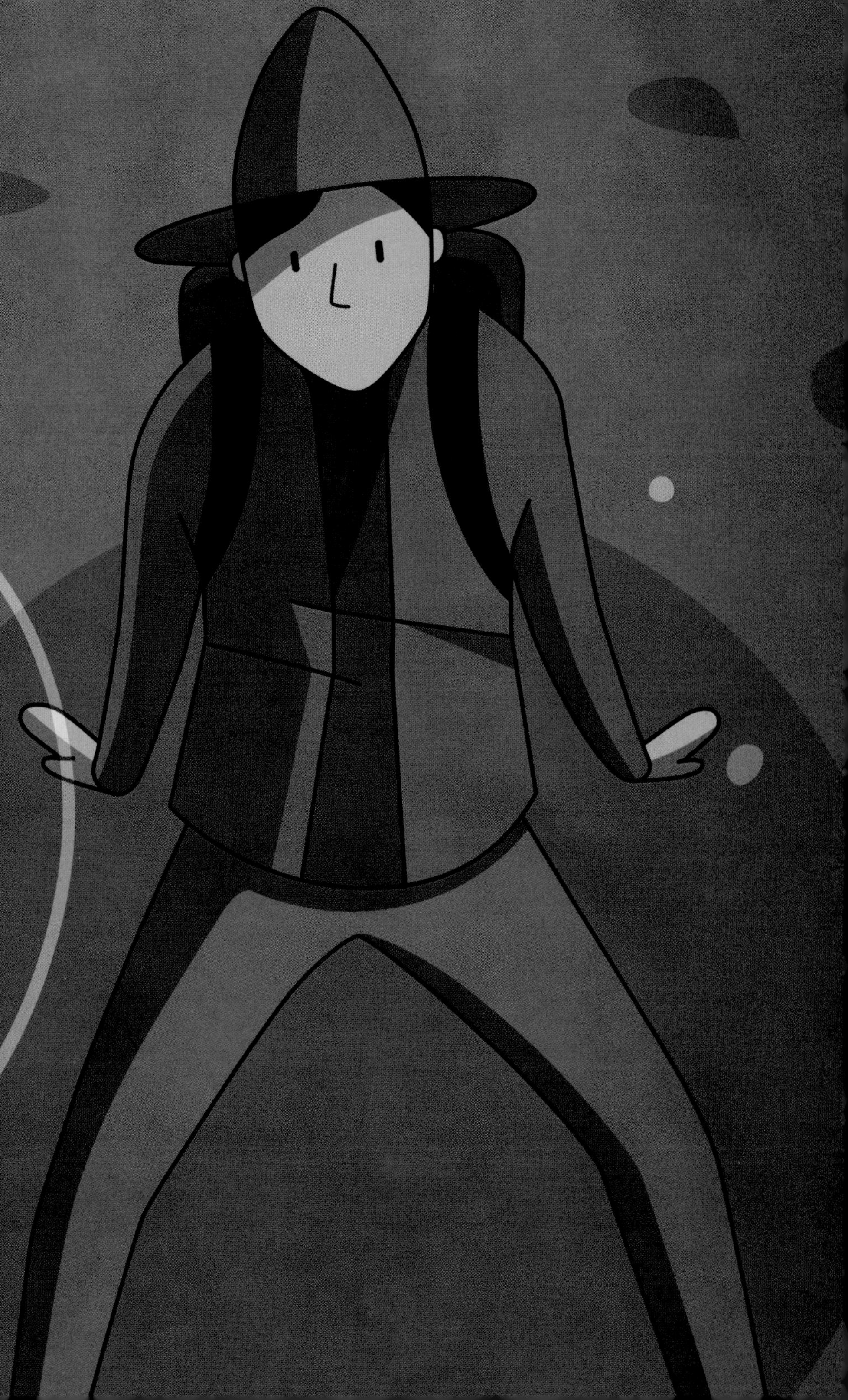

My pain led me to reflect on how things work, which helped to put things into perspective.

I saw that everything that happens is a result of causes that make it happen—and that all things that happen cause other things to happen so that reality works like a perpetual motion machine that goes on into eternity.

That is literally true.

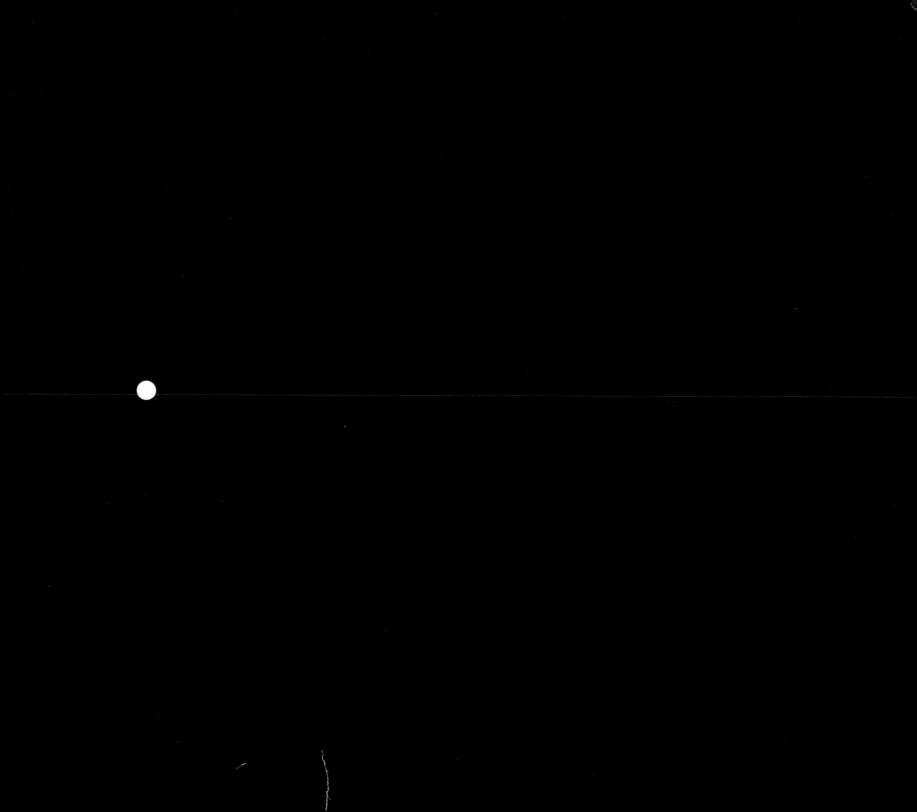

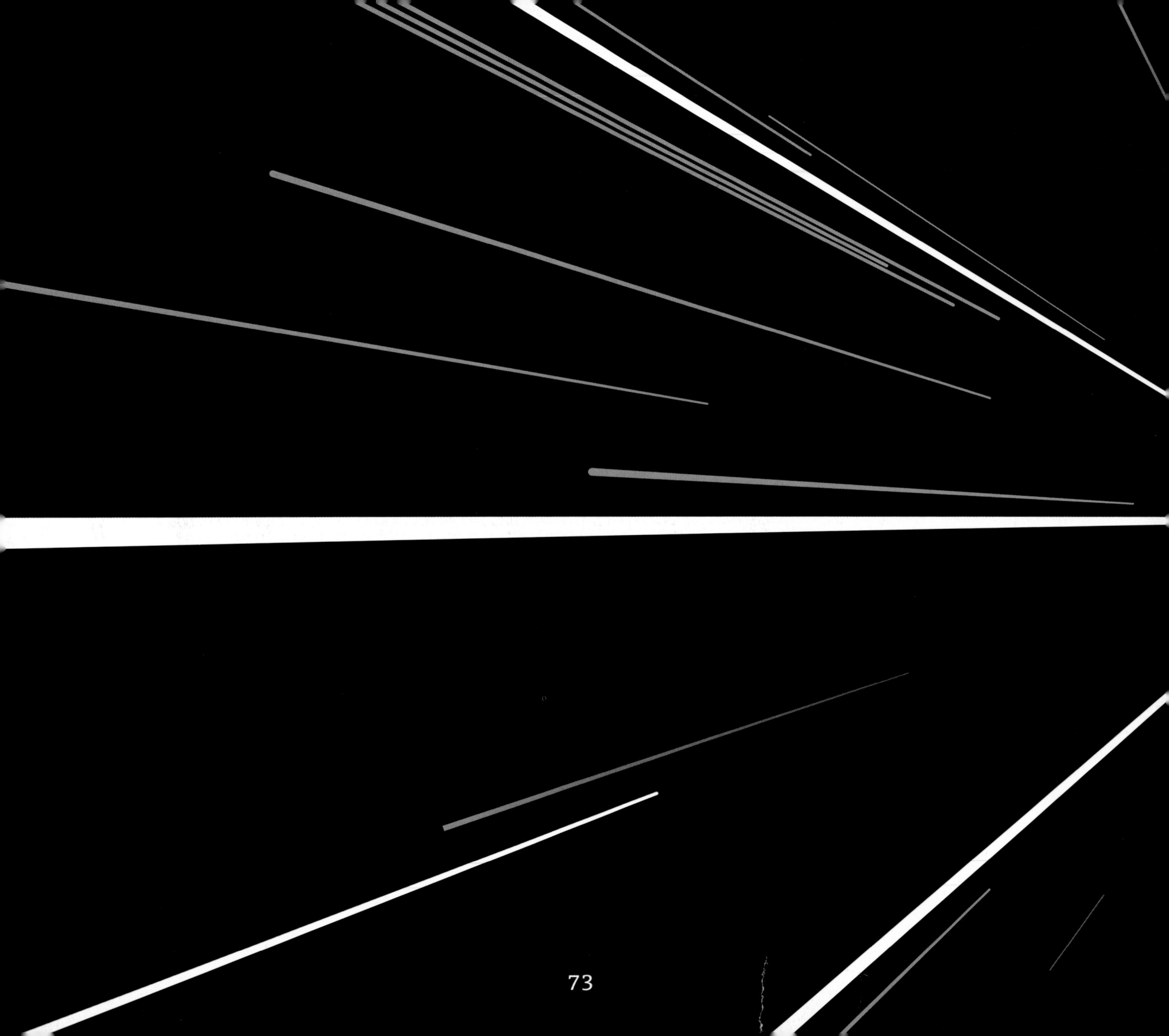

At the Big Bang, all the laws and forces of the universe were propelled forward, interacting with each other as a perpetual motion machine in which all the bits and pieces formed machines that worked for a while, fell apart, and then formed new machines.

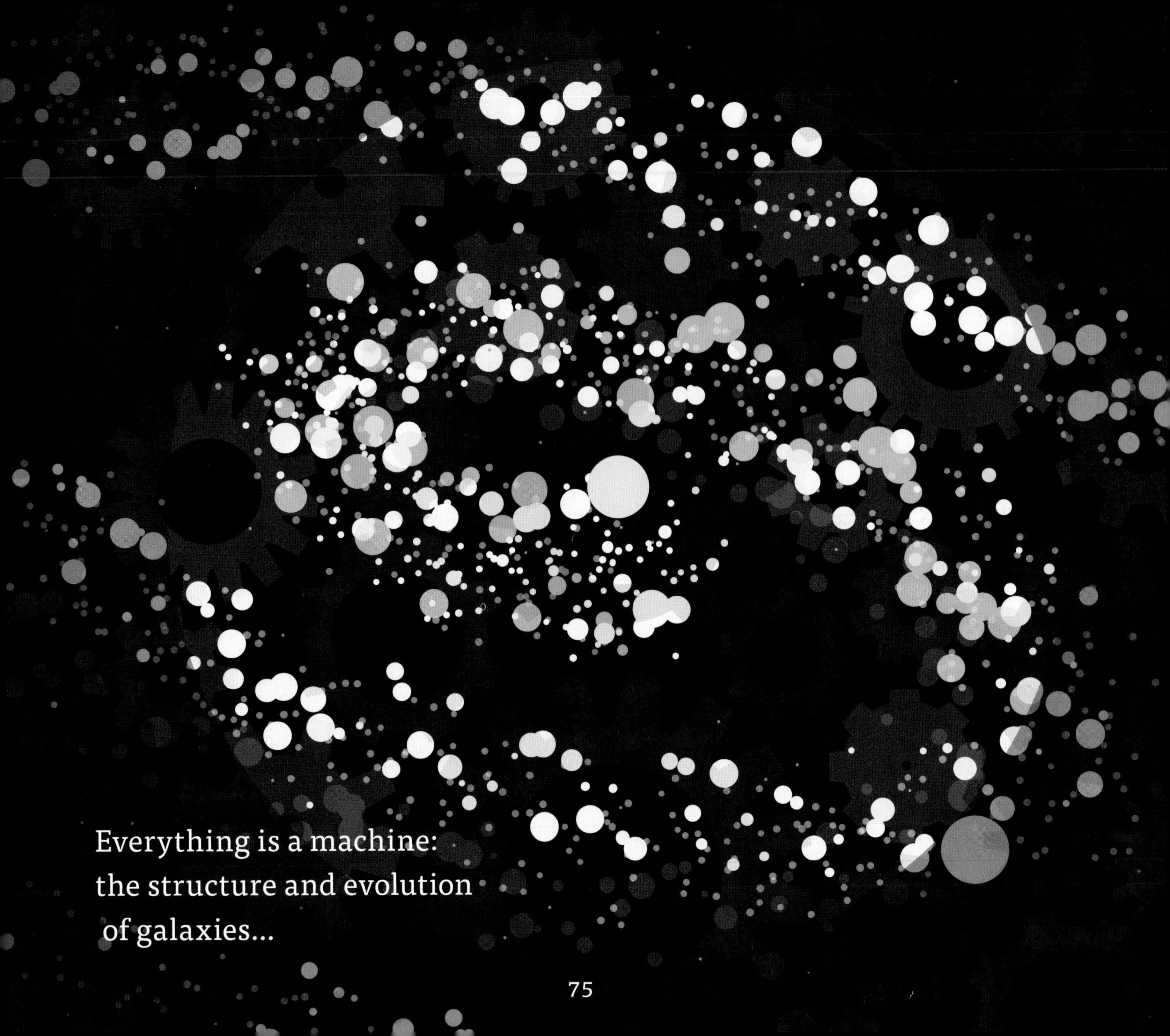

Everything is a machine:
the structure and evolution
of galaxies...

...the formation of our solar system, the make-up of Earth's geography and ecosystems...

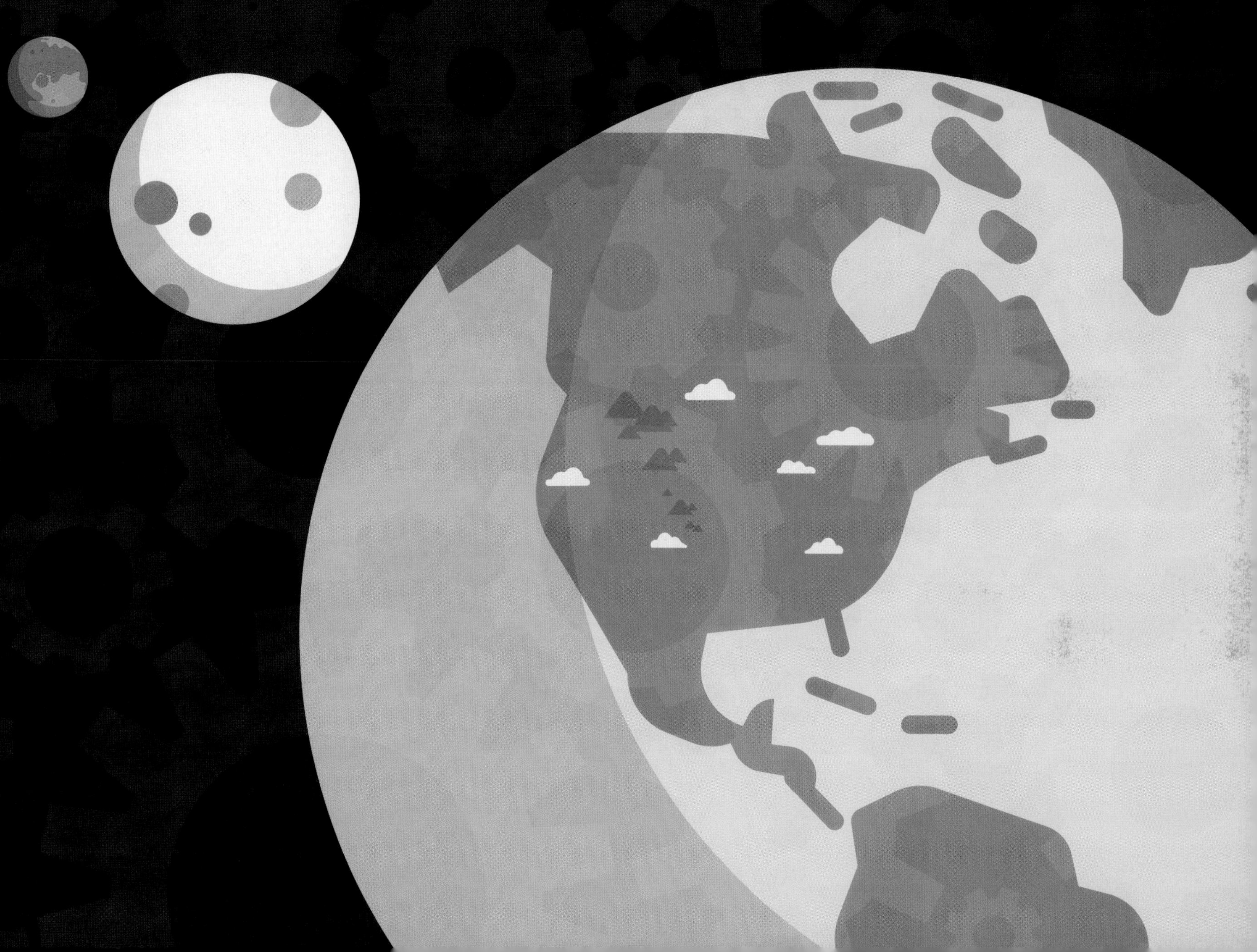

...our economies and markets...

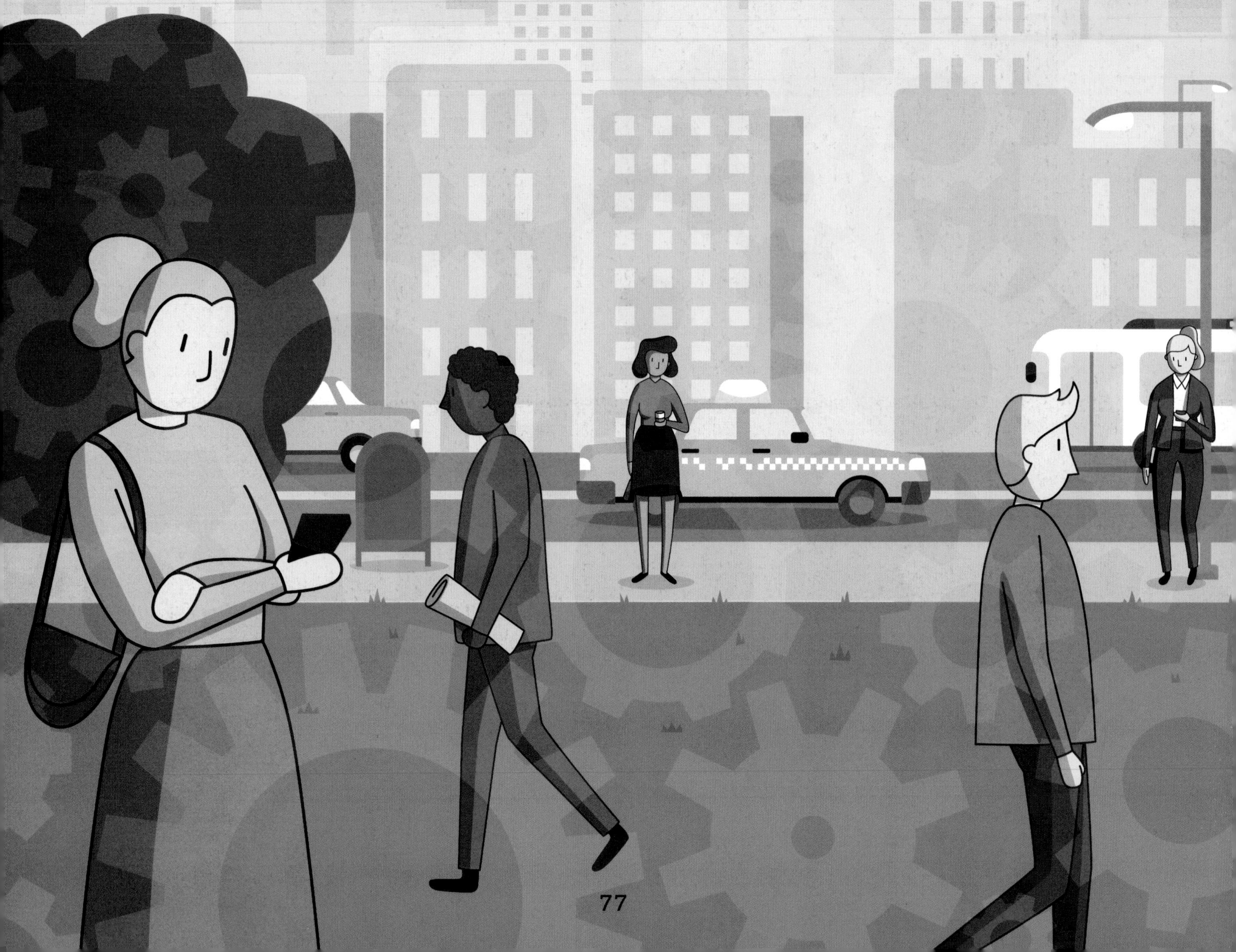

...and each of us.

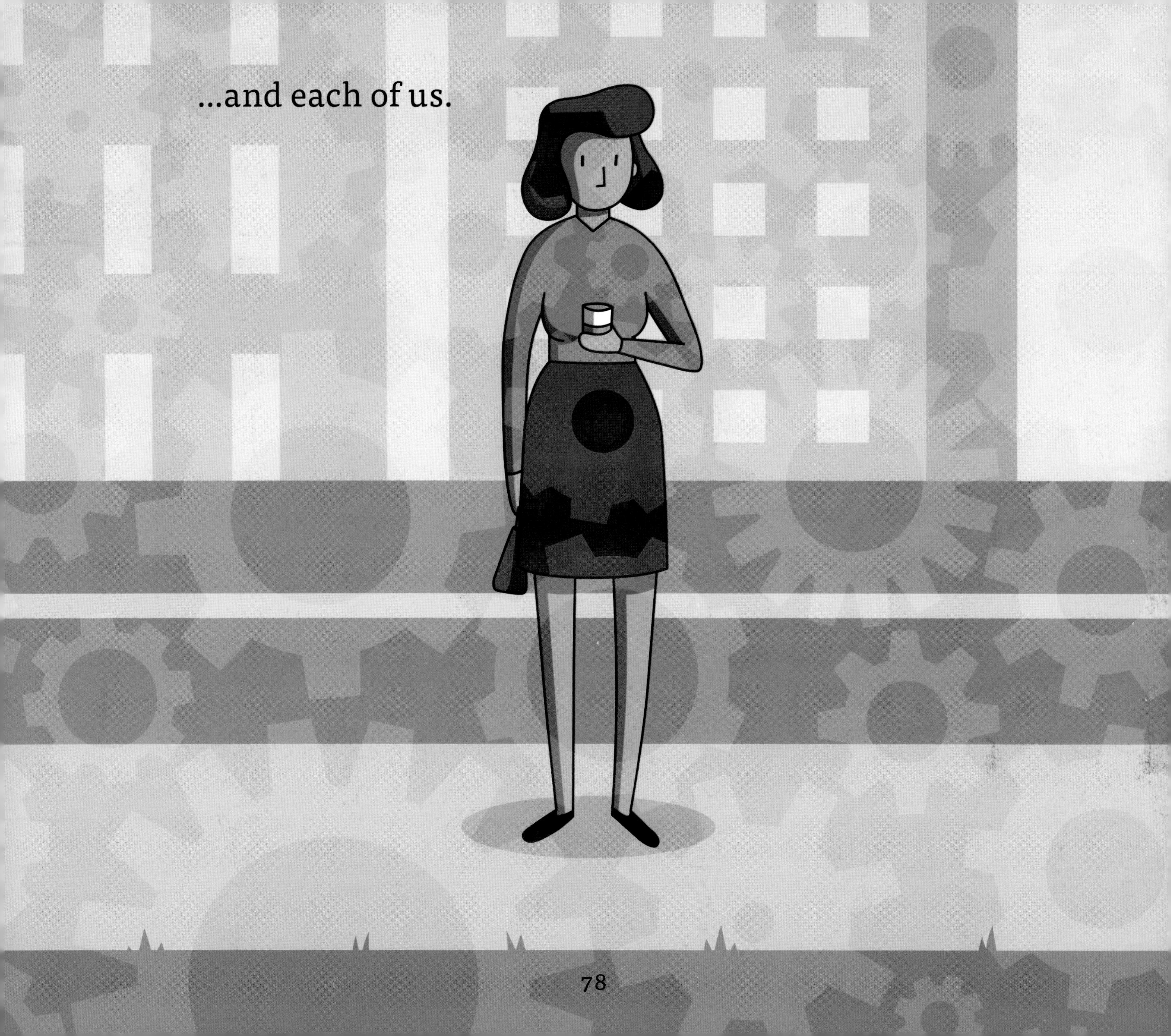

We are machines made up of machines—our circulatory system, our nervous system, etc.—that produce thoughts, dreams, emotions, and everything else.

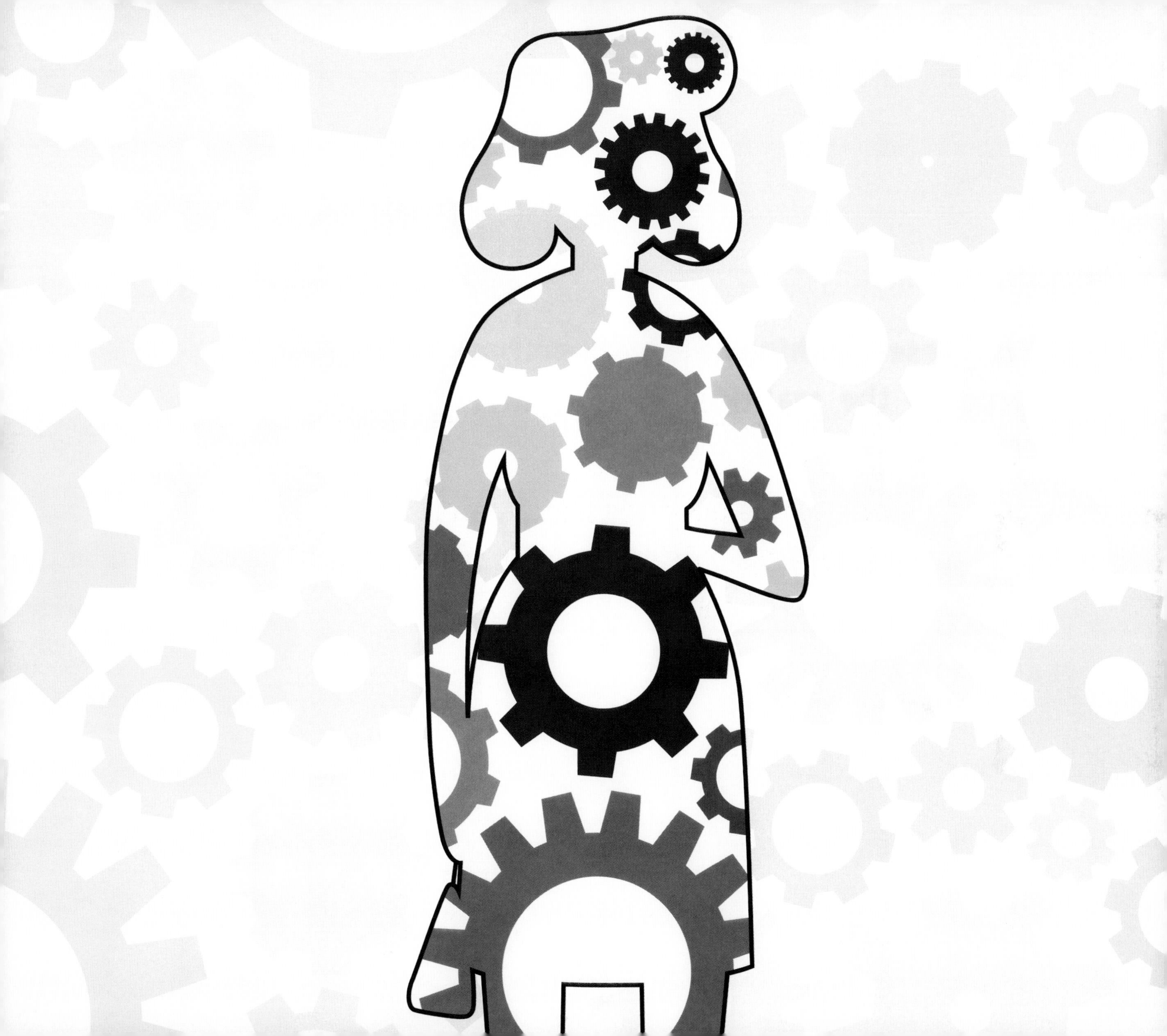

All of these machines evolve together to produce the realities we encounter every day.

That sounds philosophical, but I found it practical because it put things in perspective and helped me deal with my realities in a better way.

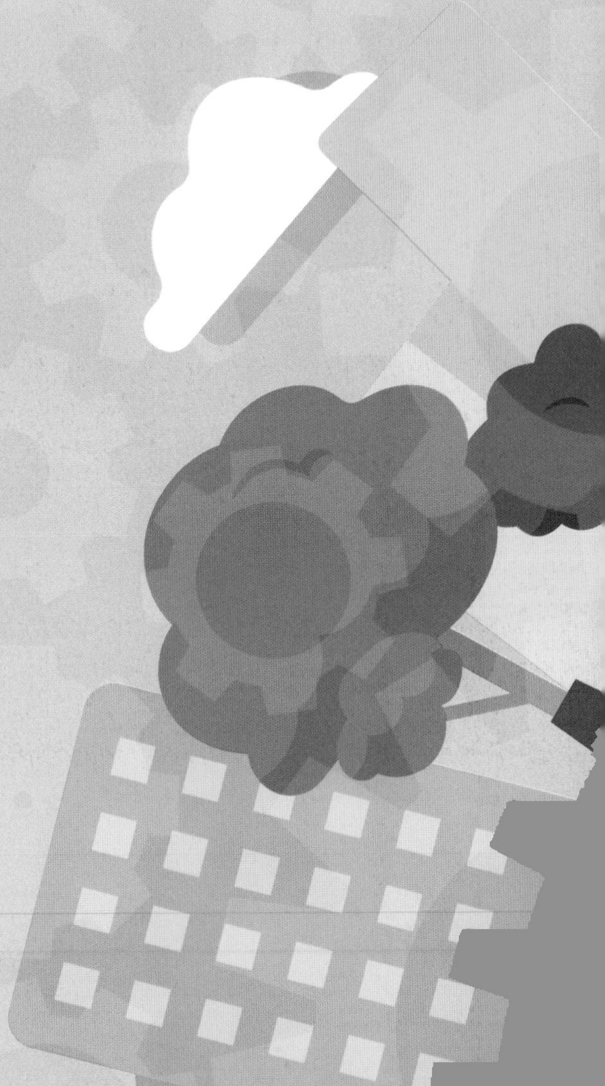

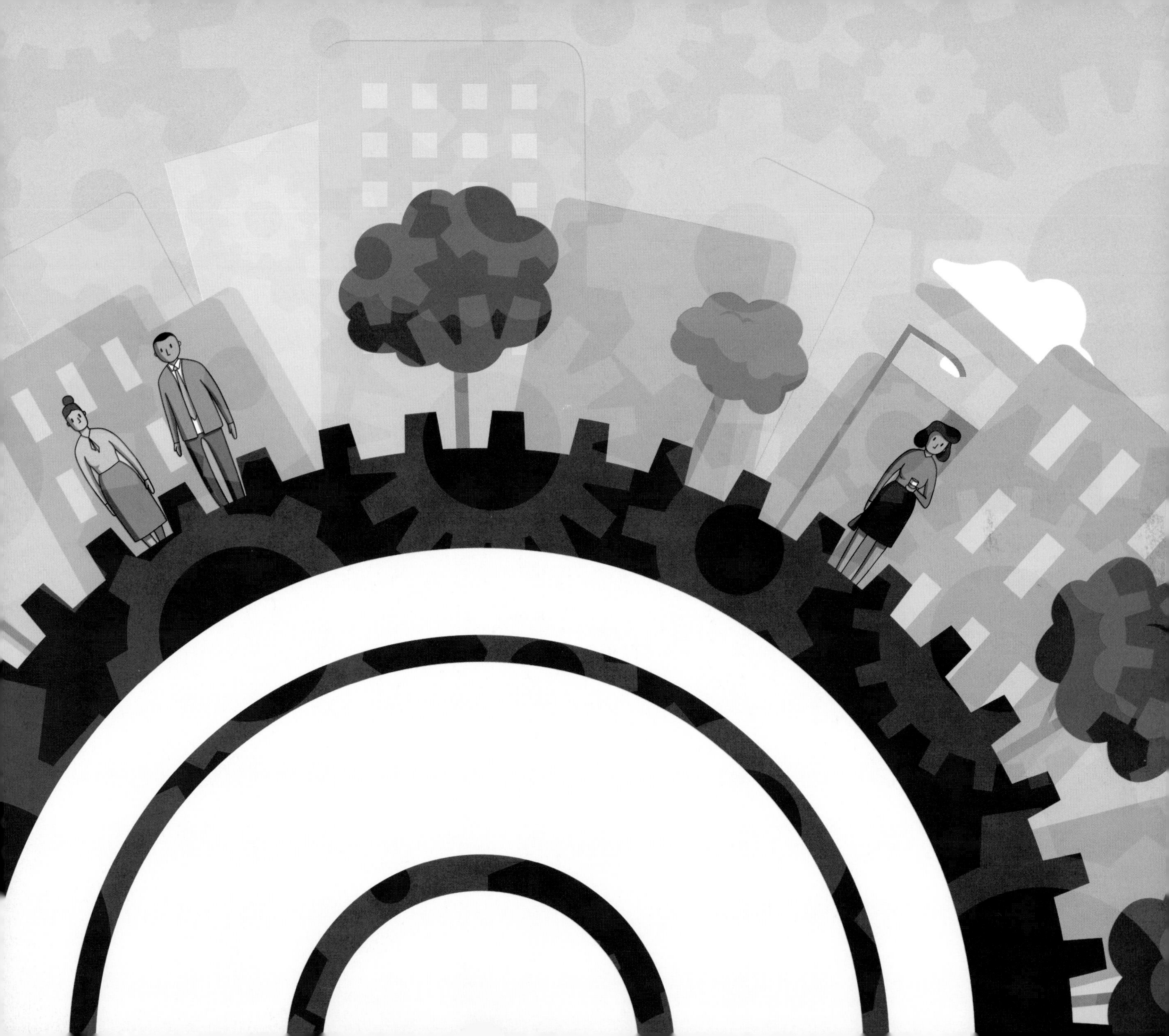

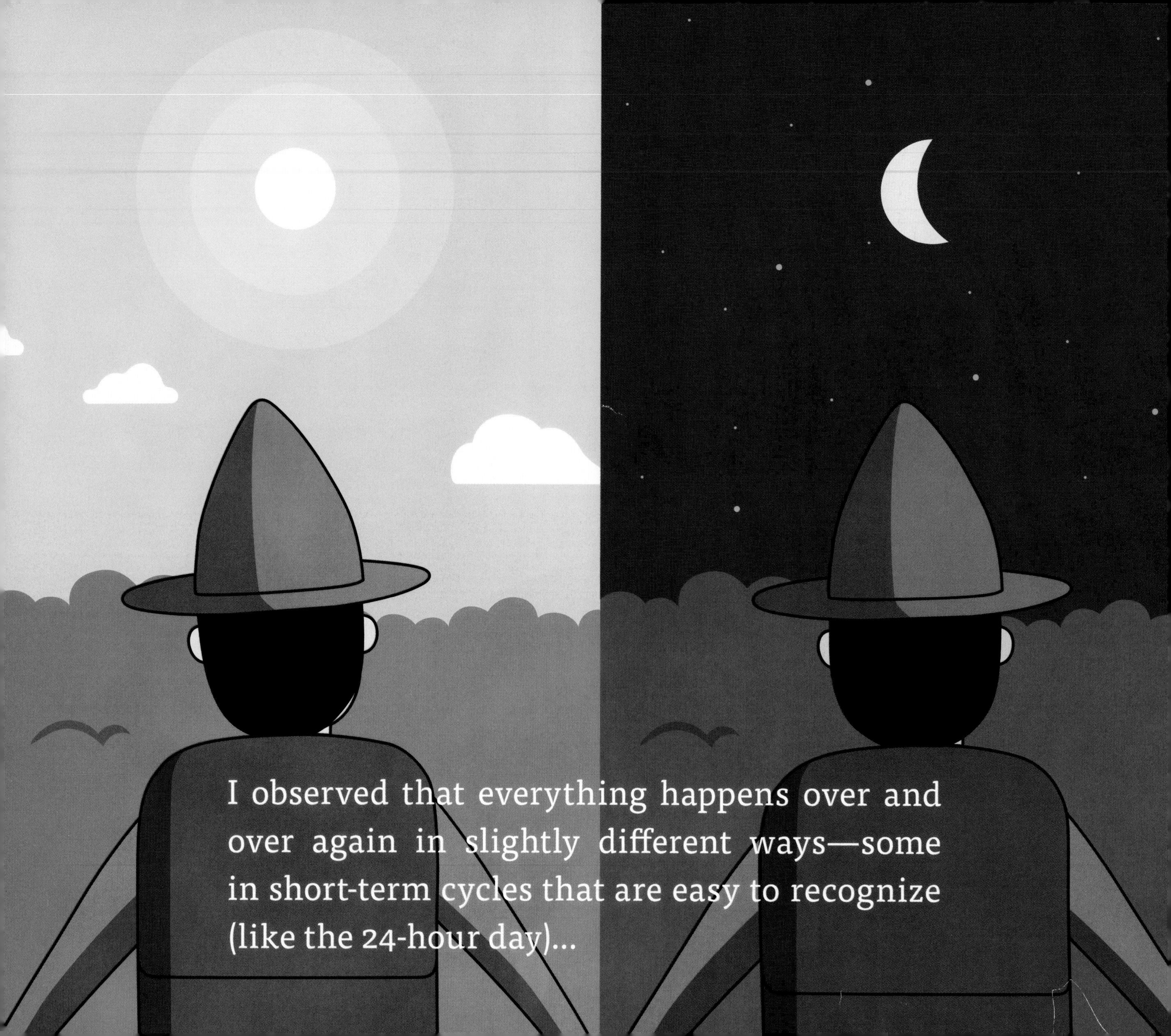

I observed that everything happens over and over again in slightly different ways—some in short-term cycles that are easy to recognize (like the 24-hour day)...

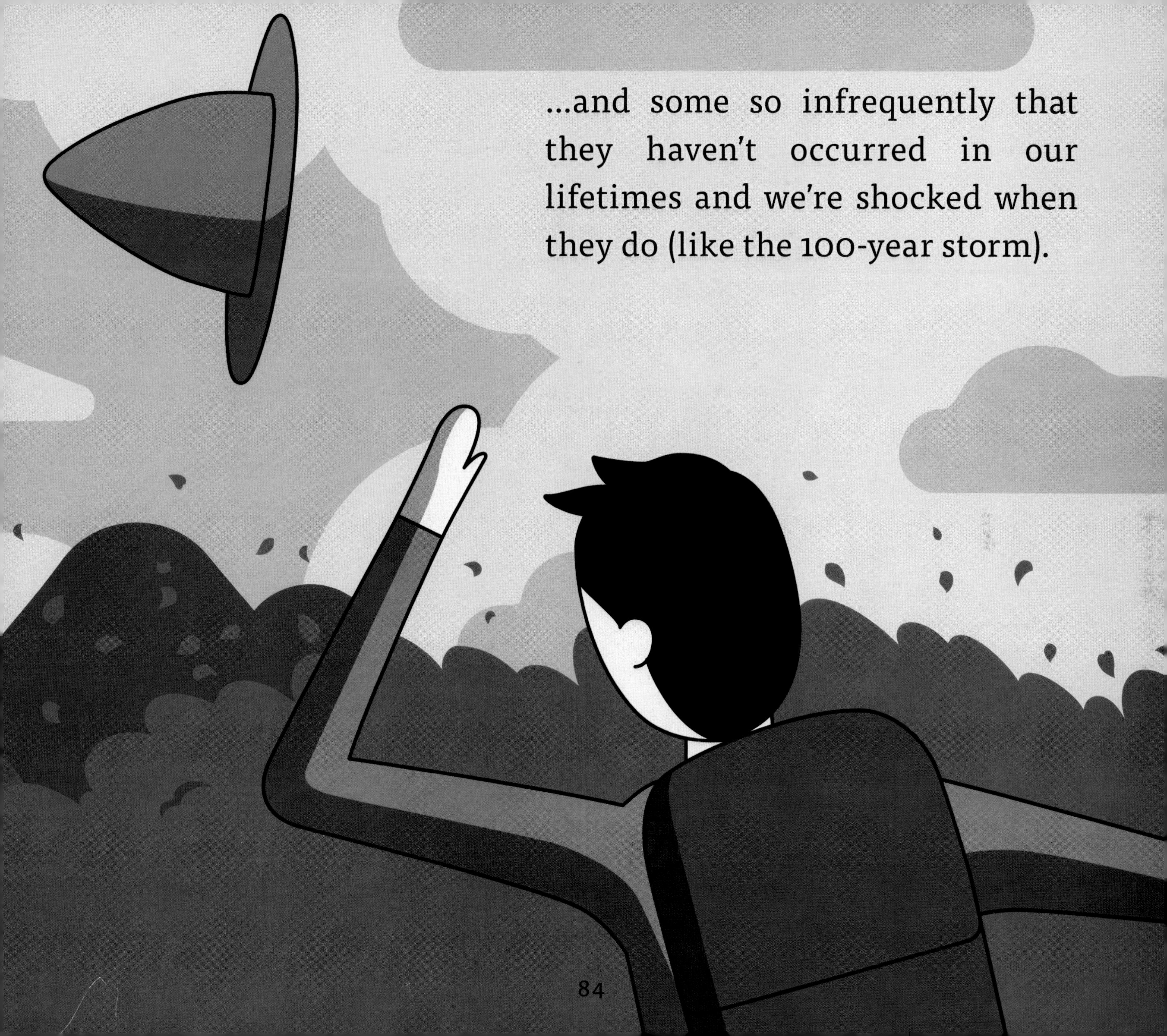

...and some so infrequently that they haven't occurred in our lifetimes and we're shocked when they do (like the 100-year storm).

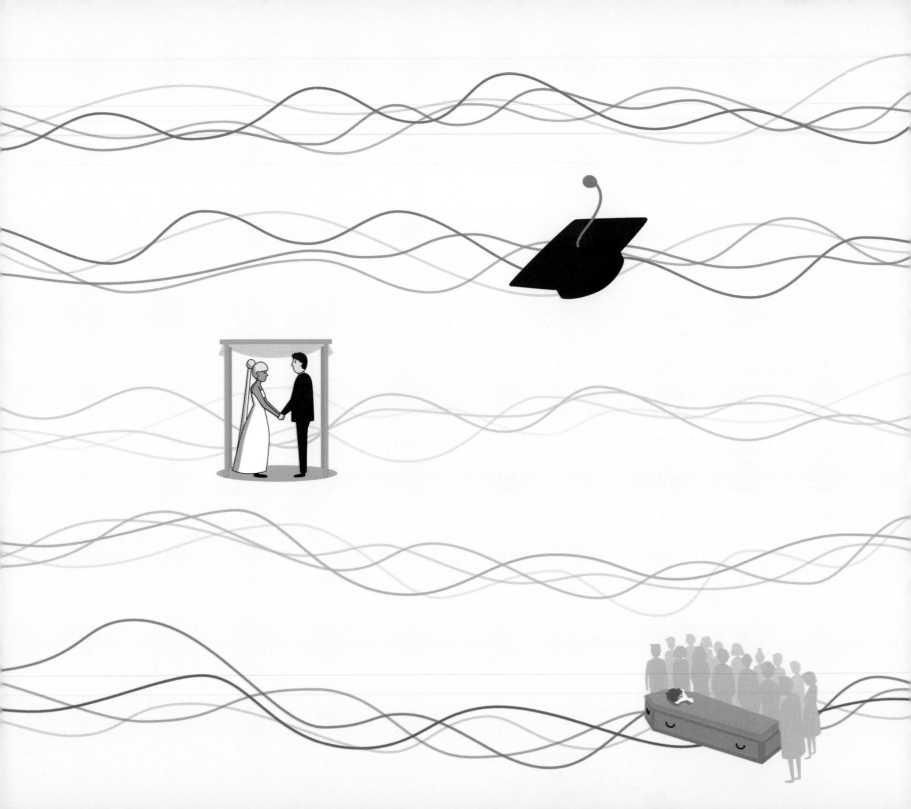

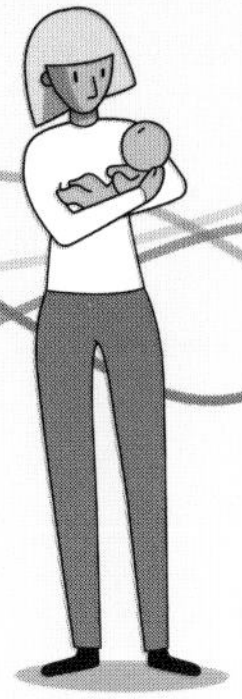

Rather than seeing a whole lot of things coming at me, I could see each one as "just another one of those." And I could see the cause-effect relationships that governed them and develop principles for dealing with them that I could express in both words and computer code.

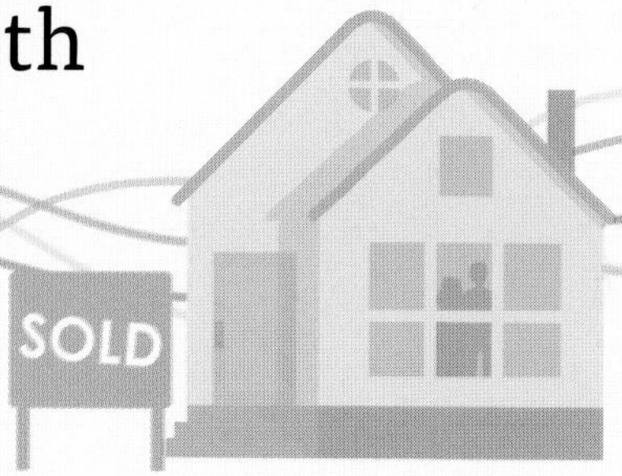
SOLD

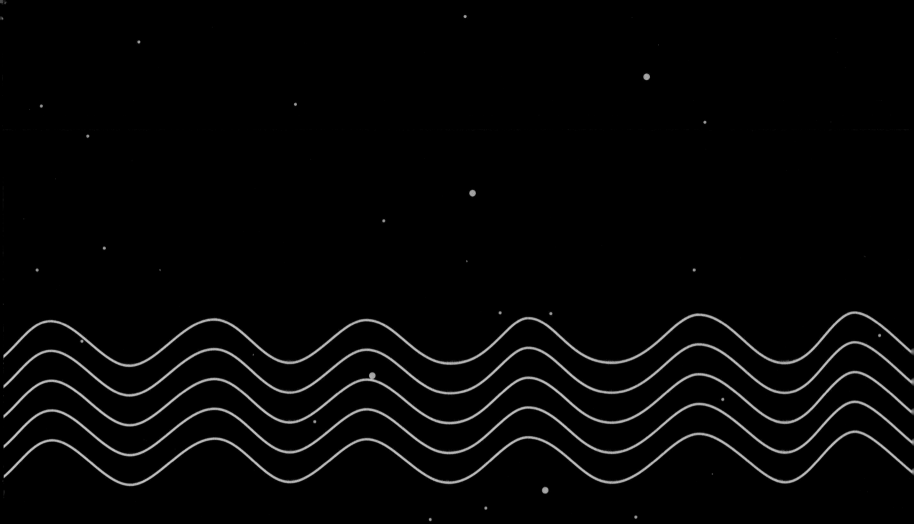

I observed that people are biased by recent history and overlook events that haven't happened in a long time, especially if they haven't happened to them.

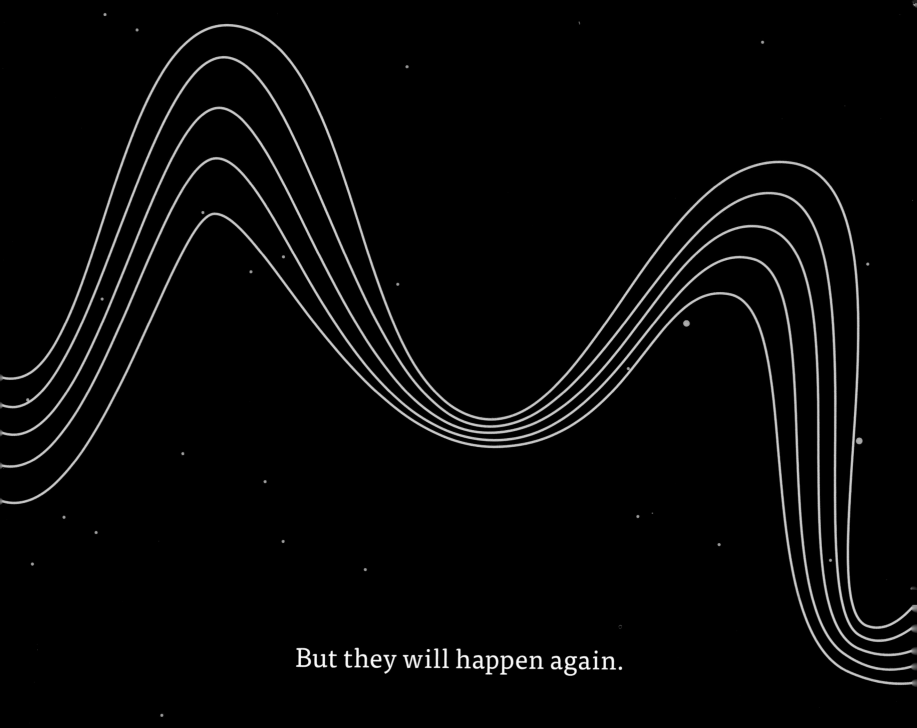

But they will happen again.

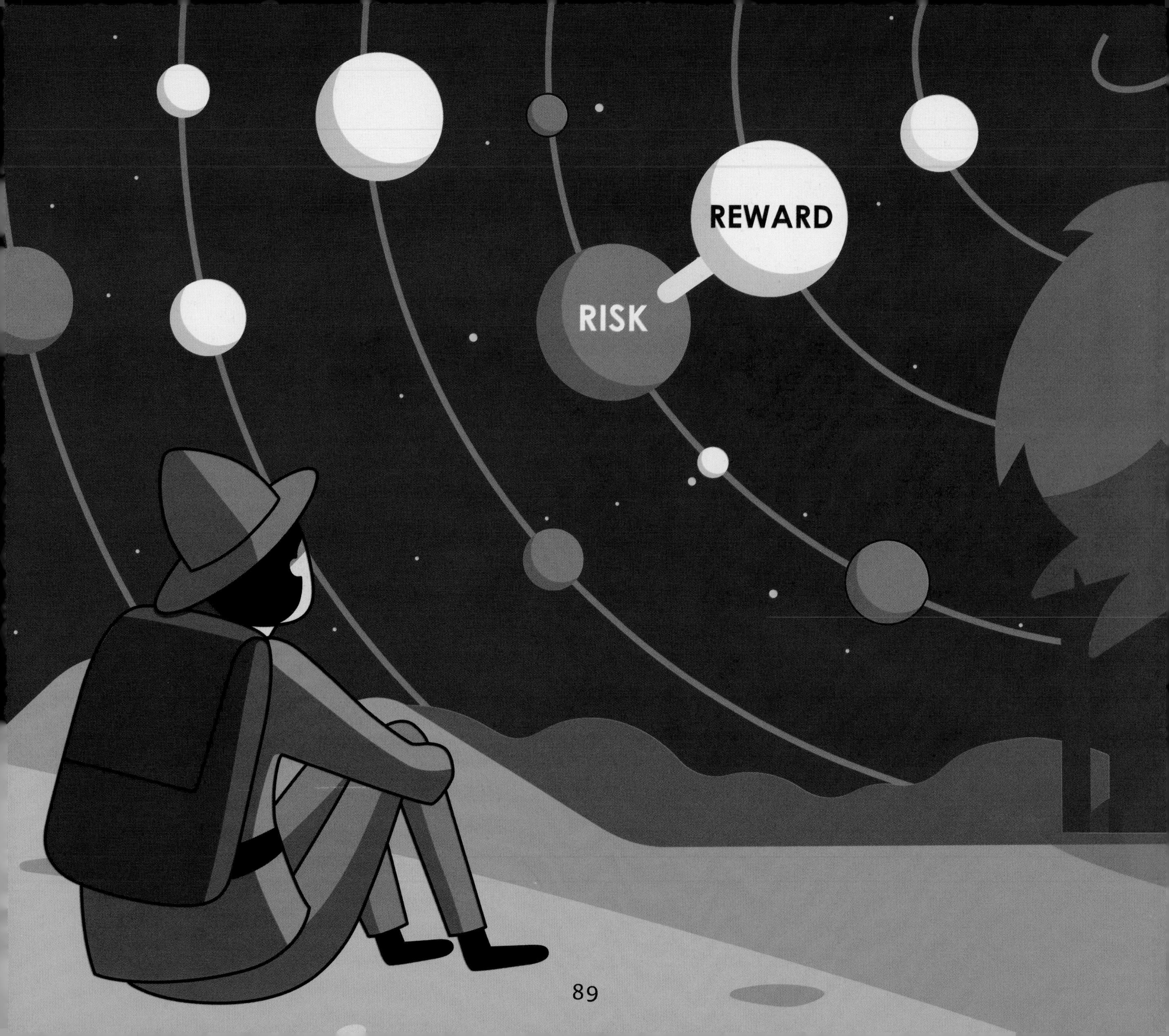
REWARD
RISK

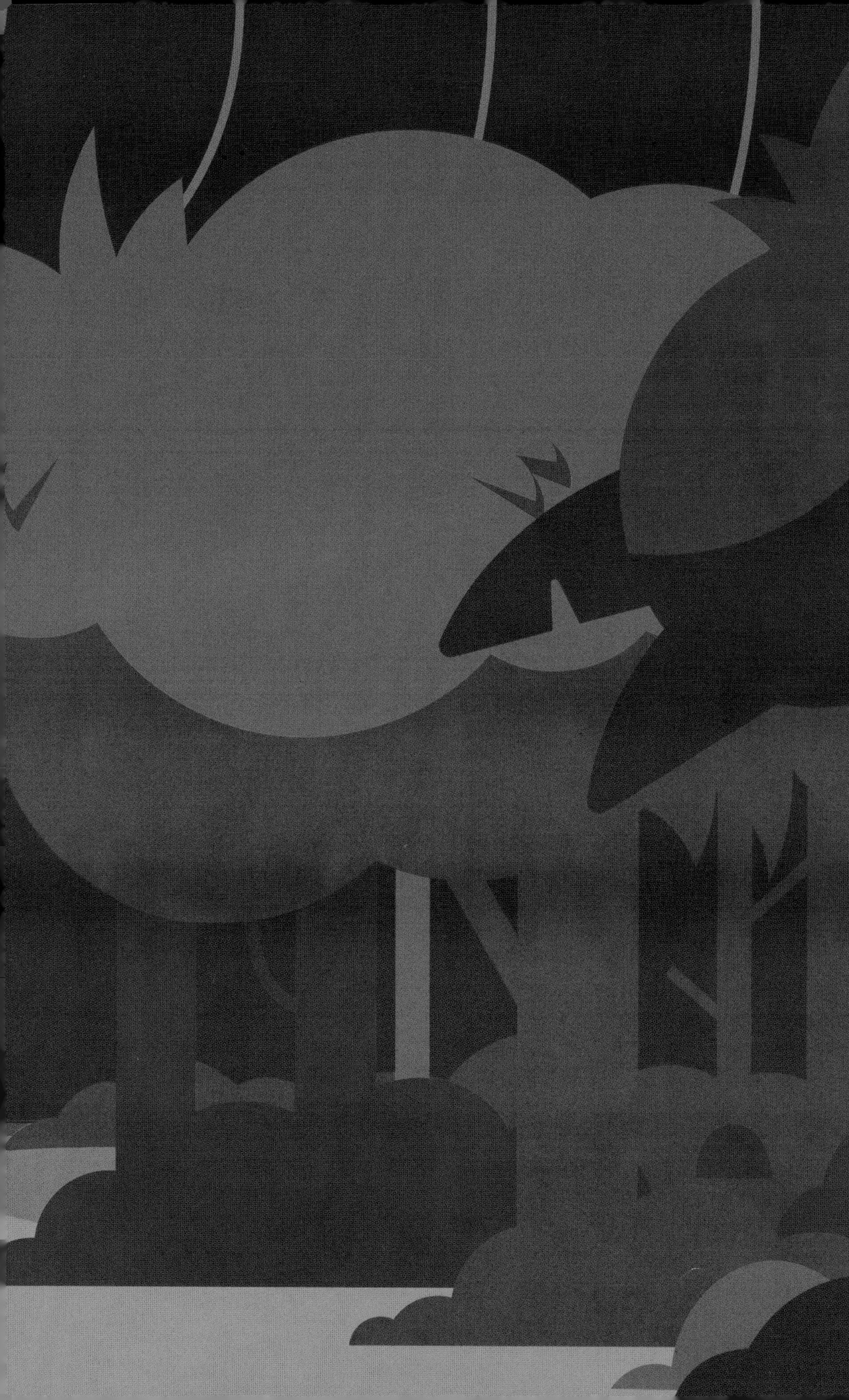

And when I thought about my challenge balancing risk and reward...I realized that risk and reward naturally go together.

I could see that to get more out of life one has to take more risk...and that knowing how to appropriately balance risk and reward is essential to having the best life possible.

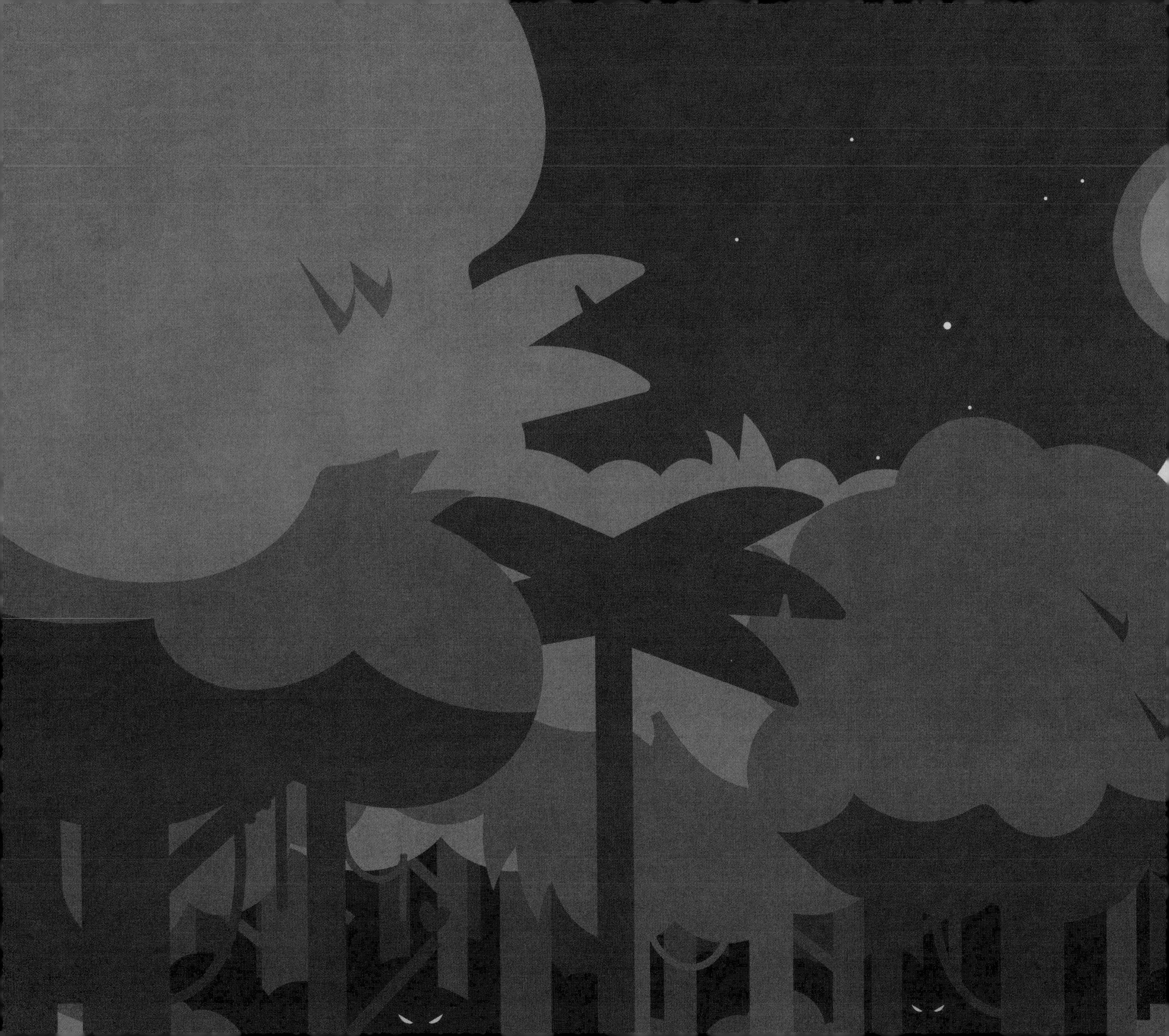

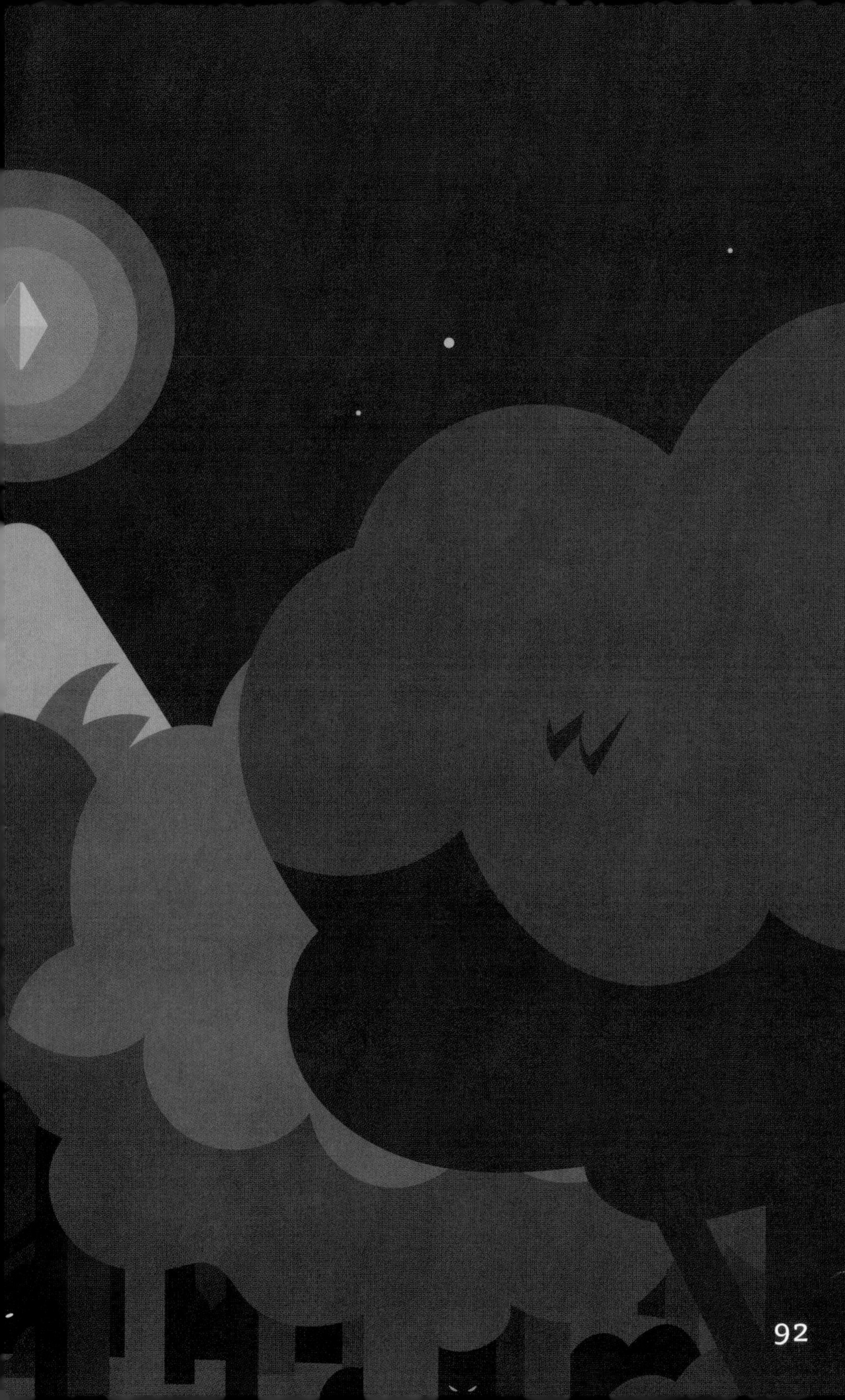

Imagine you are faced with a choice. You can have a safe, ordinary life if you stay where you are or you can have a fabulous one if you can successfully cross a dangerous jungle.

How would you approach that choice?

I can't tell you which path is best for you. We each have to decide for ourselves.

As for me, I needed to have the best life possible so I needed to figure out how to successfully deal with the big risks to get the big rewards.

To cross the jungle, I needed to see more than I alone could see. But standing in my way were the two biggest barriers everyone faces...

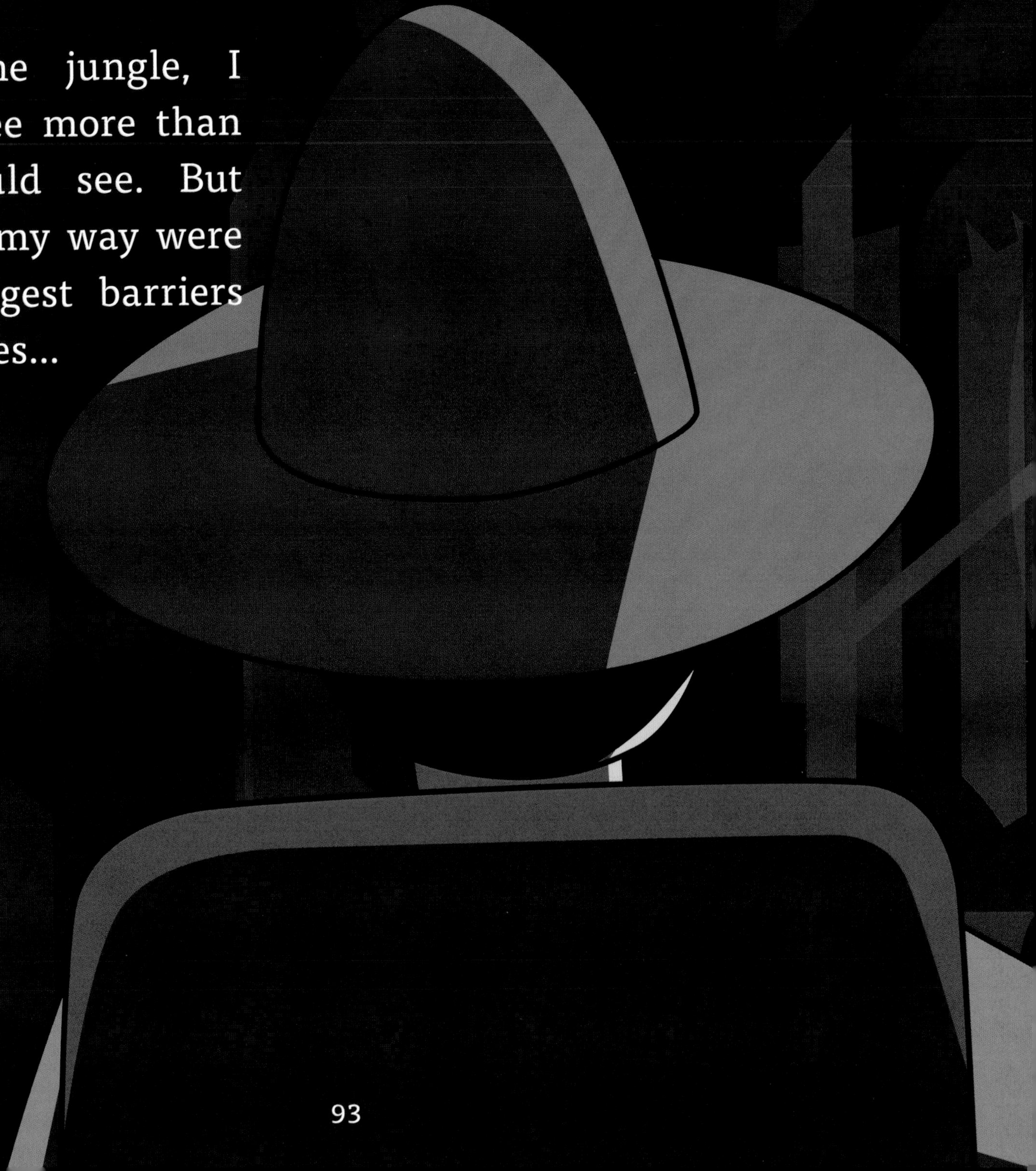

OUR EGO AND BLIND SPOT BARRIERS

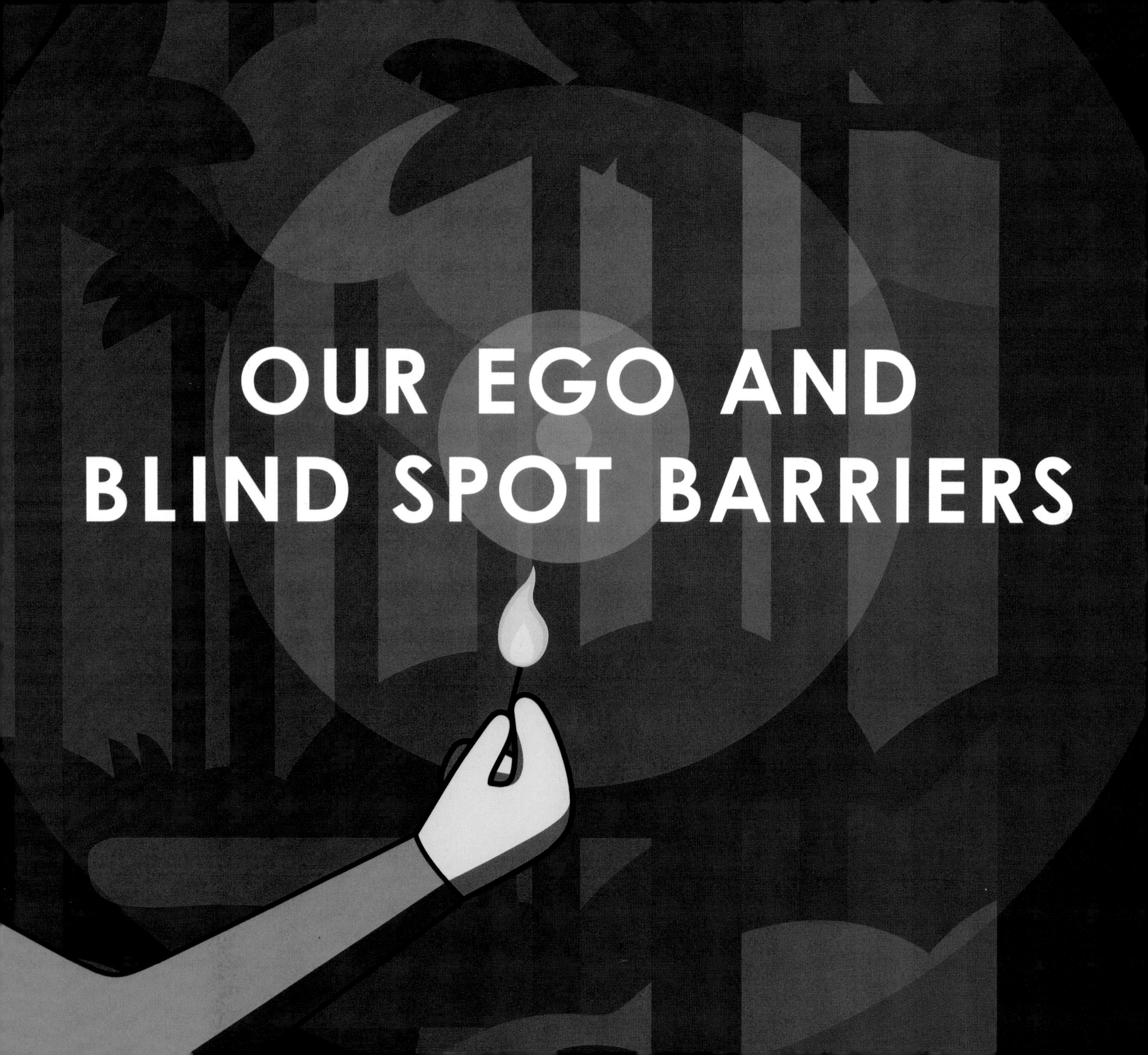

Our Ego Barrier prevents us from acknowledging our weaknesses.

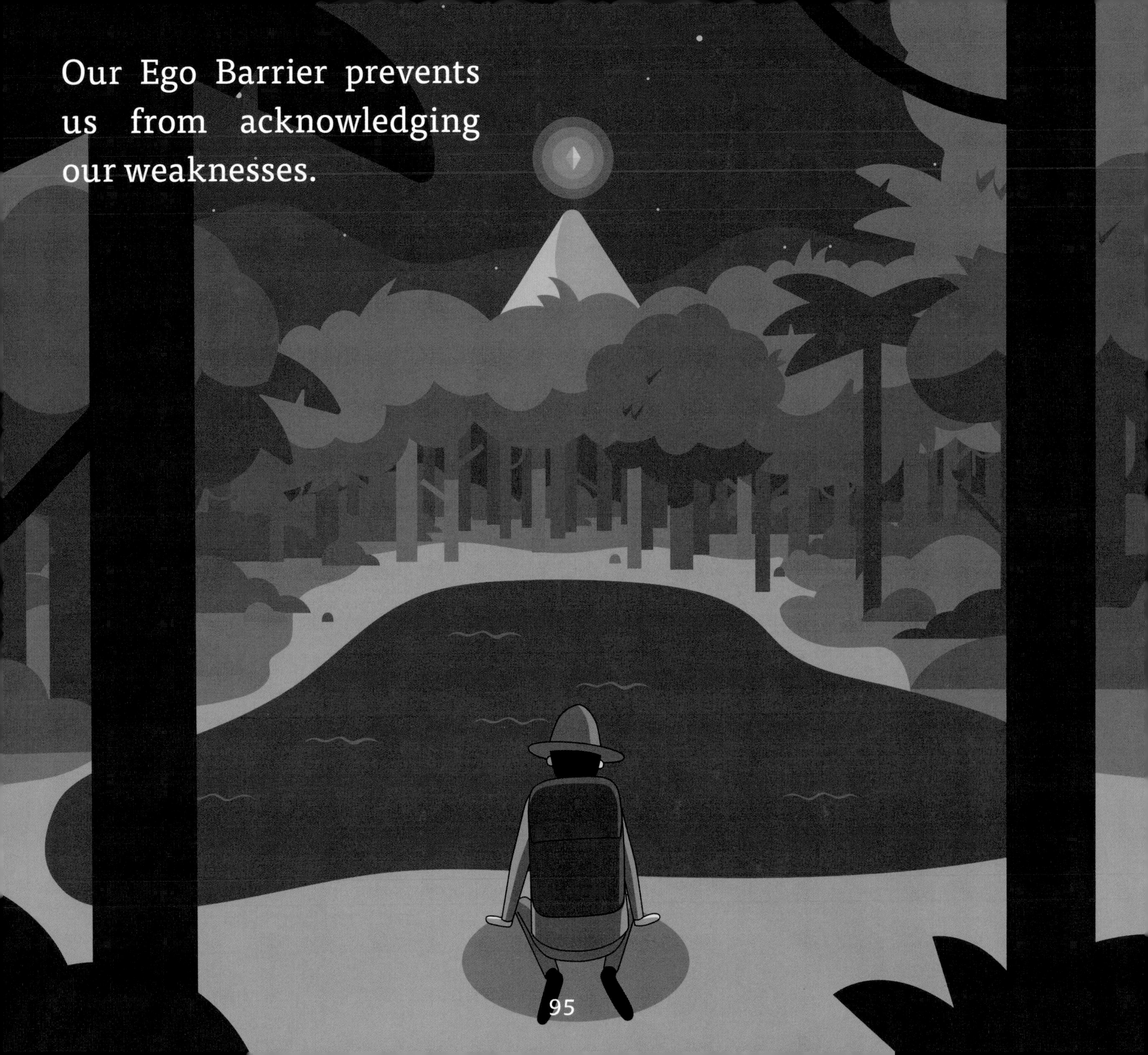

Our need to be right can come before our need to know what's true...so we believe our opinions without testing them.

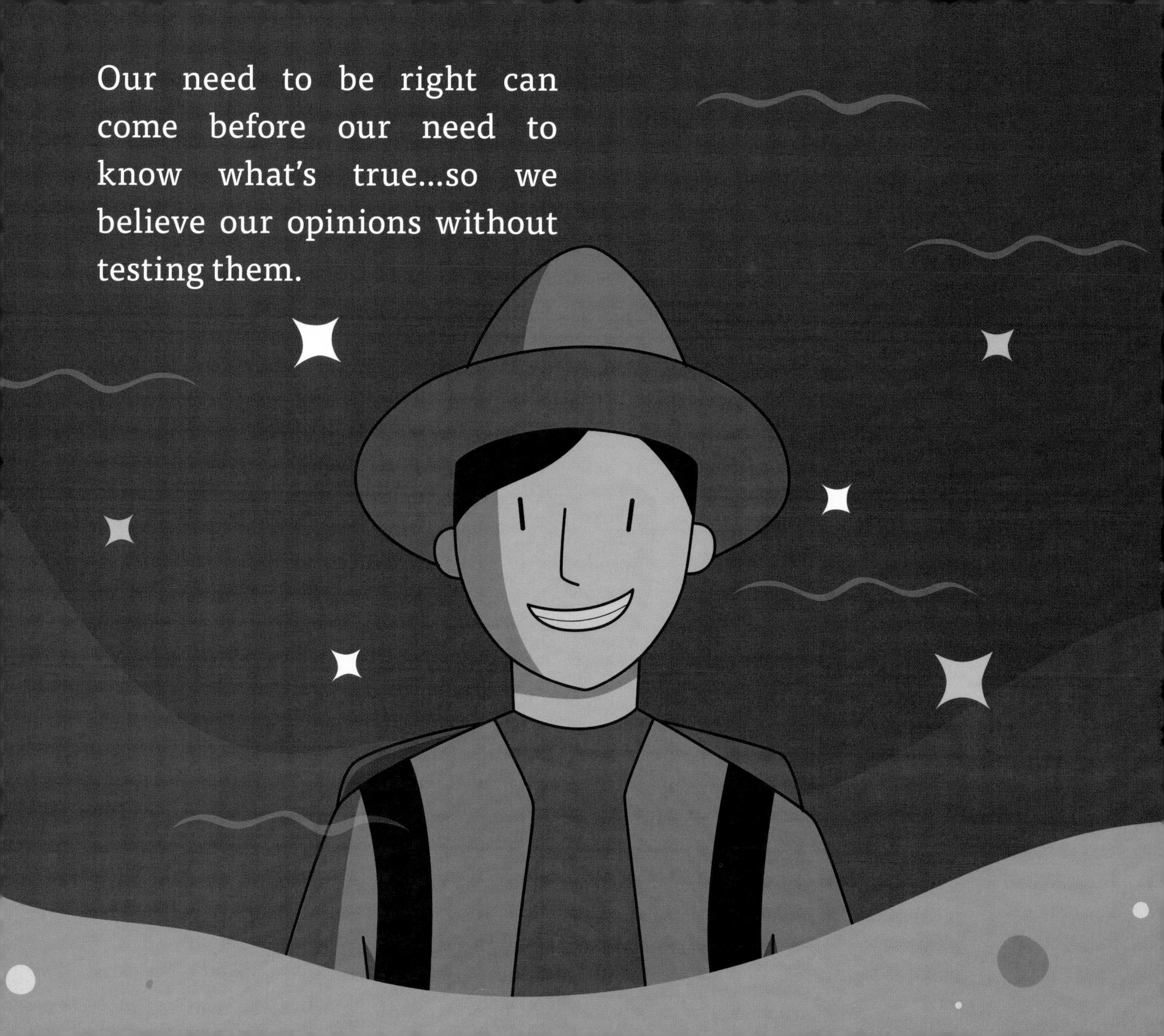

We especially don't like to look at our mistakes and weaknesses. We are instinctively prone to react to explorations of them as attacks.

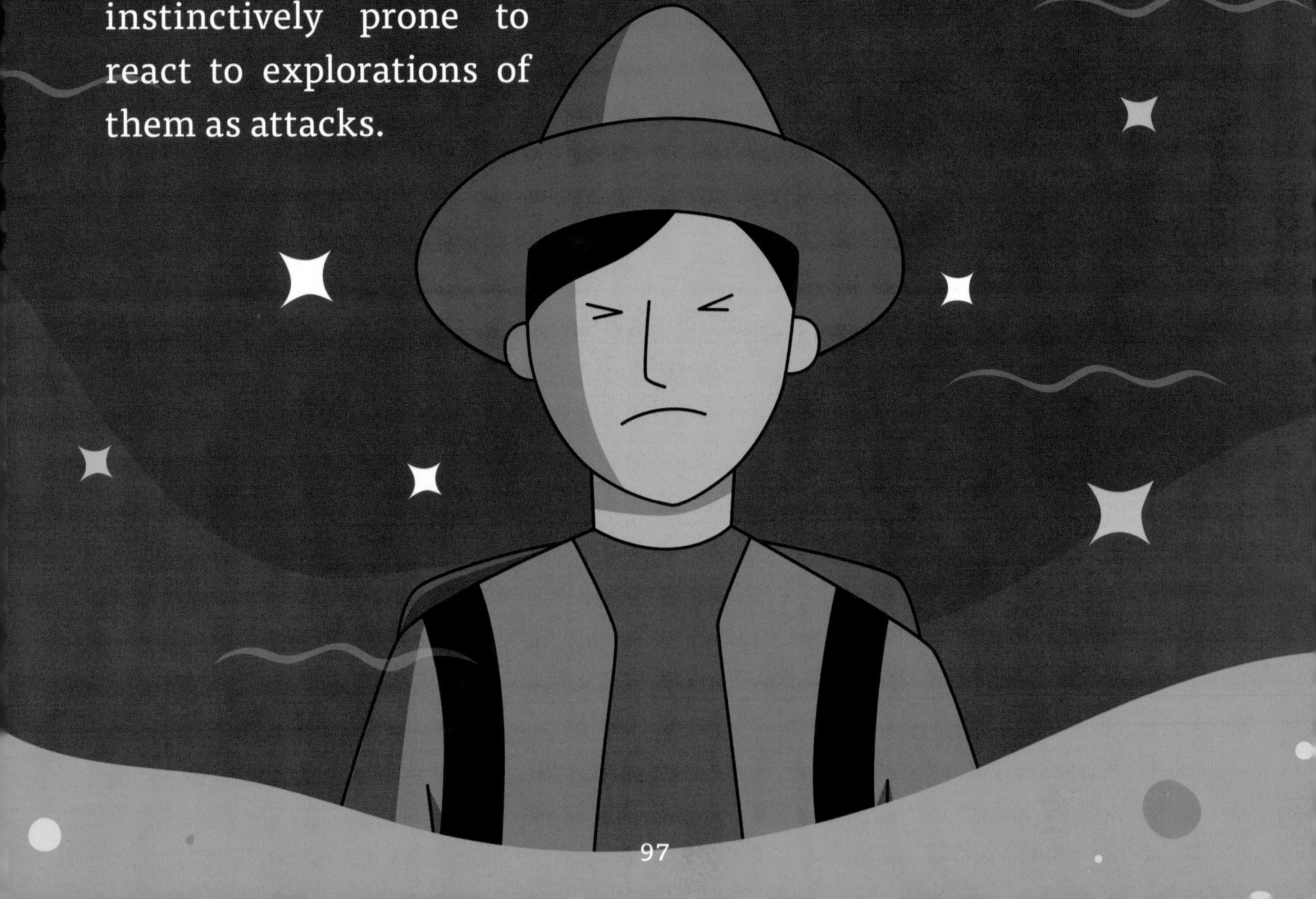

This leads to worse decisions, learning less, and falling short of our potentials.

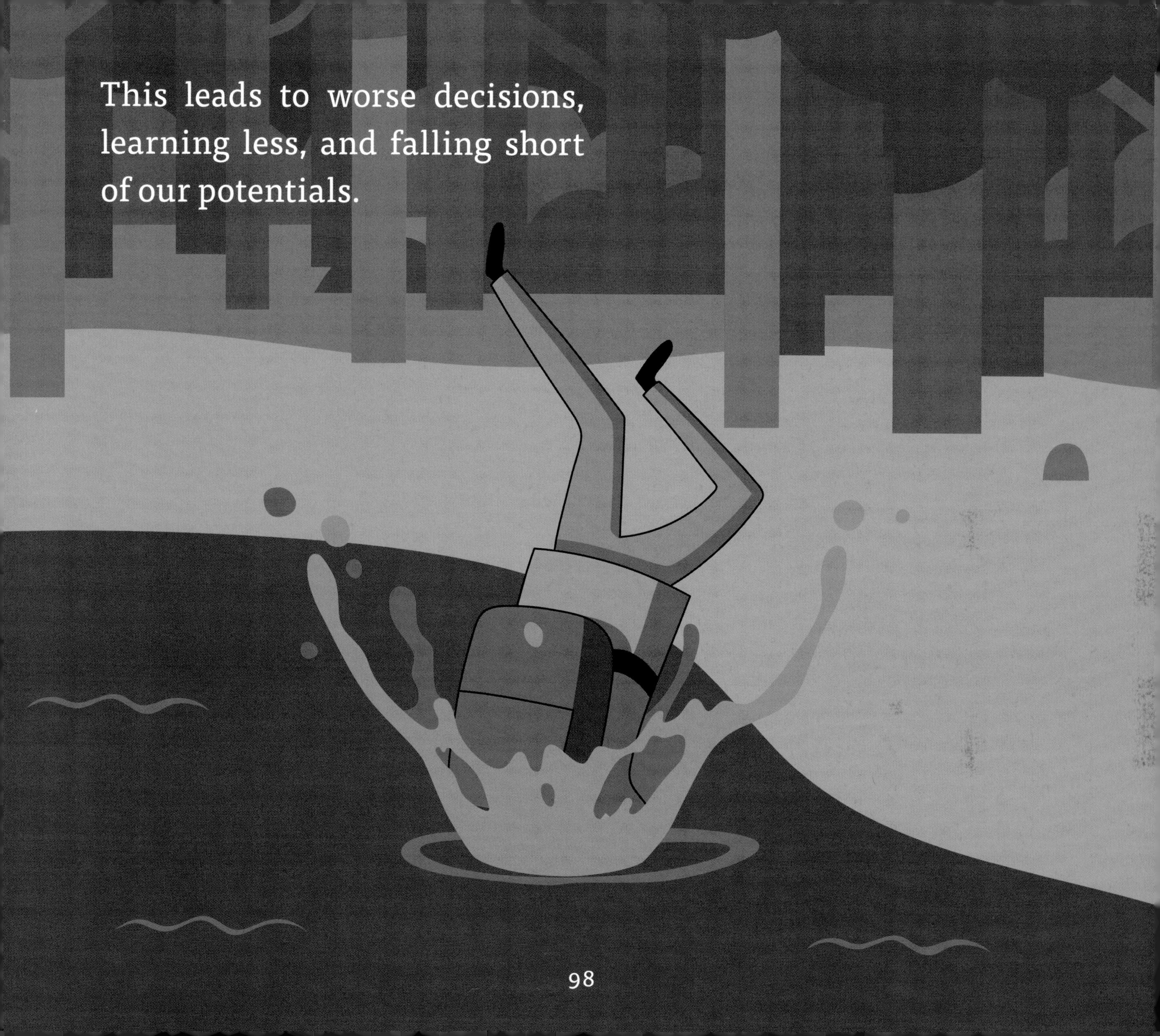

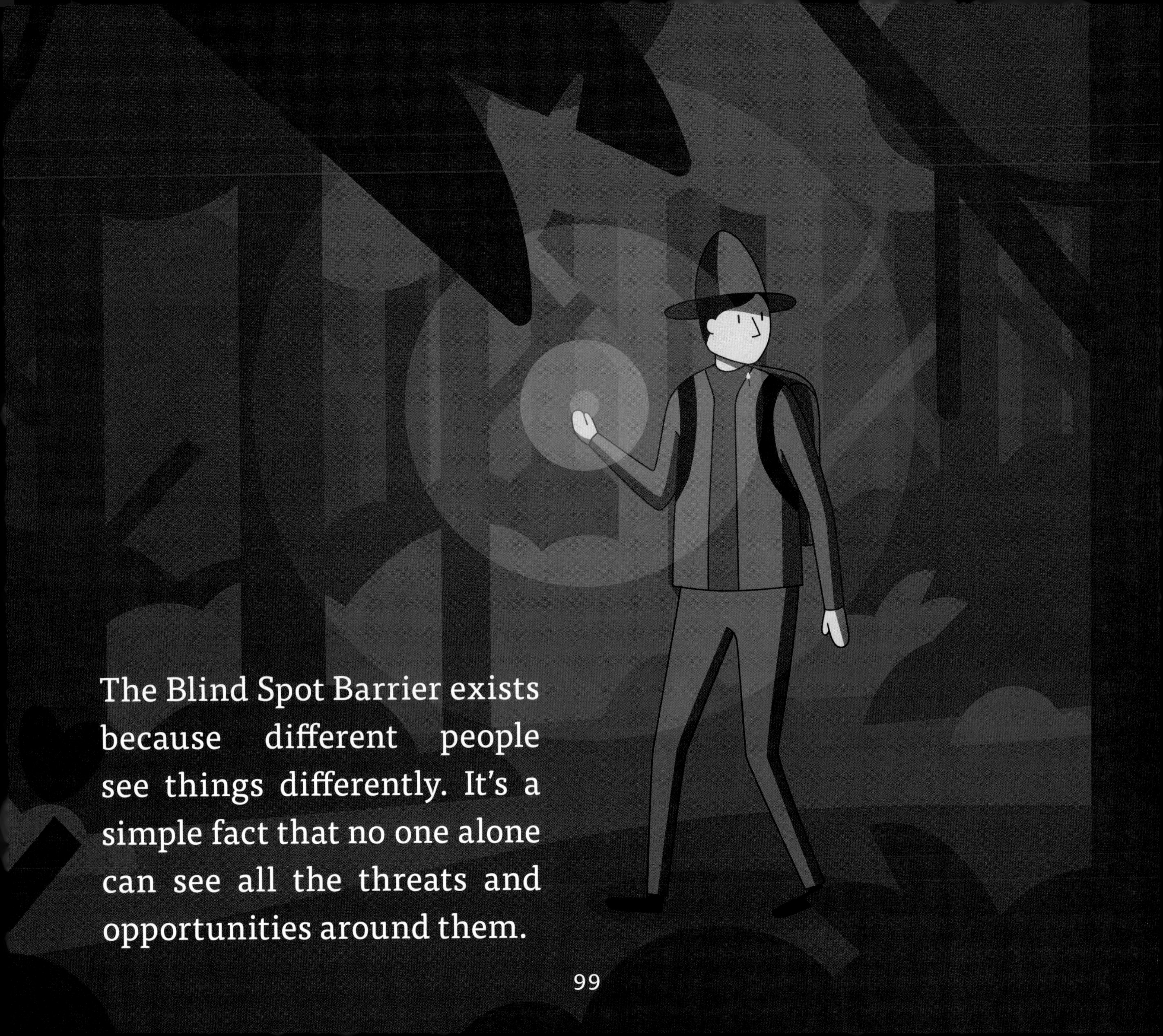

The Blind Spot Barrier exists because different people see things differently. It's a simple fact that no one alone can see all the threats and opportunities around them.

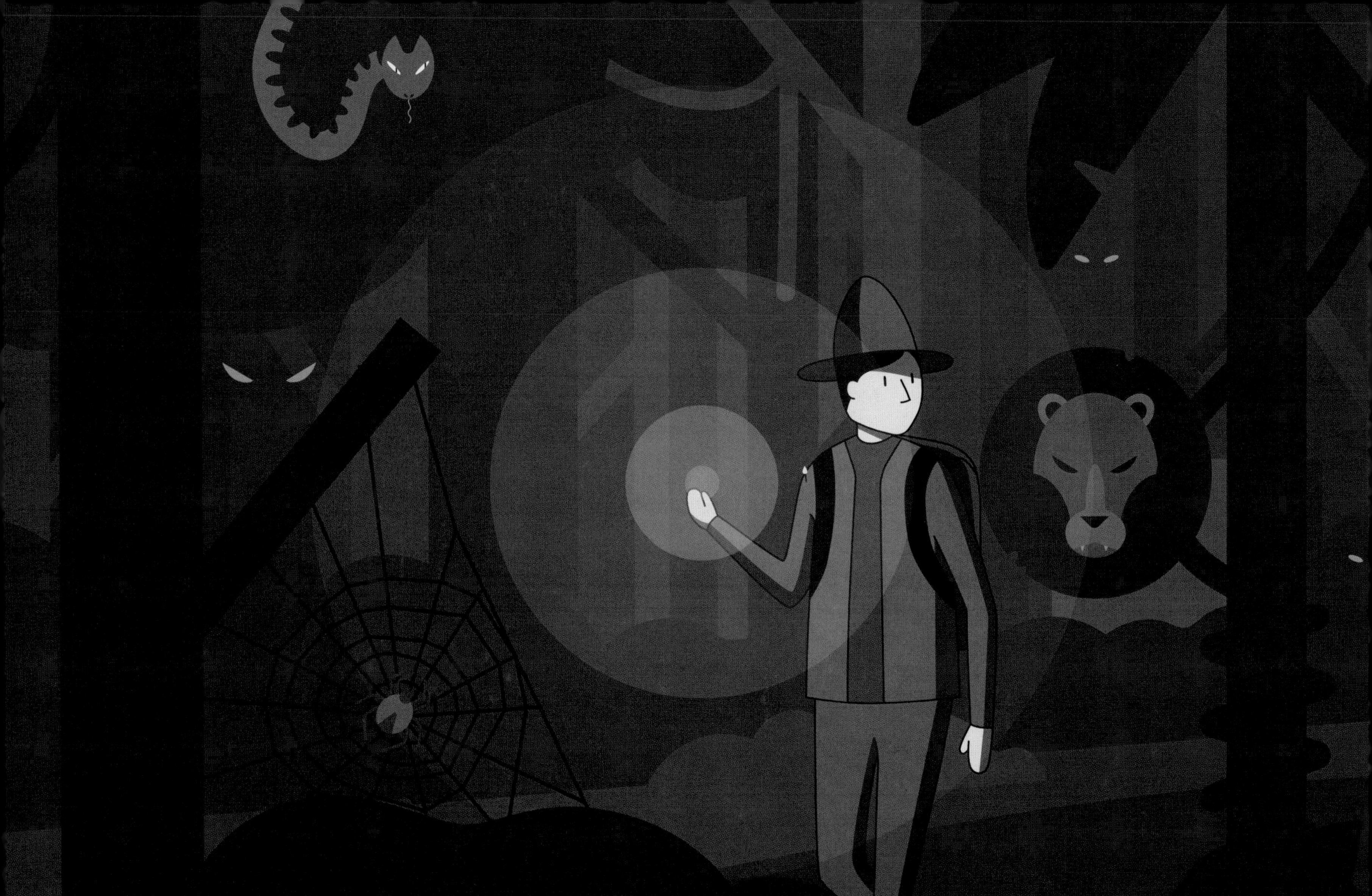

If you can look at things with the help of others who can see what you are blind to, you'll see much more than you can alone.

I learned that doing this was essential for my successfully seeing the dangers and the opportunities in the jungle of life.

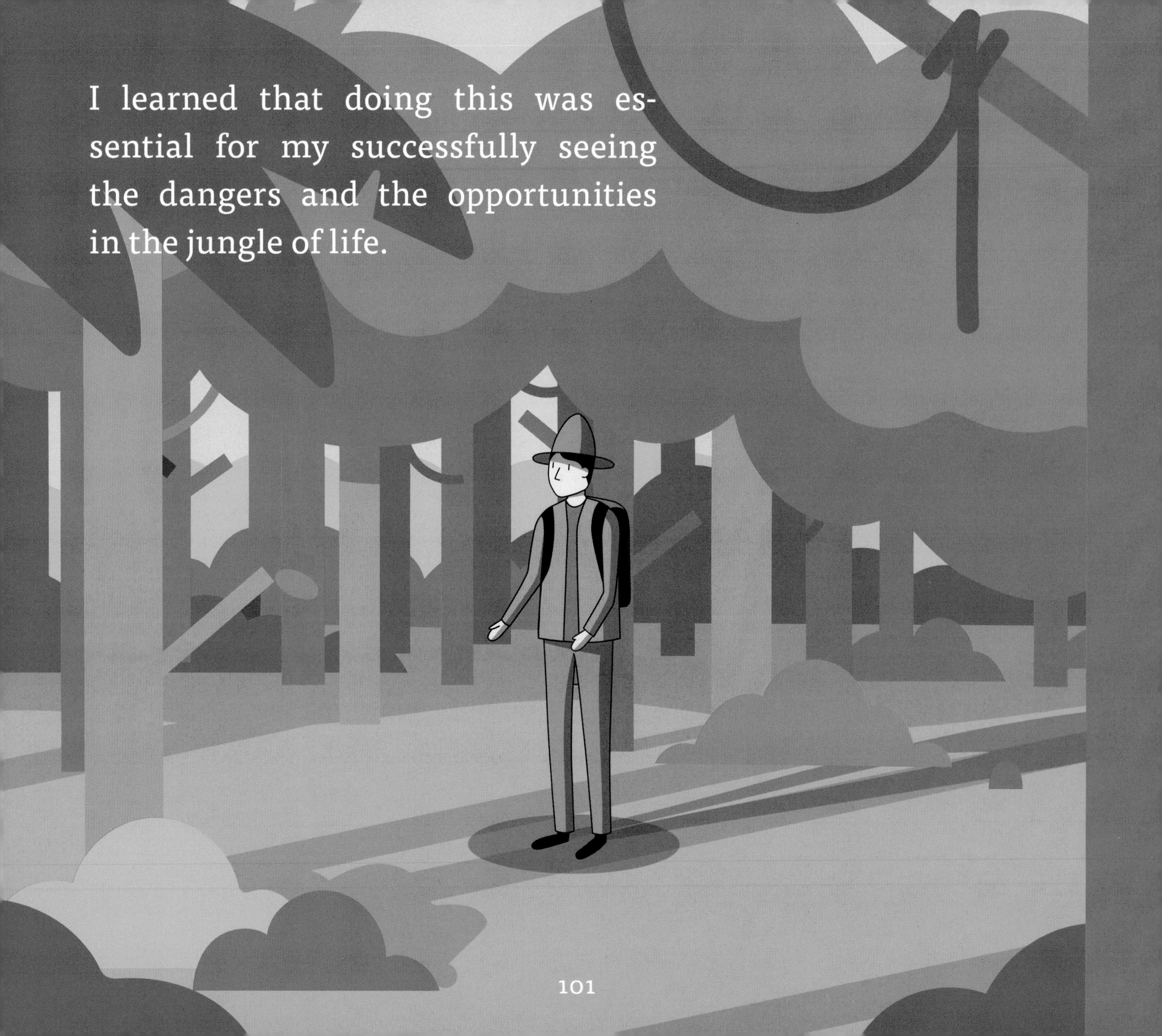

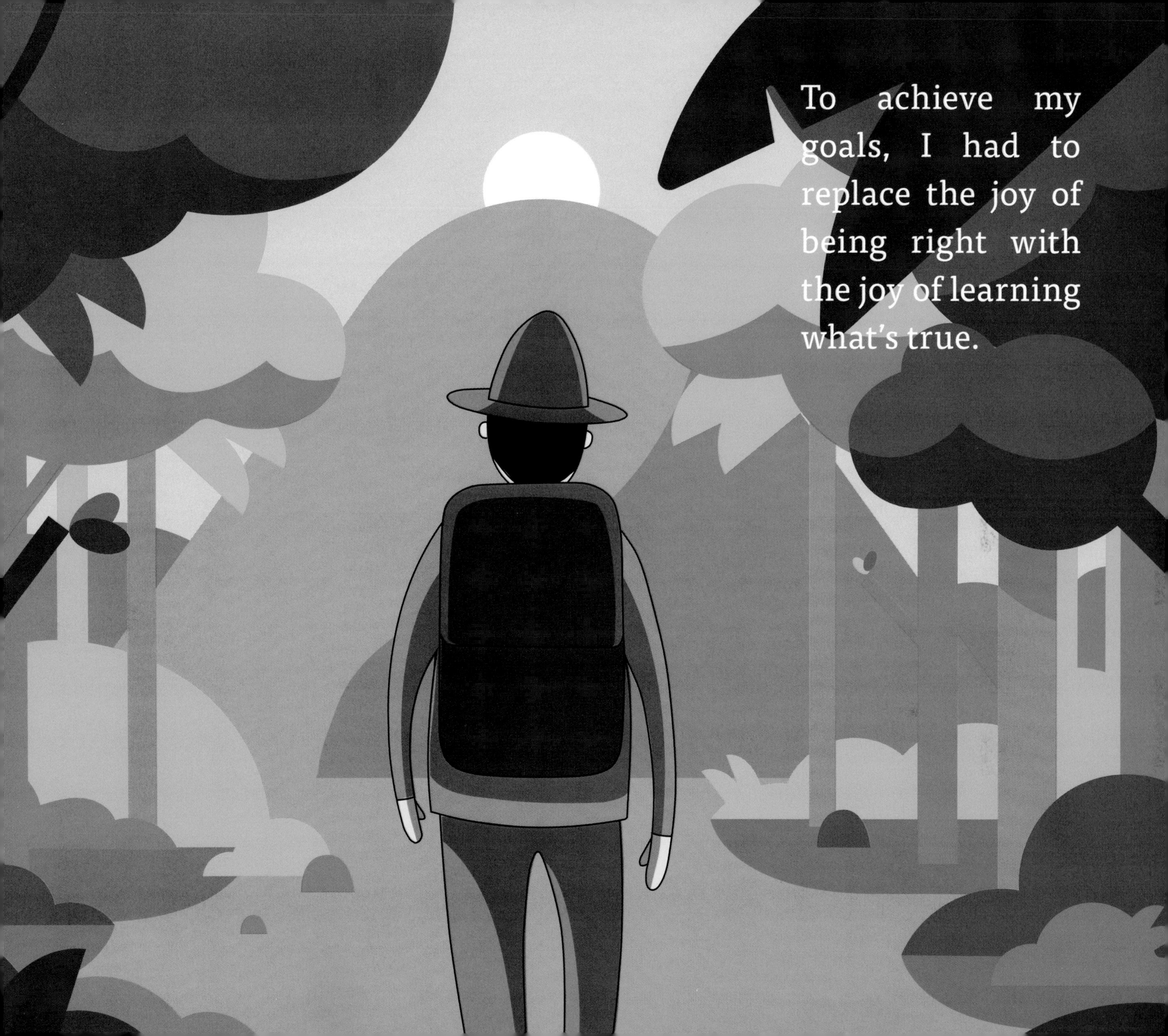

To achieve my goals, I had to replace the joy of being right with the joy of learning what's true.

So I looked for the most thoughtful people who disagreed with me.

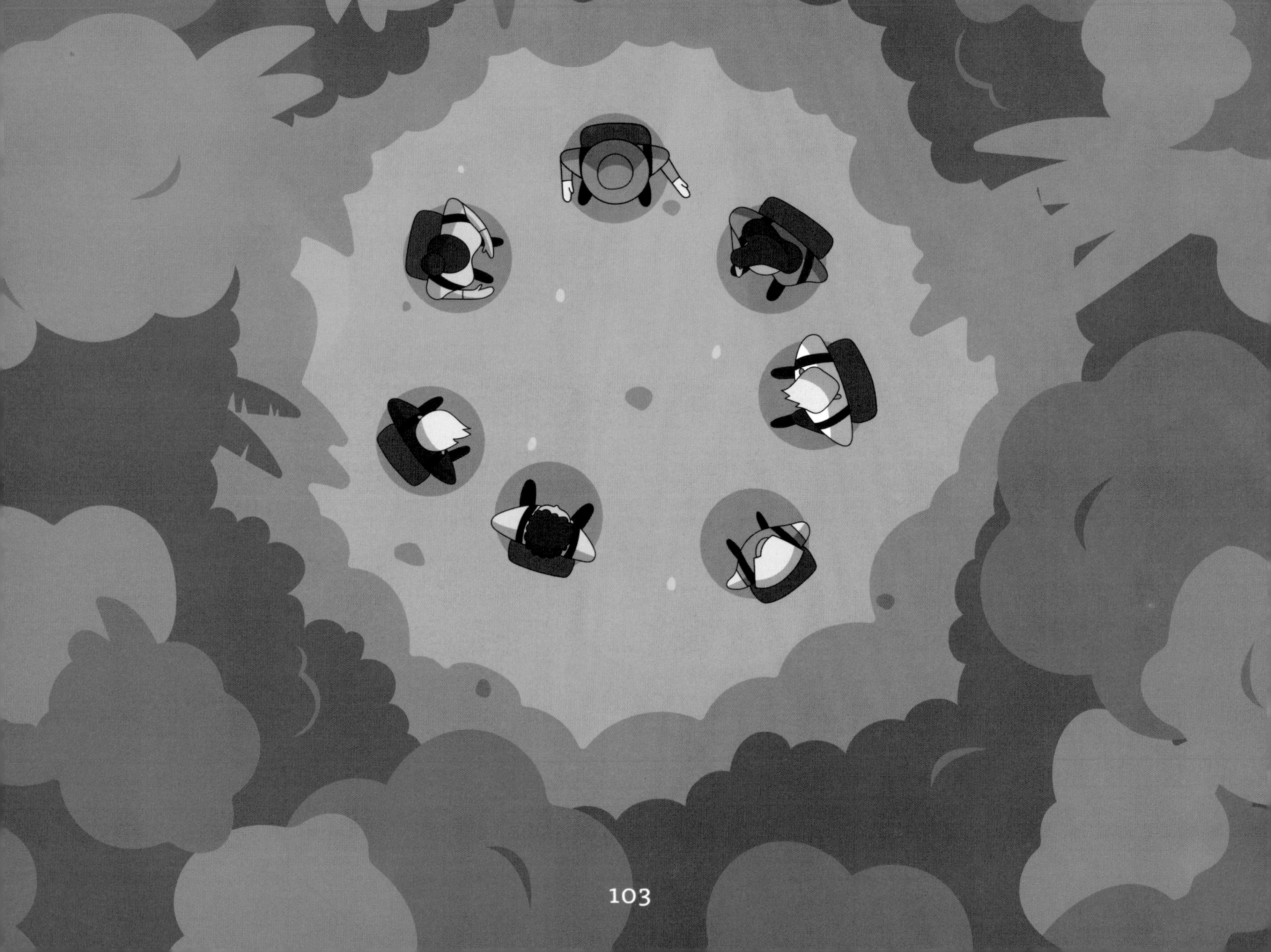

I wanted to see through their eyes and have them see through mine... so that we could together find what's true and how to deal with it. I wanted to learn the art of thoughtful disagreement.

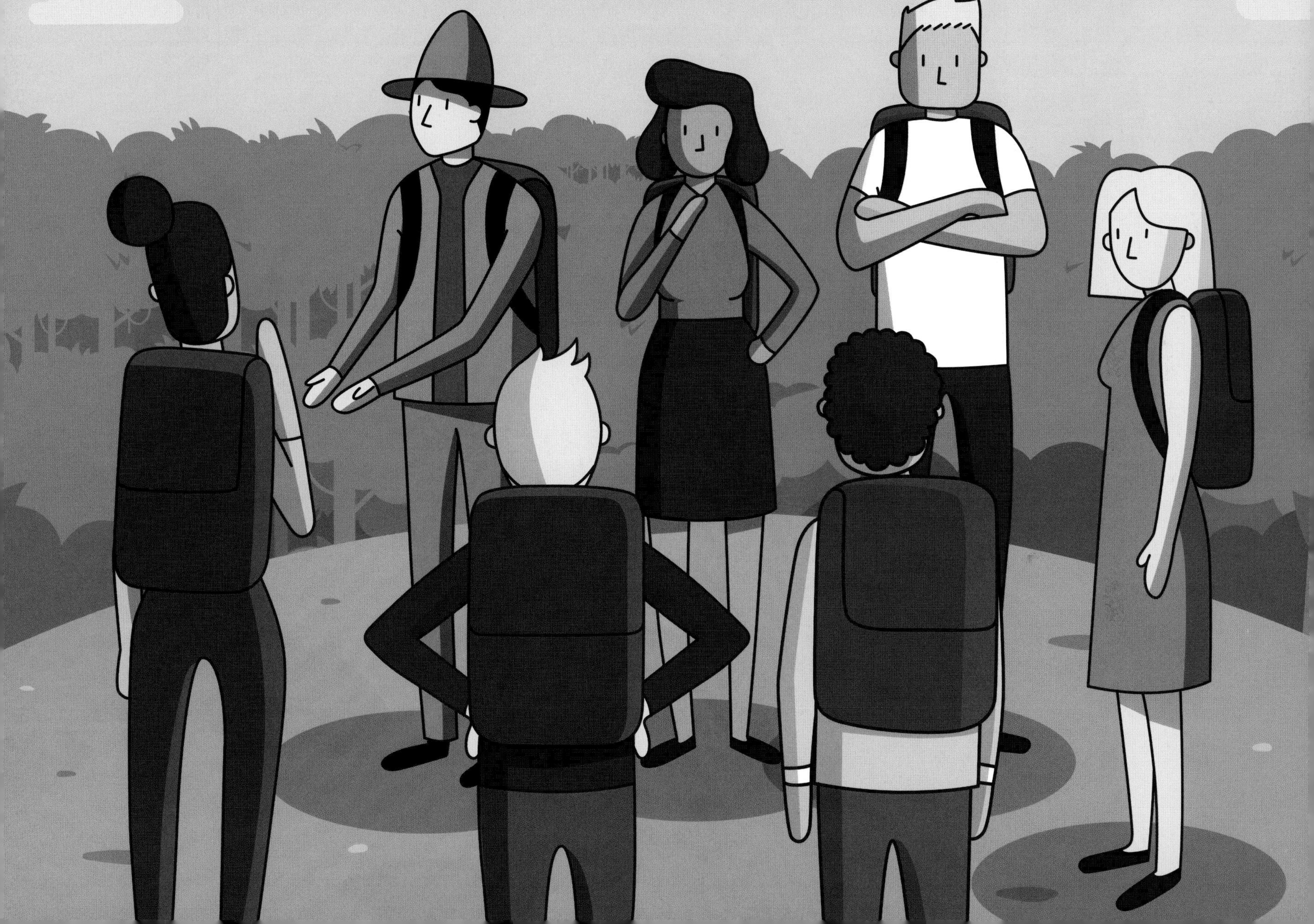

going from seeing things through just my eyes...to seeing them through the eyes of these thoughtful people...

...was like going from seeing things in black and white...

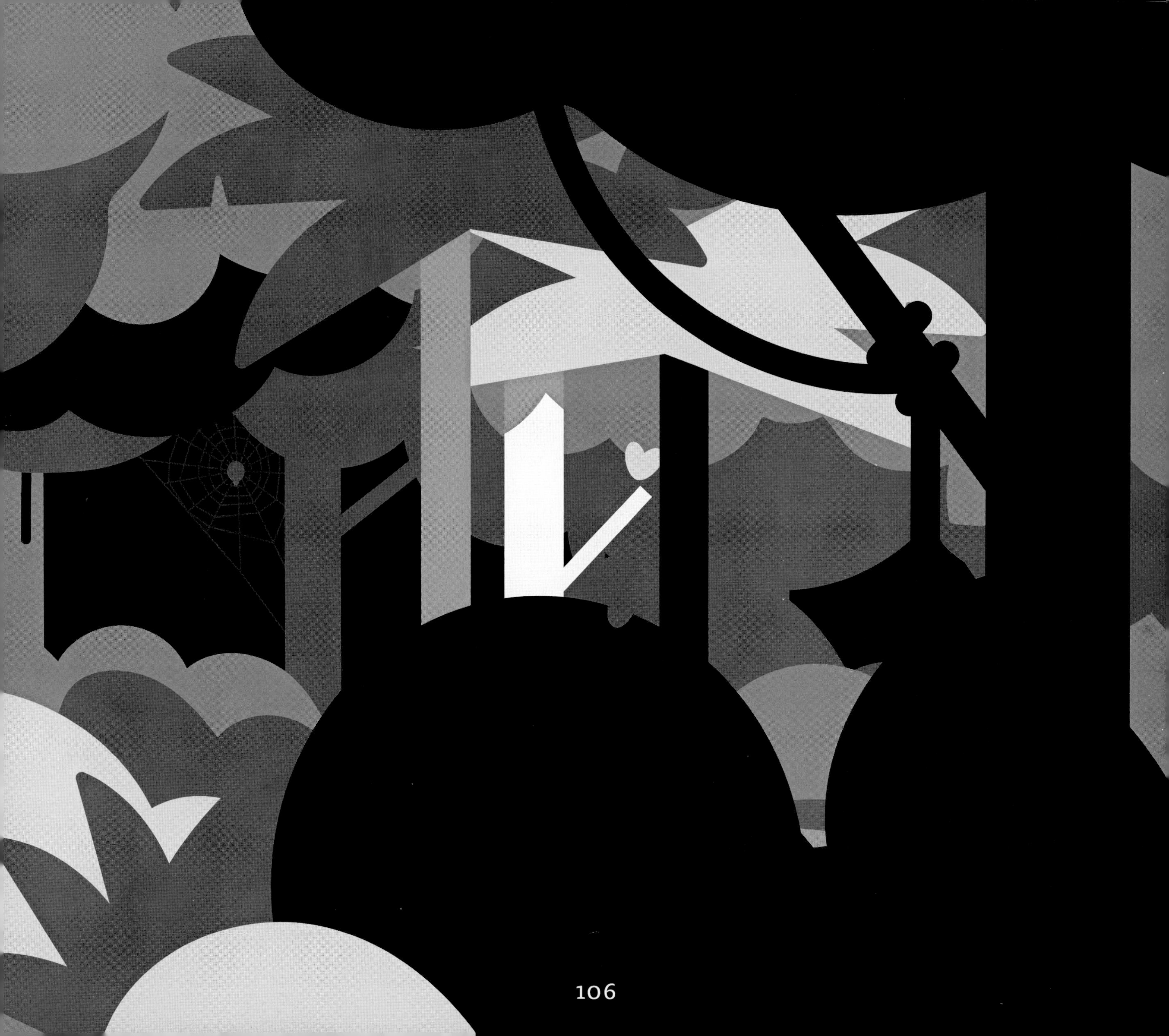

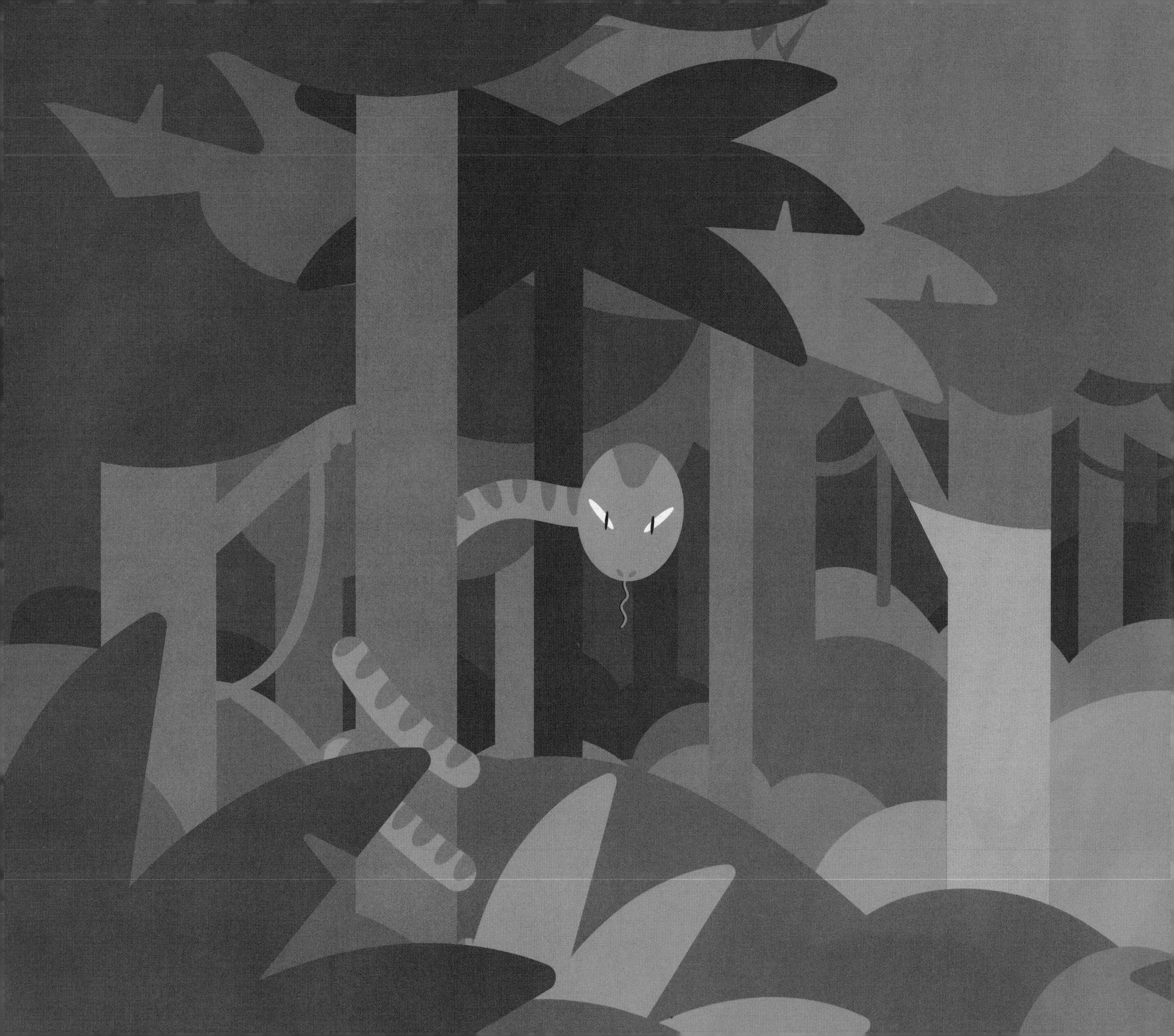

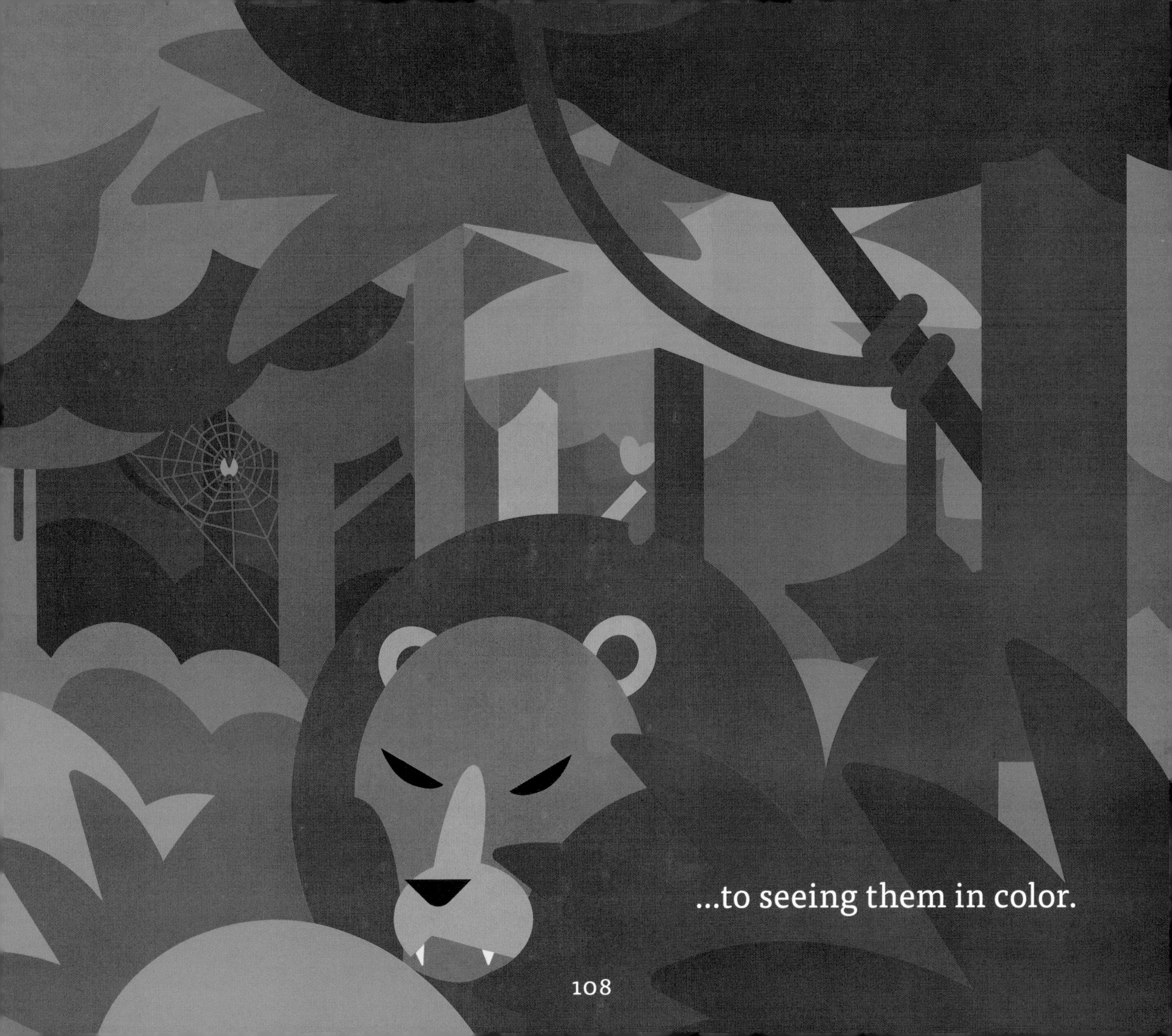
...to seeing them in color.

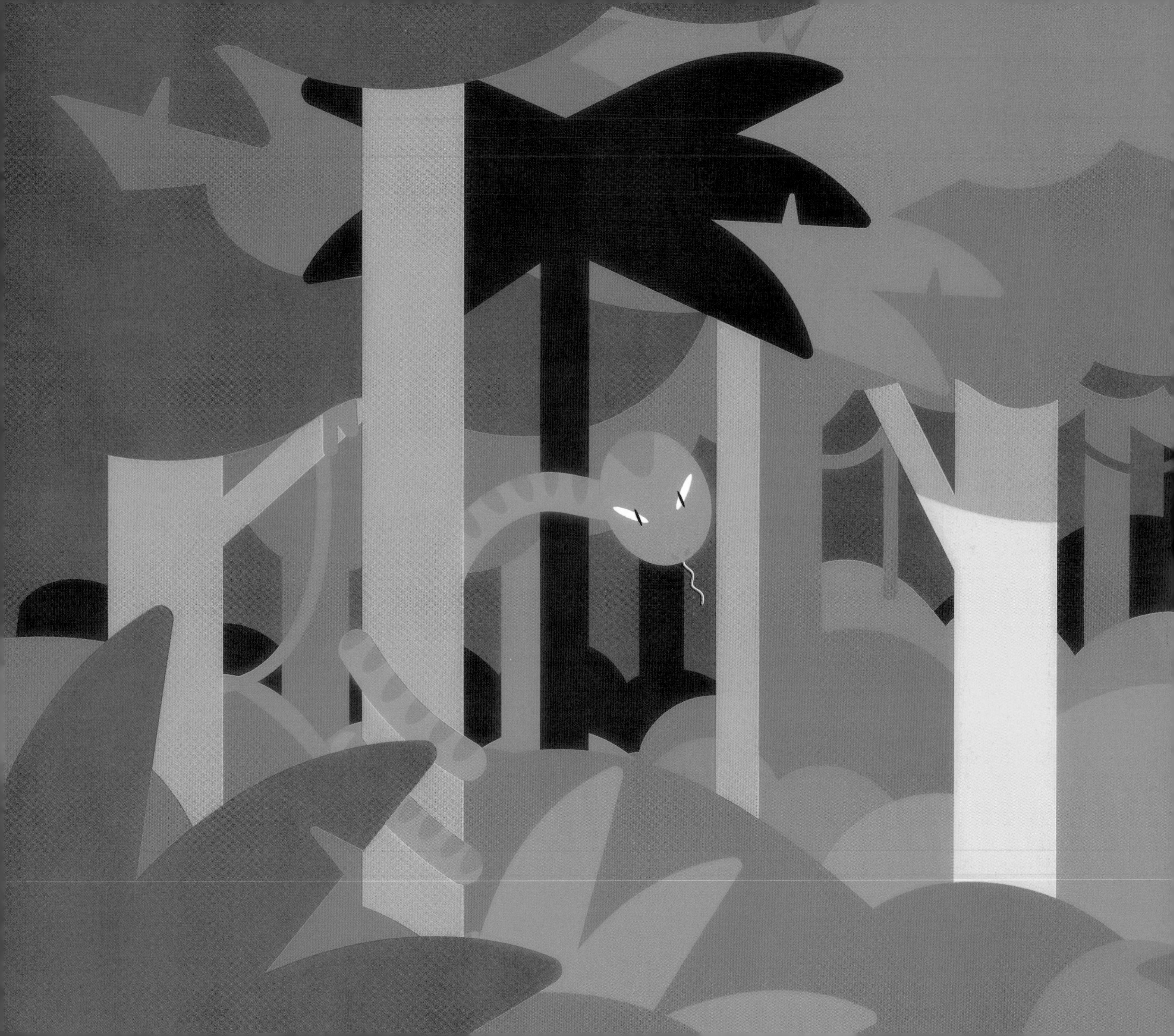

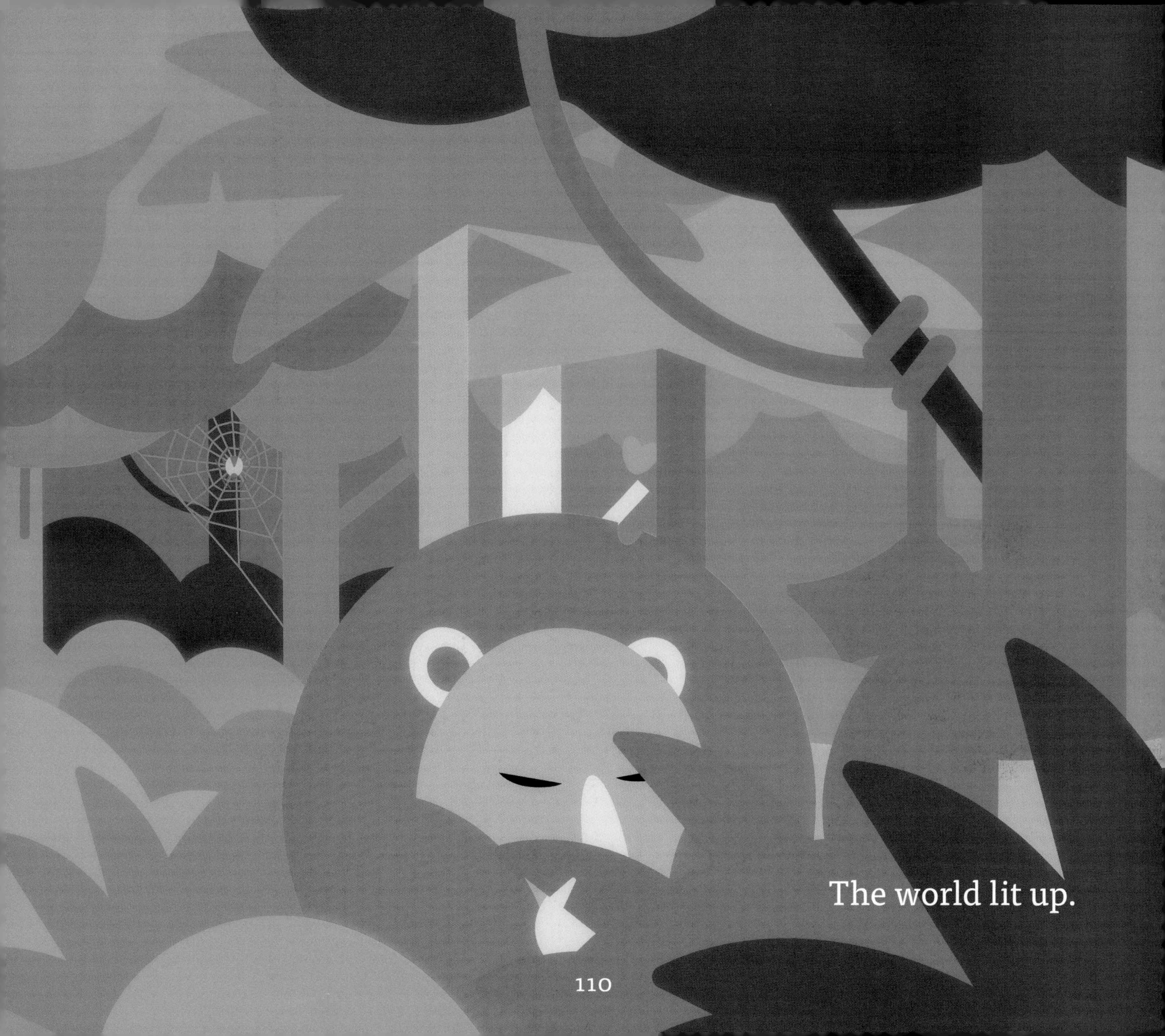

The world lit up.

That's when I realized that the best way to go through the jungle of life is with insightful people who see things differently from me.

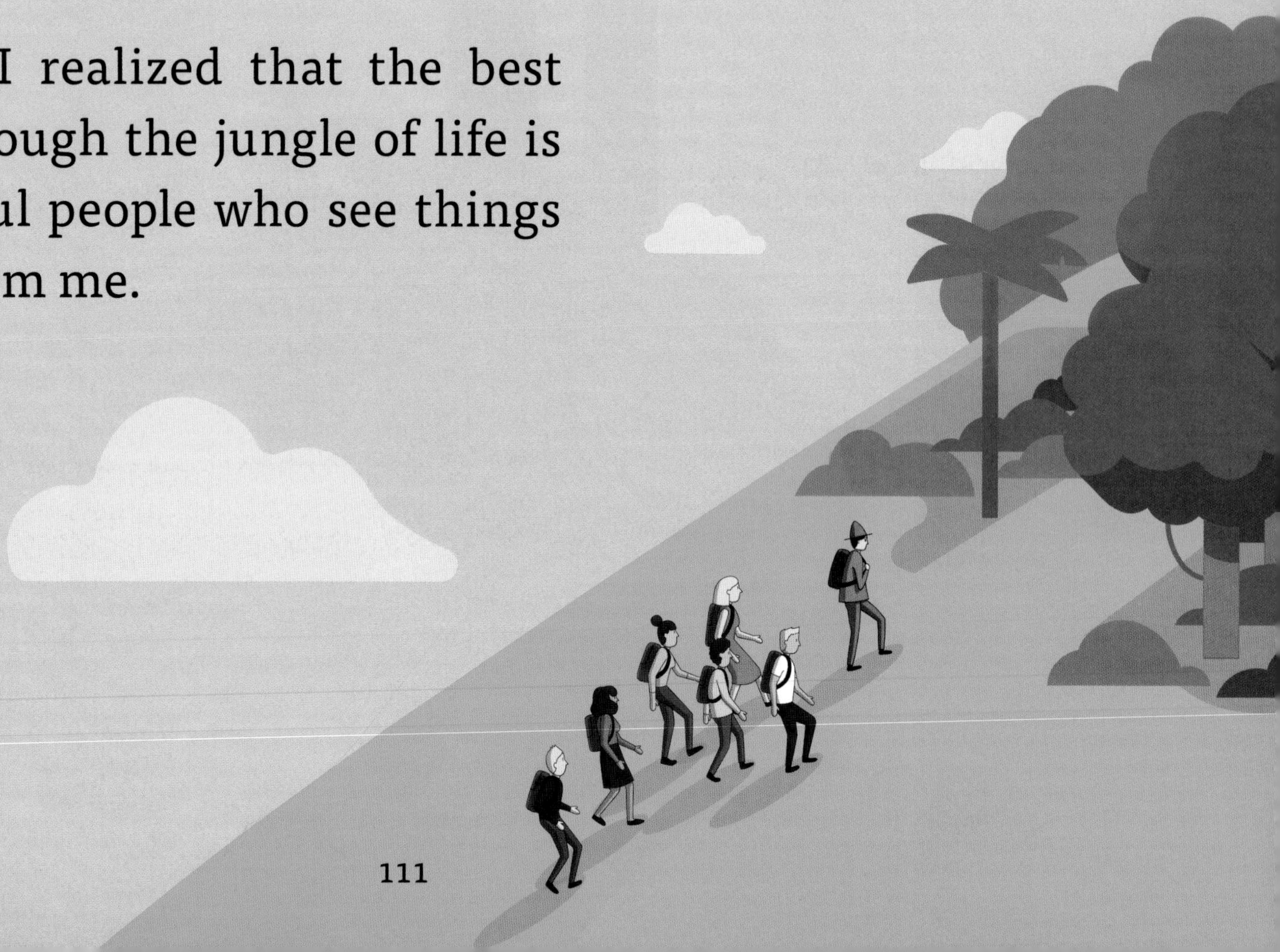

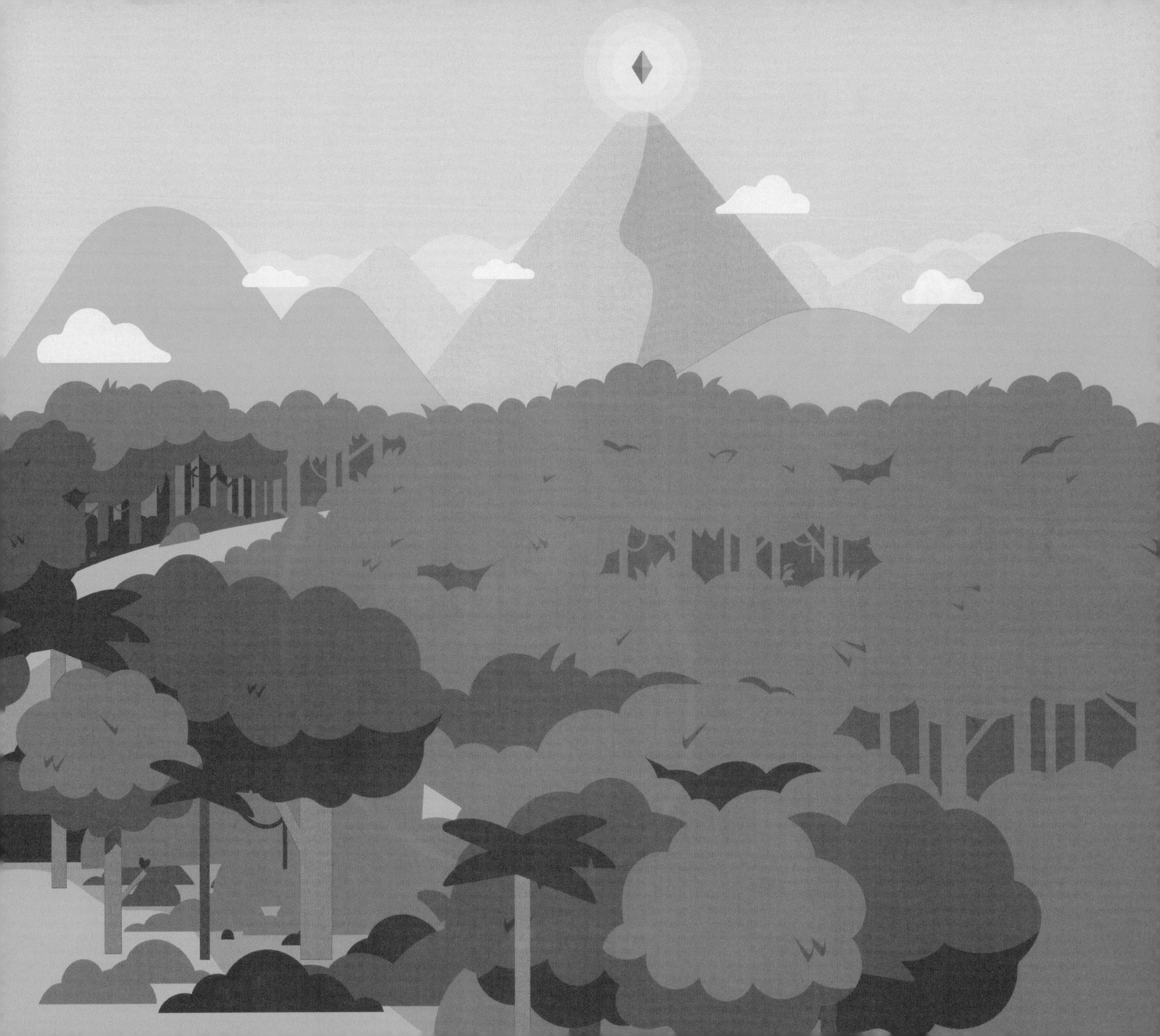

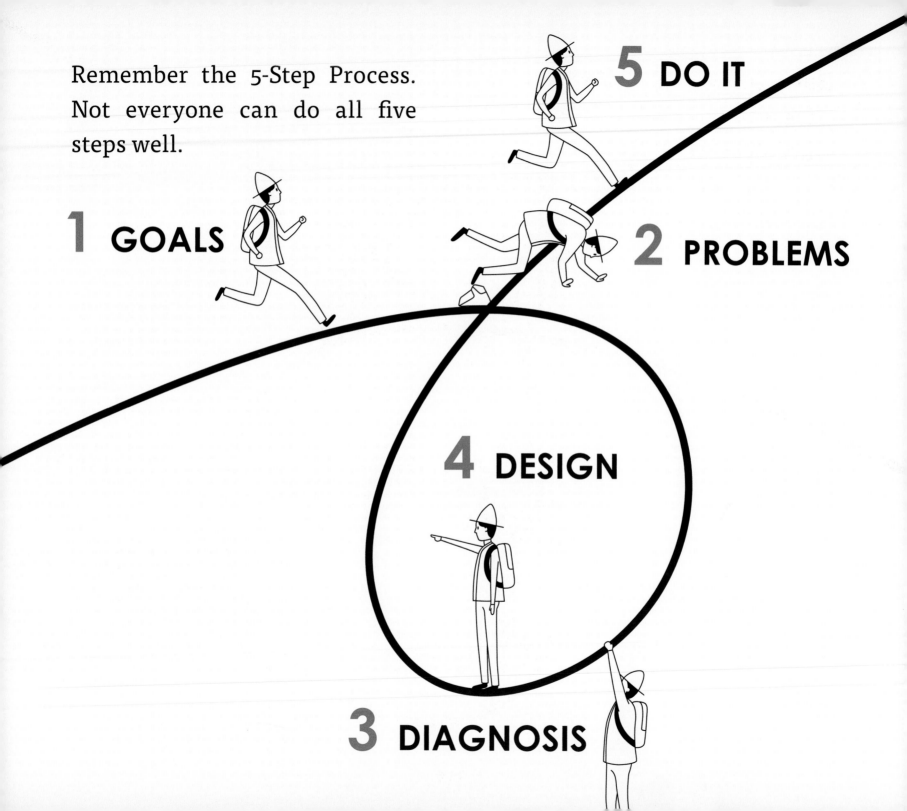

Remember the 5-Step Process.
Not everyone can do all five
steps well.

1 GOALS

5 DO IT

2 PROBLEMS

4 DESIGN

3 DIAGNOSIS

But you can get help from others who can see and do things you can't.

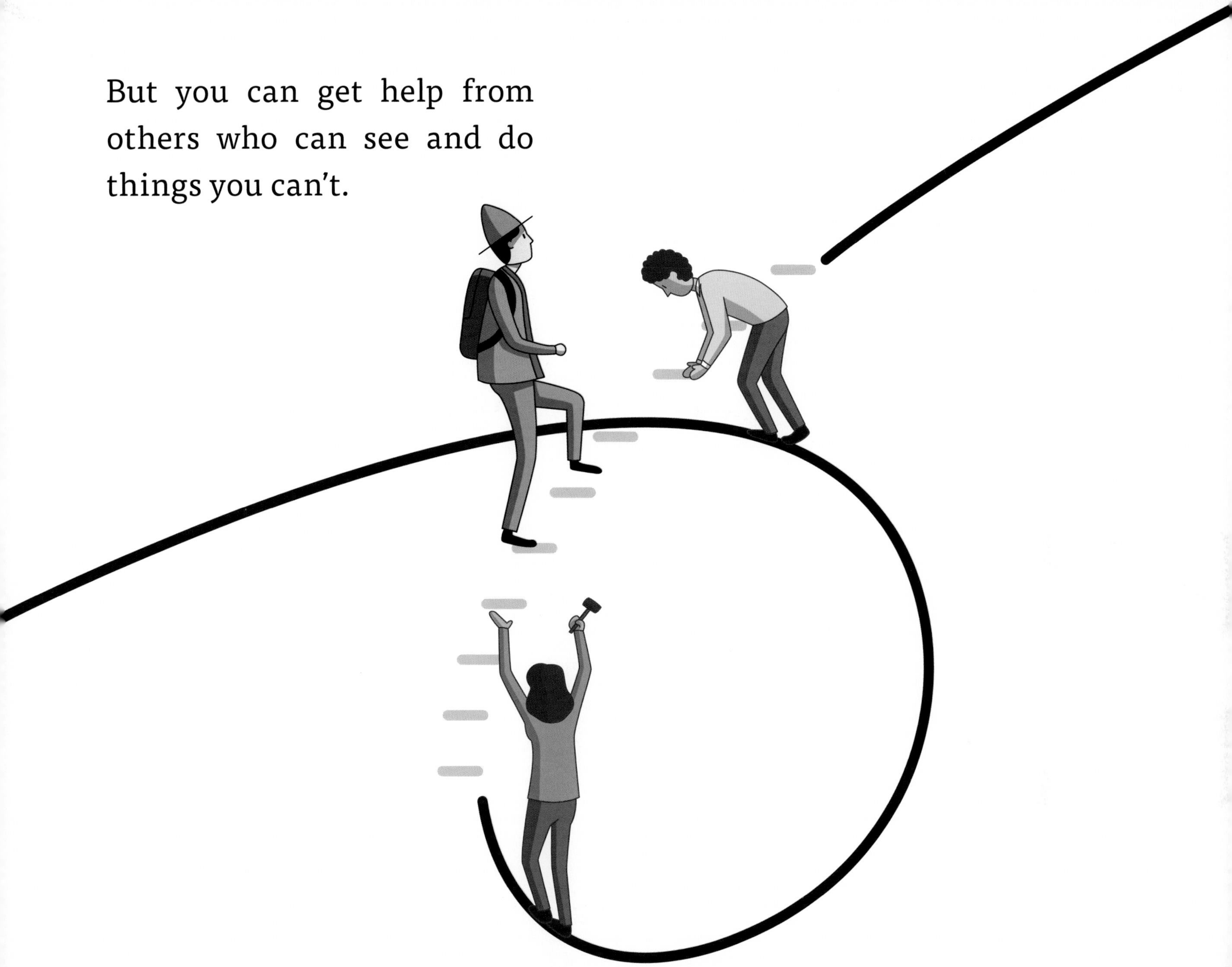

You just need to let go of your attachment to having the right answers yourself and become open-minded to these other views. This radically open-minded approach significantly improved my decision making.

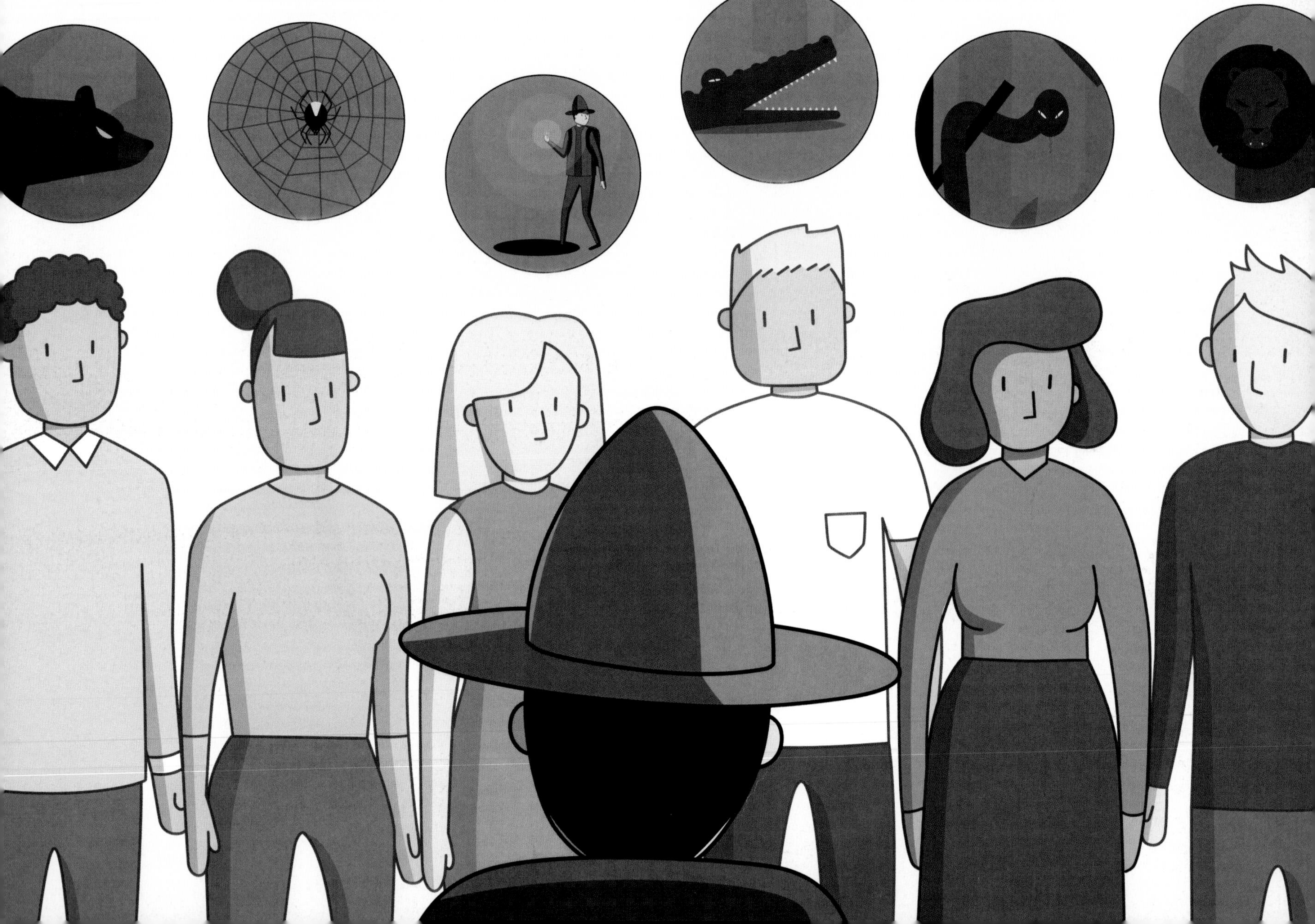

I also learned that there is nothing better than to be on a shared mission with people you care about who can be radically truthful and radically transparent with each other.

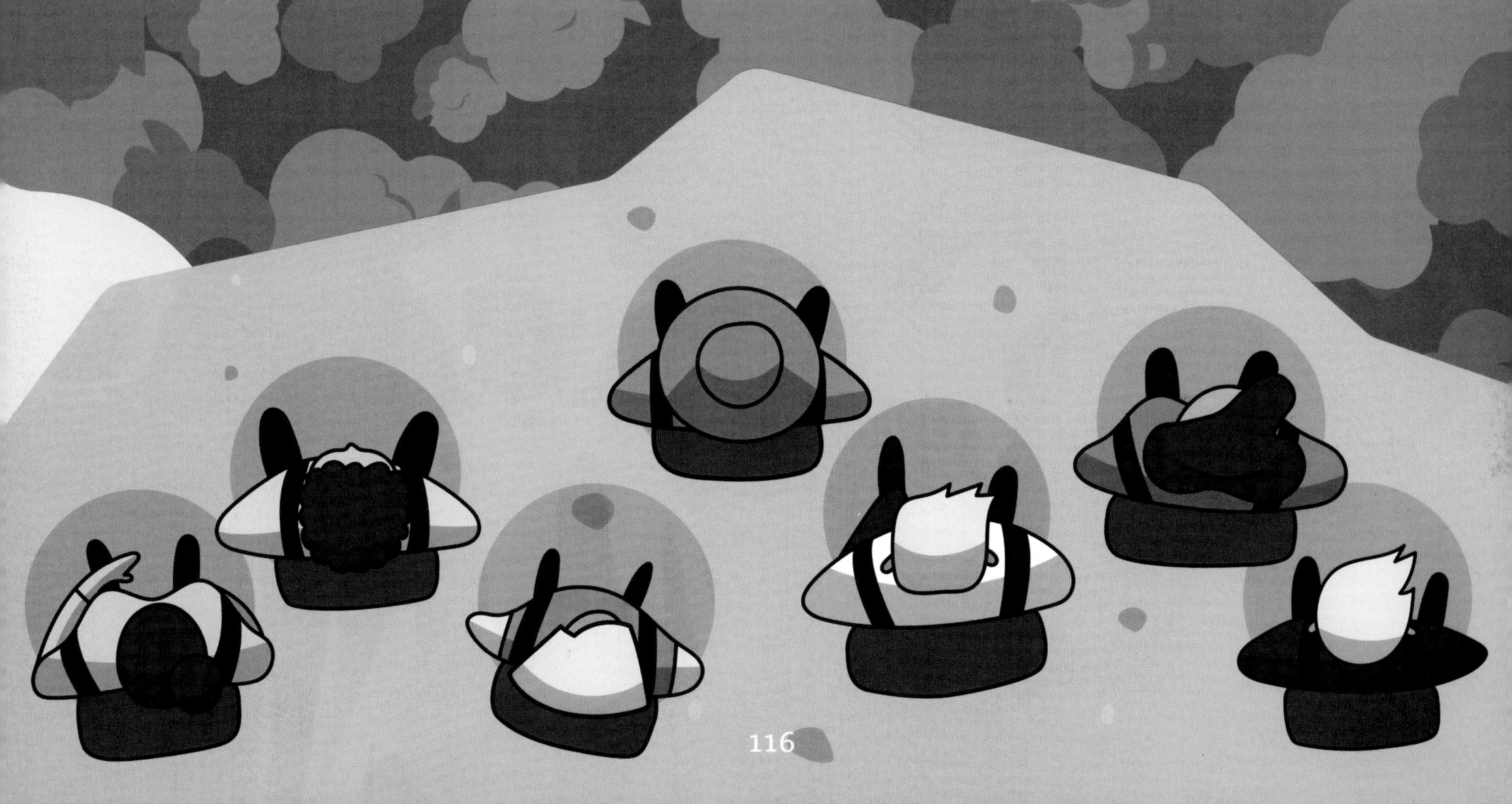

This led me to create a company with a unique idea meritocracy, operating in a way that has produced remarkable successes. That's because in an idea meritocracy, you get the best from everybody.

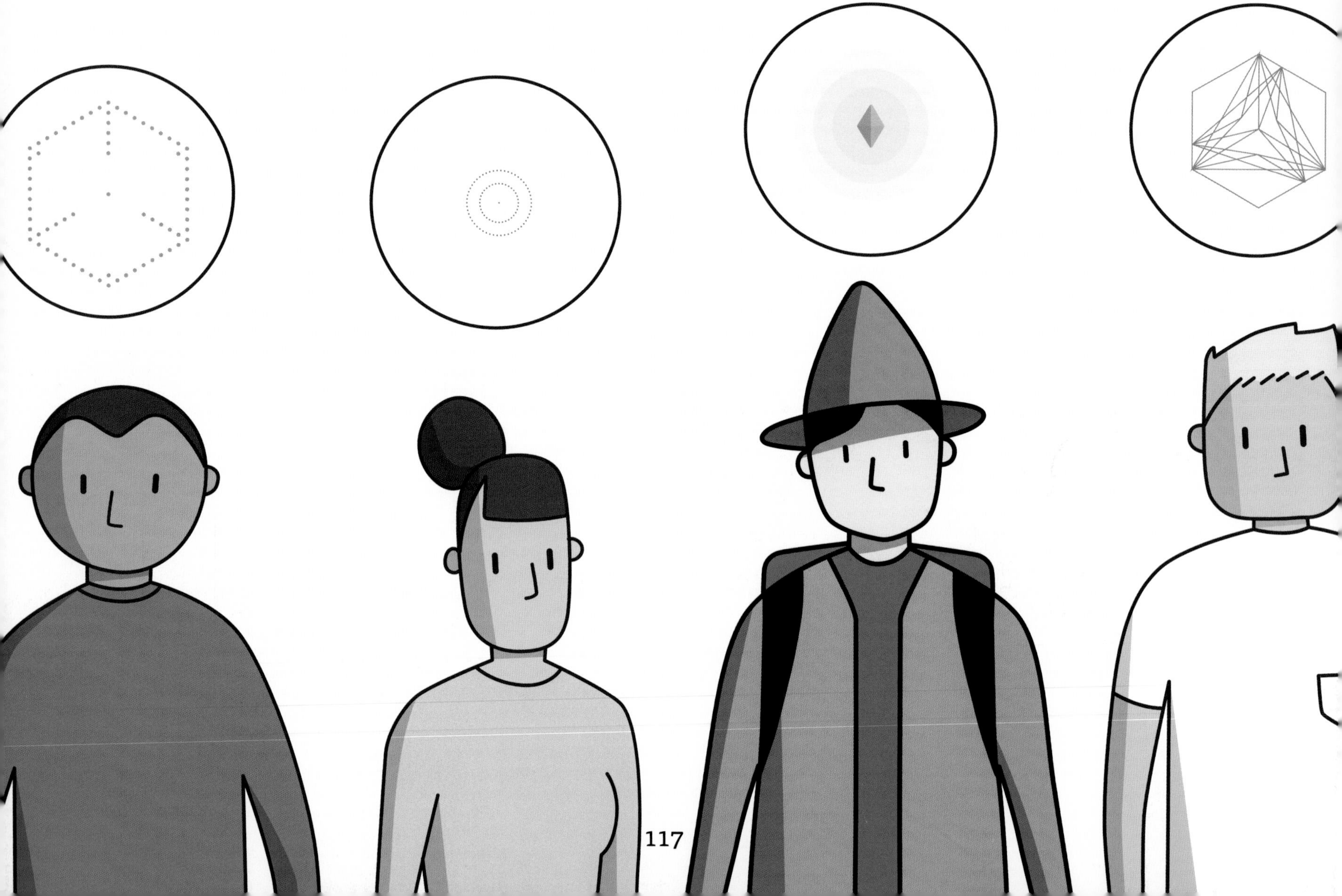

Independent thinking is welcome, and there is an efficient process for working through our disagreements to get at what is best.

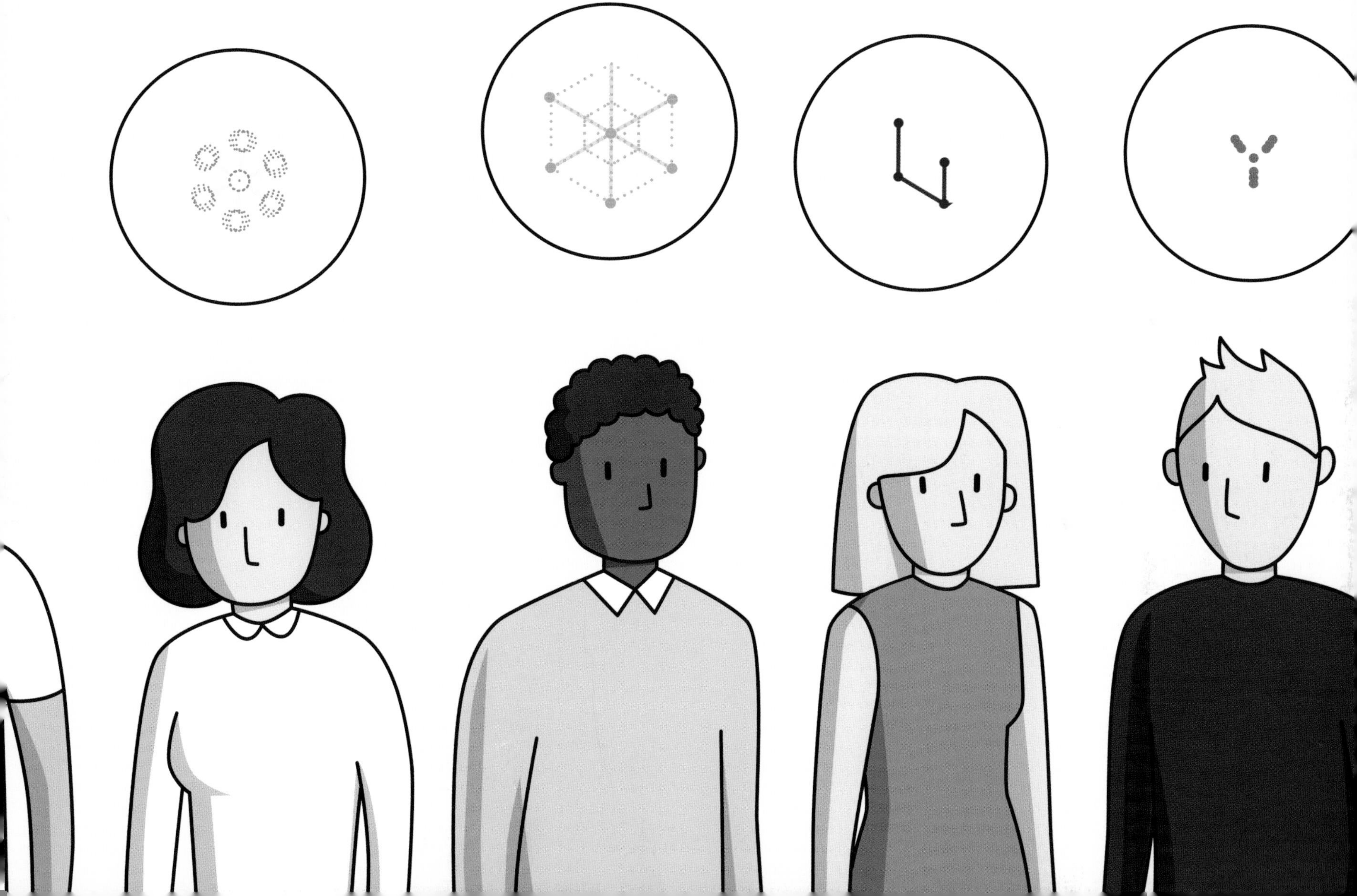

When I met other successful people, I found their journeys were similar to mine.

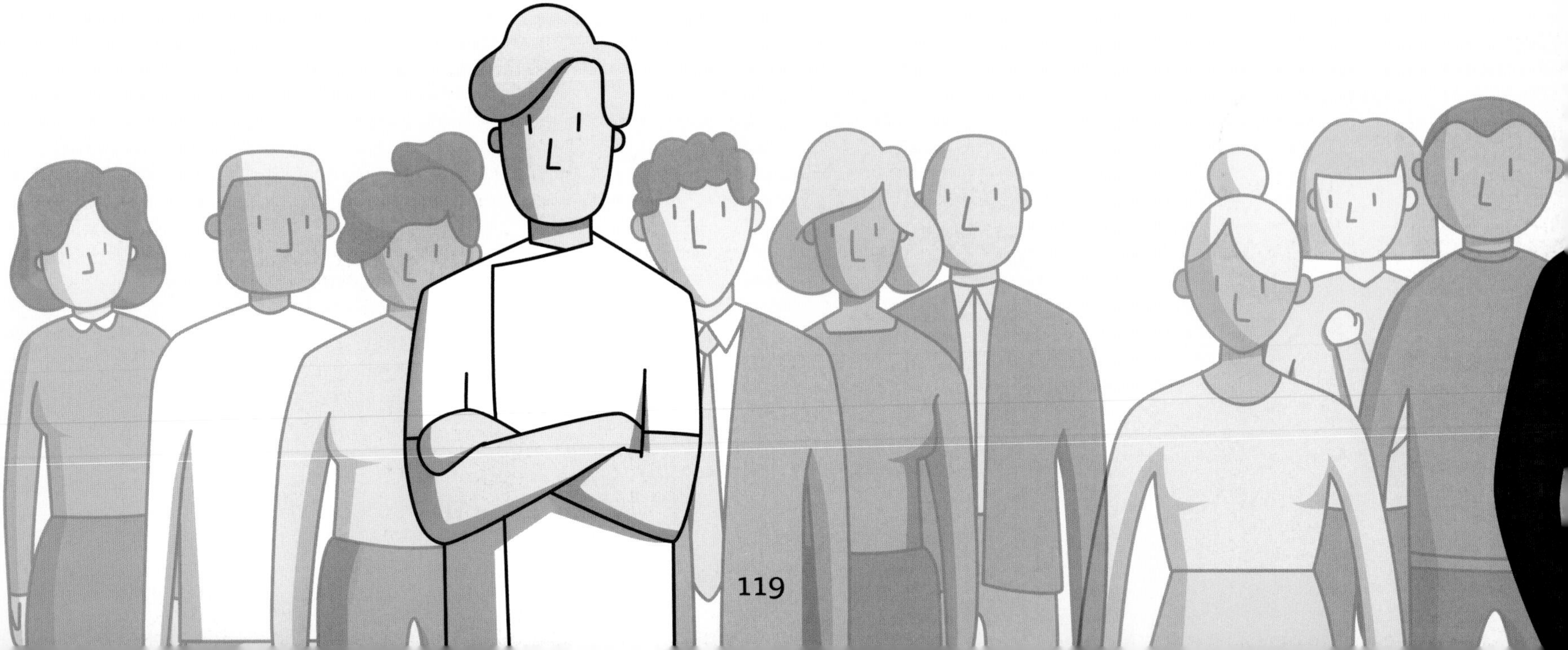

They all struggle, and they all have weaknesses that they get around by working with people who see risks and opportunities that they would miss.

Striving hard for big things is bound to lead you to painful falls. These setbacks will test you.

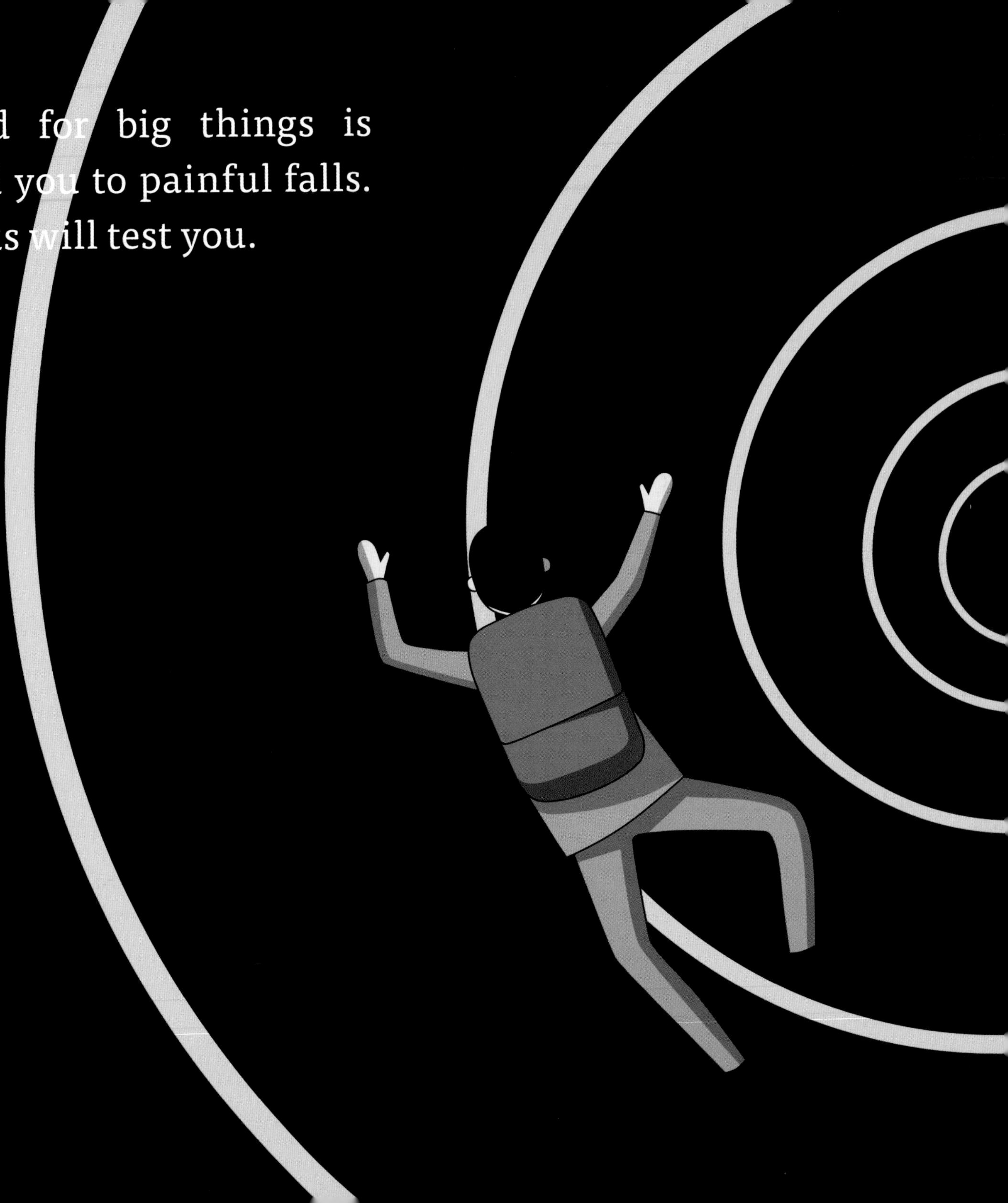

They sort people.

Some think hard about what caused these setbacks and learn valuable lessons...

...while others decide that this game is not for them and get off the field.

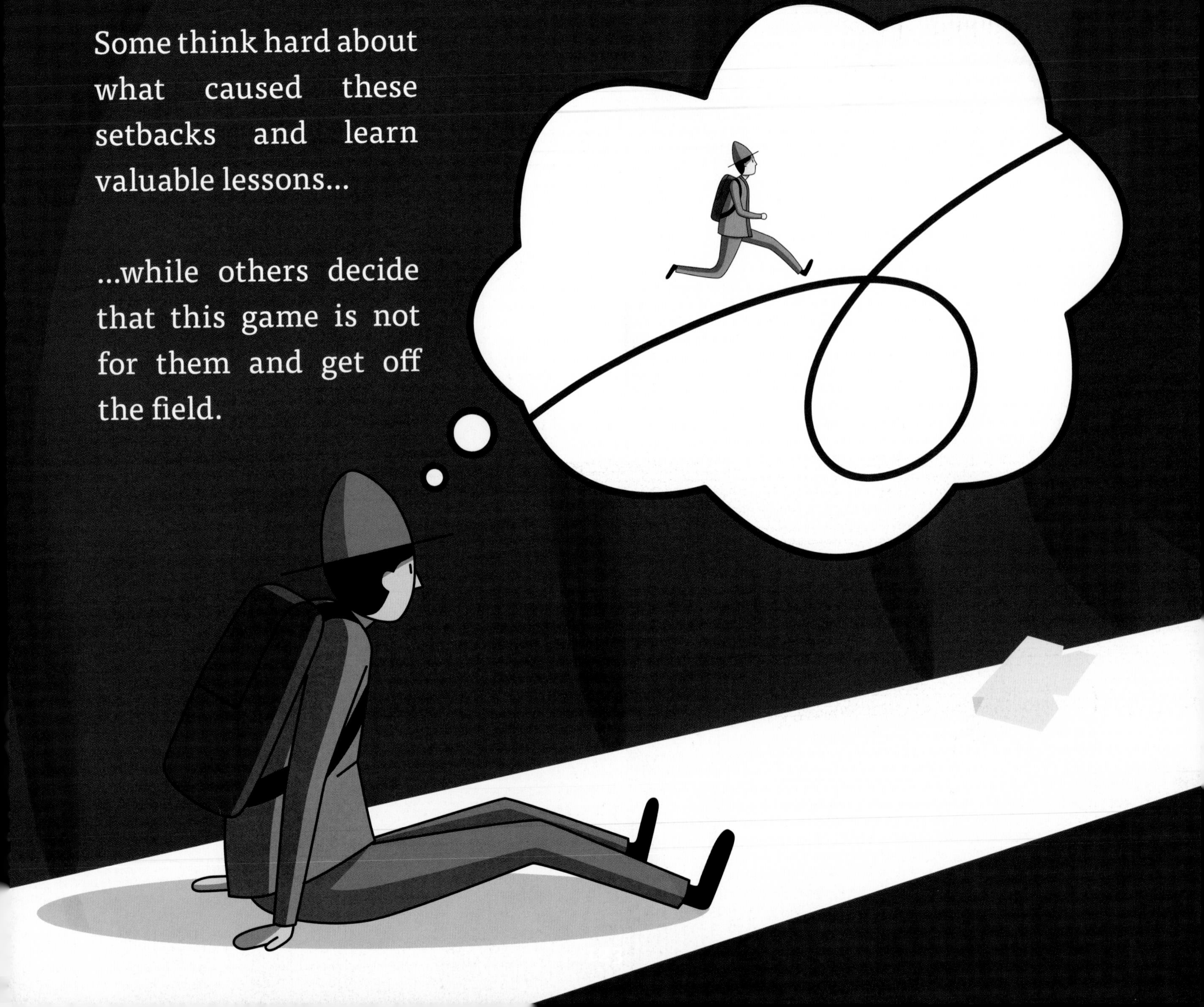

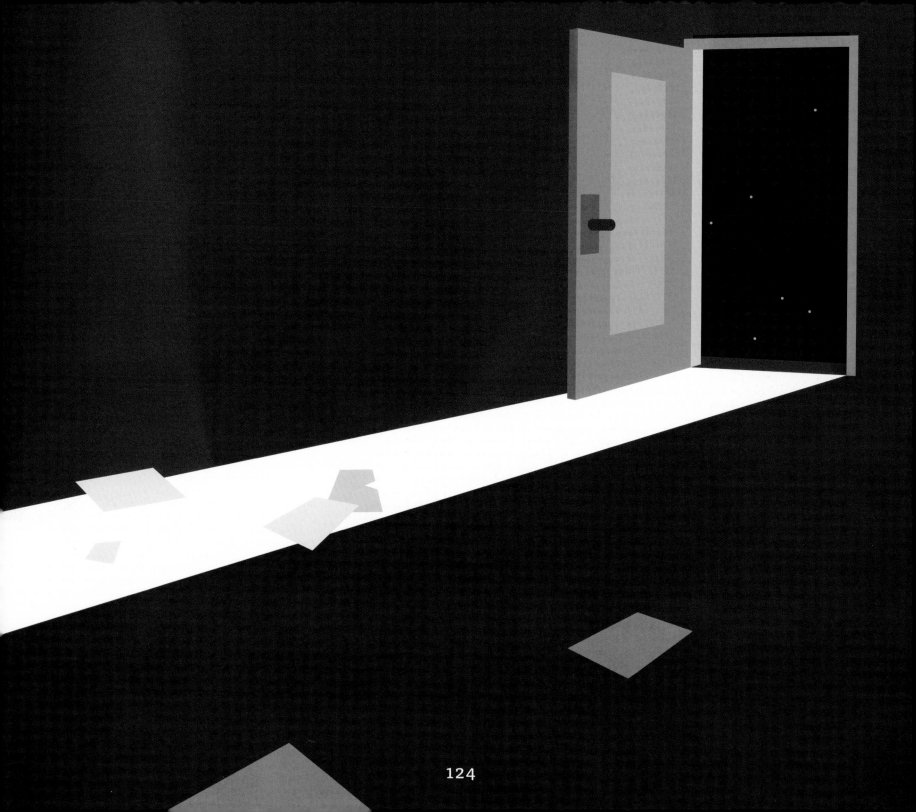

With time I made another even more amazing discovery. I learned that success is not a matter of achieving one's goals.

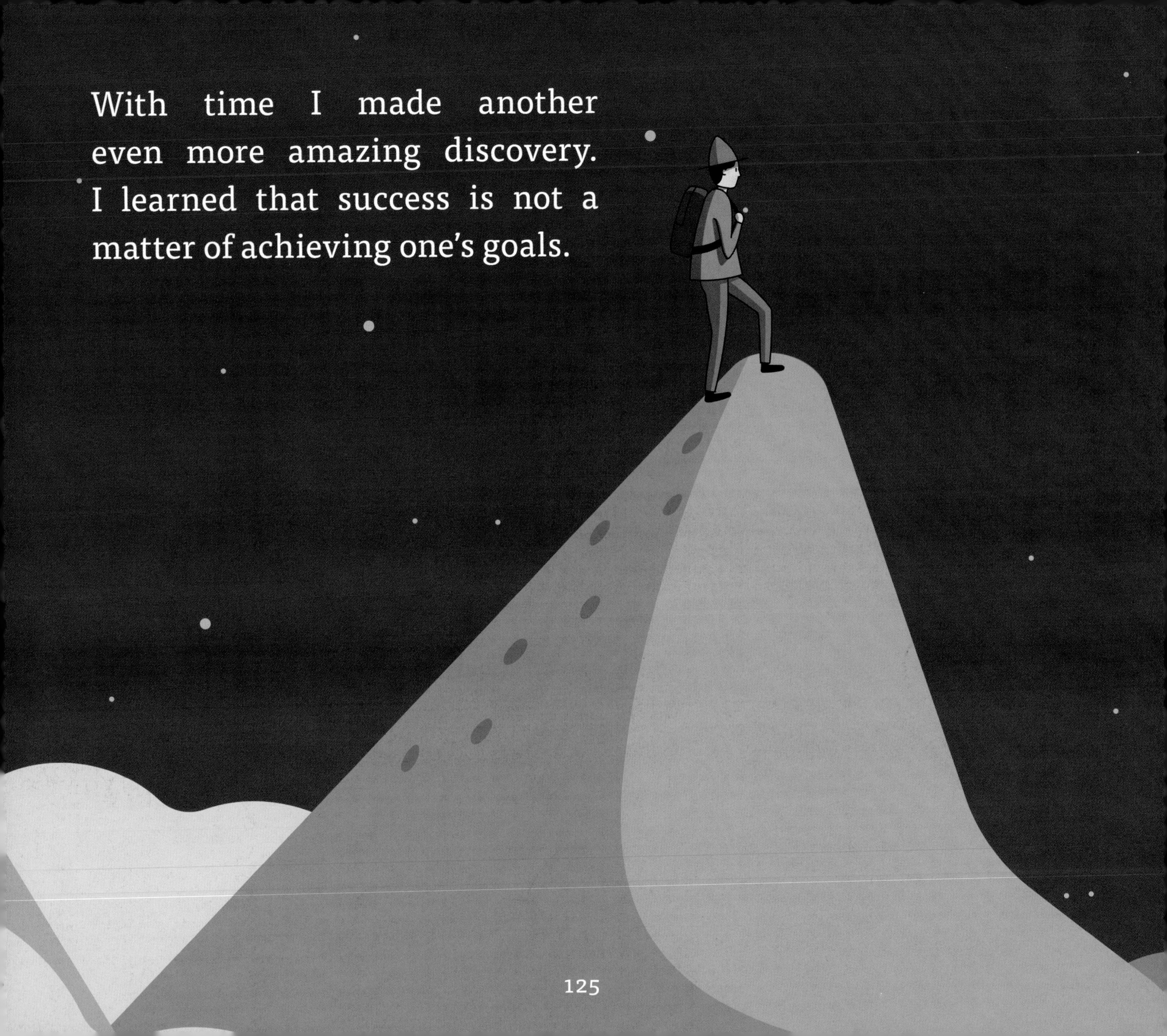

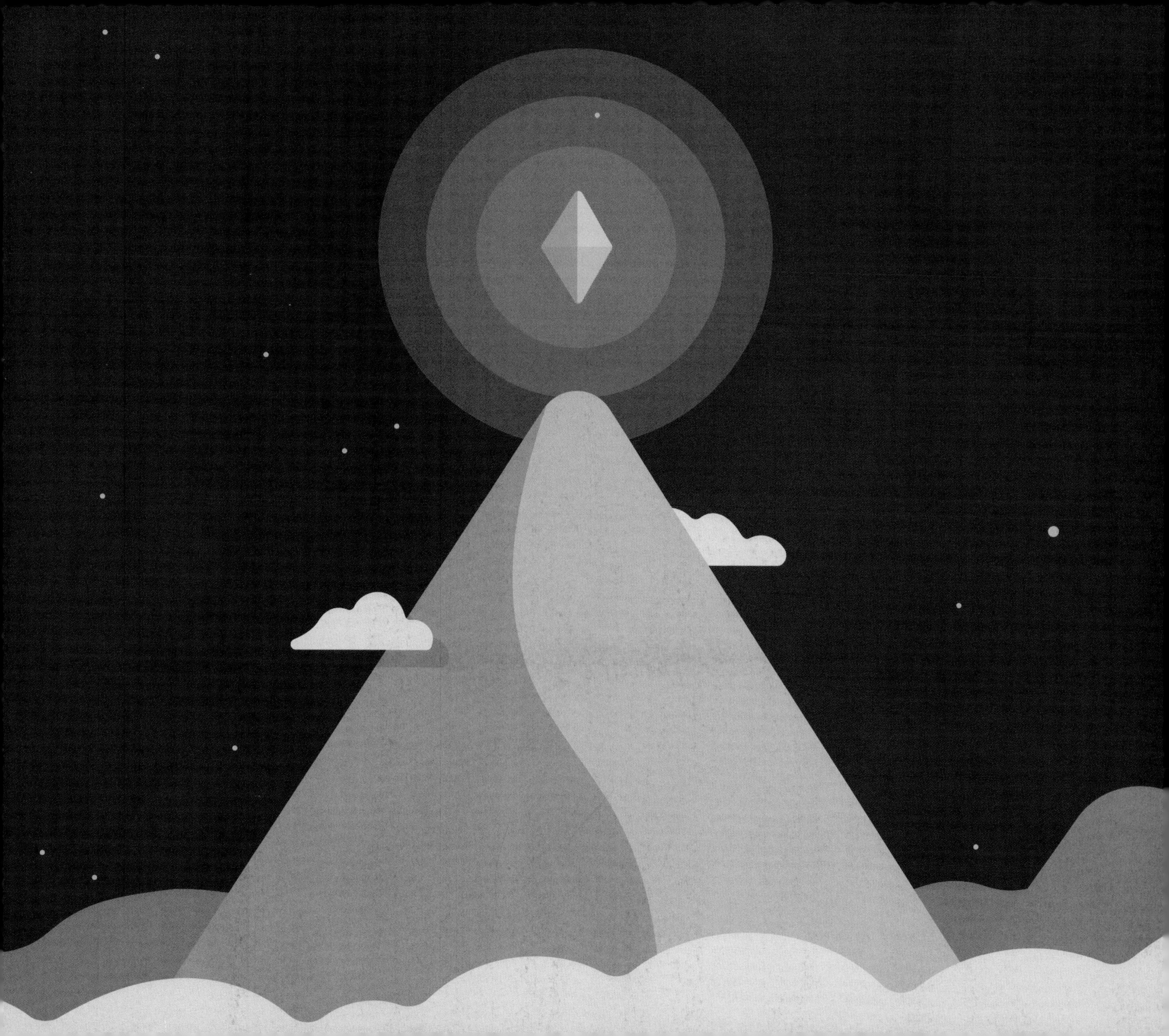

The things we strive for are just the bait...the struggle to get them with people that we care about gives us the personal evolution and the meaningful relationships that are the real rewards.

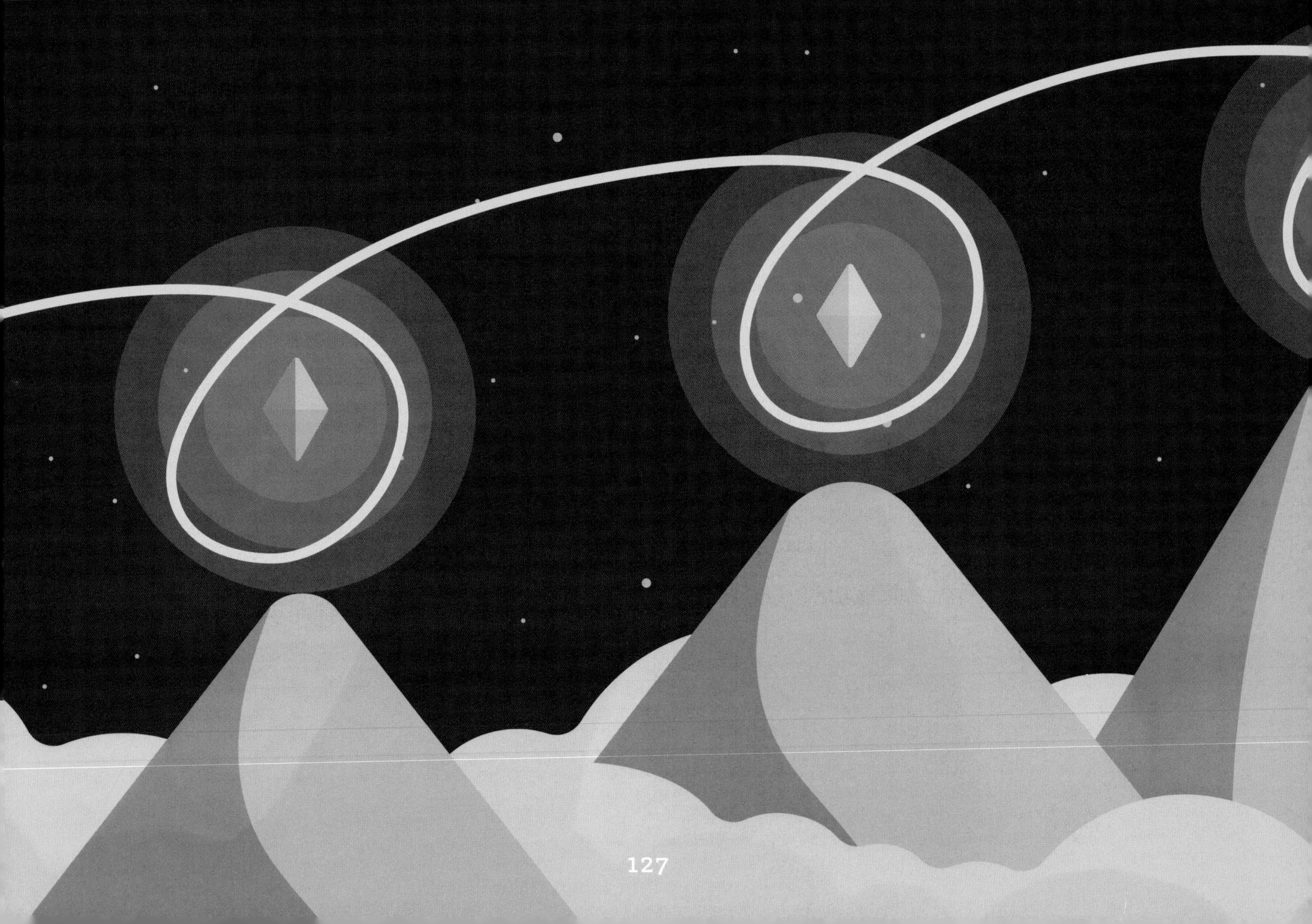

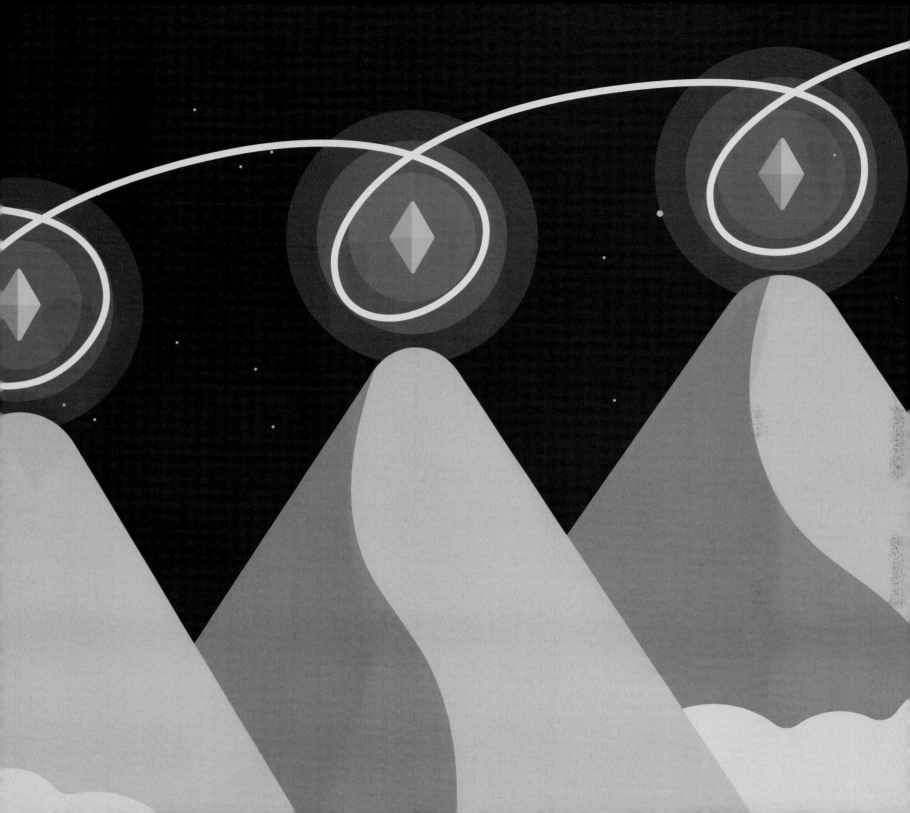

I no longer wanted to get to the other side of the jungle to reach the rewards. I instead wanted to stay in the jungle, struggling to be successful with people I cared about.

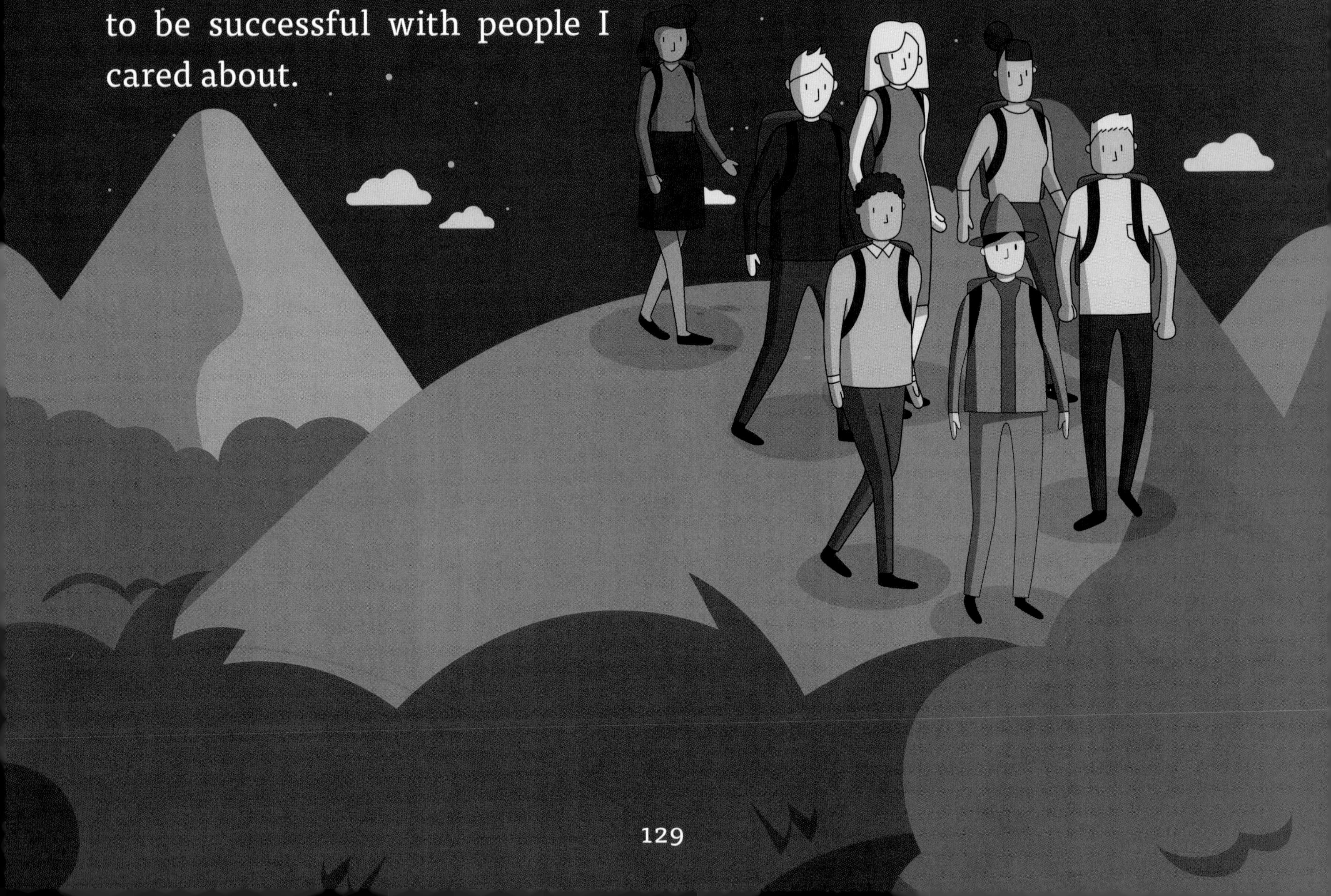

With time, the success of the mission and the well-being of other people became more important than my own success.

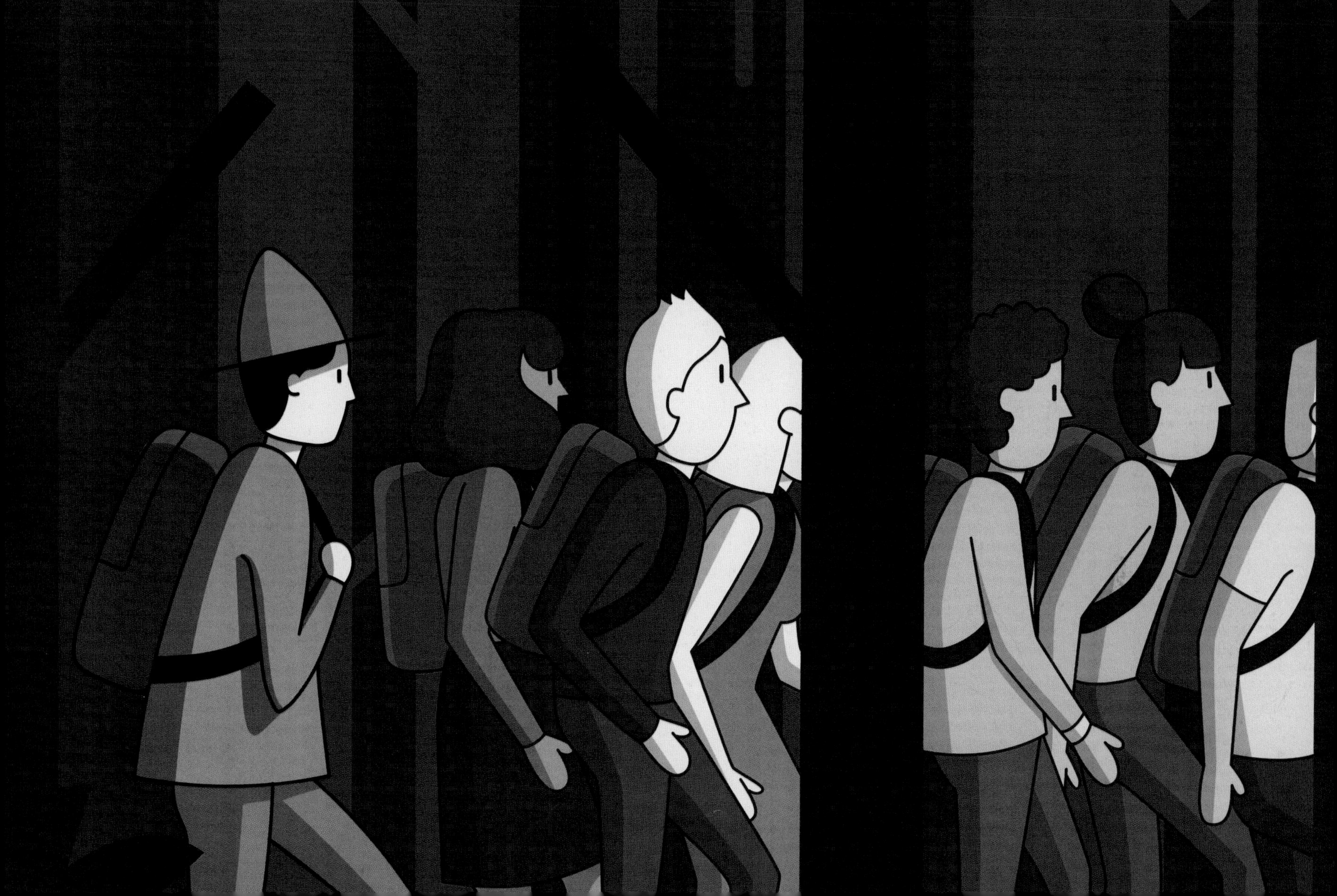

Then I started to see my life arc and to see beyond myself. That led me to want others to be successful beyond me.

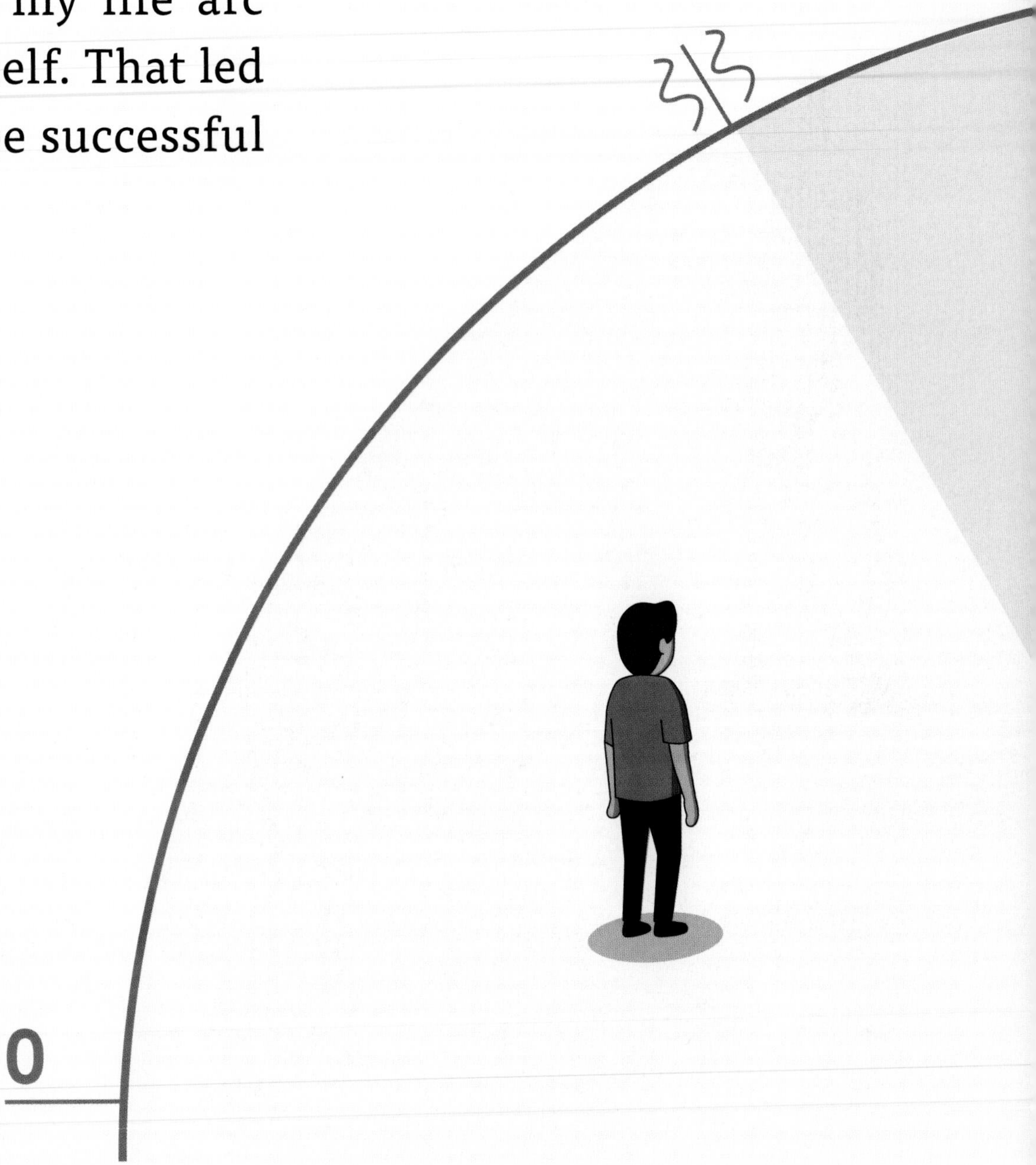
33
0

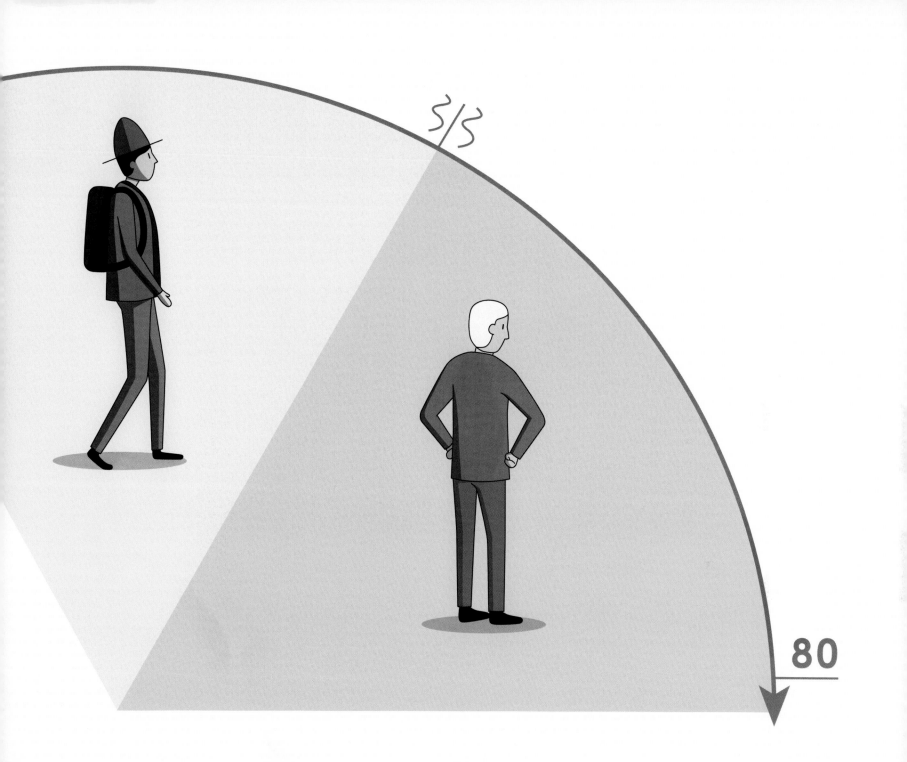

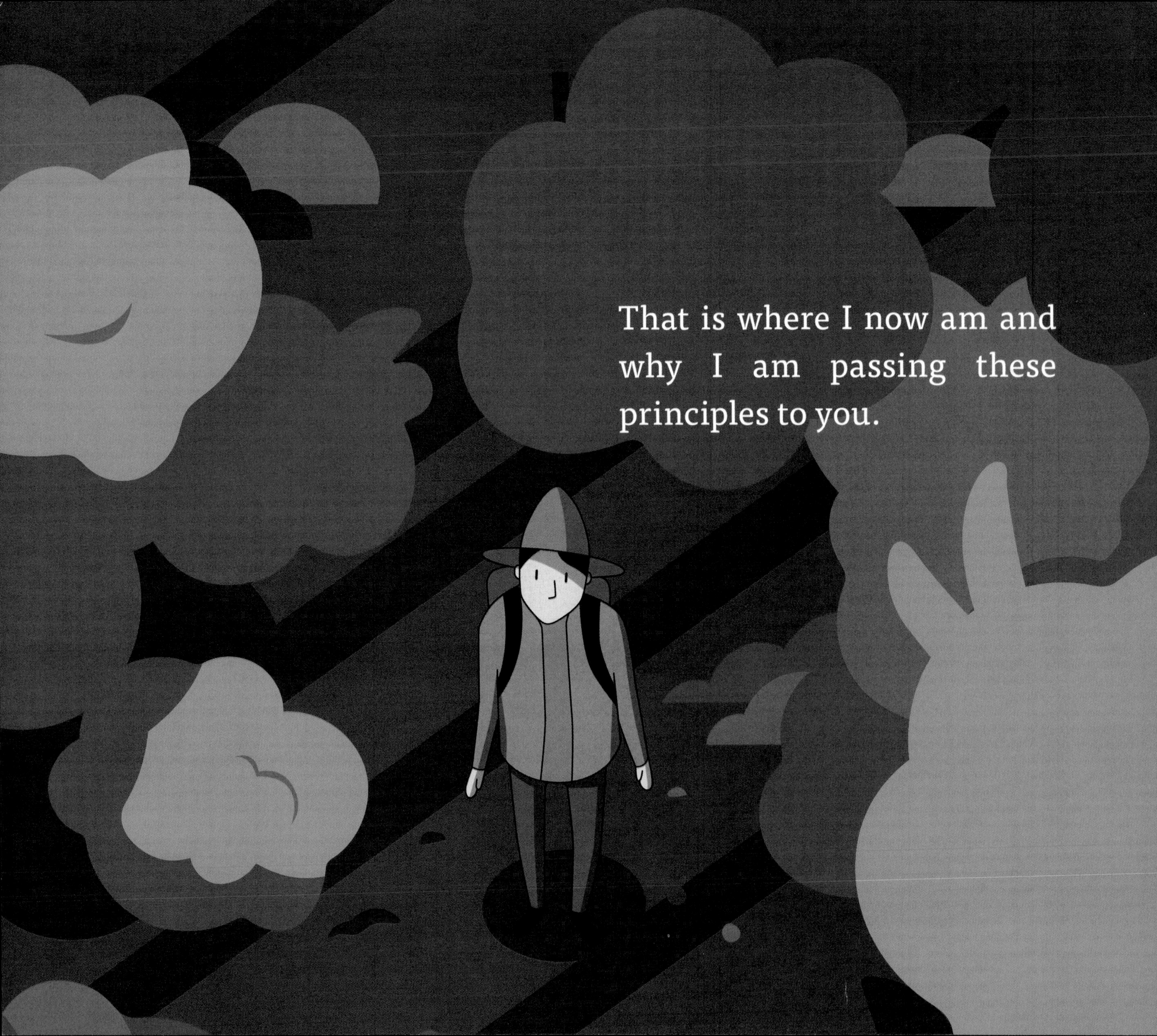

That is where I now am and why I am passing these principles to you.

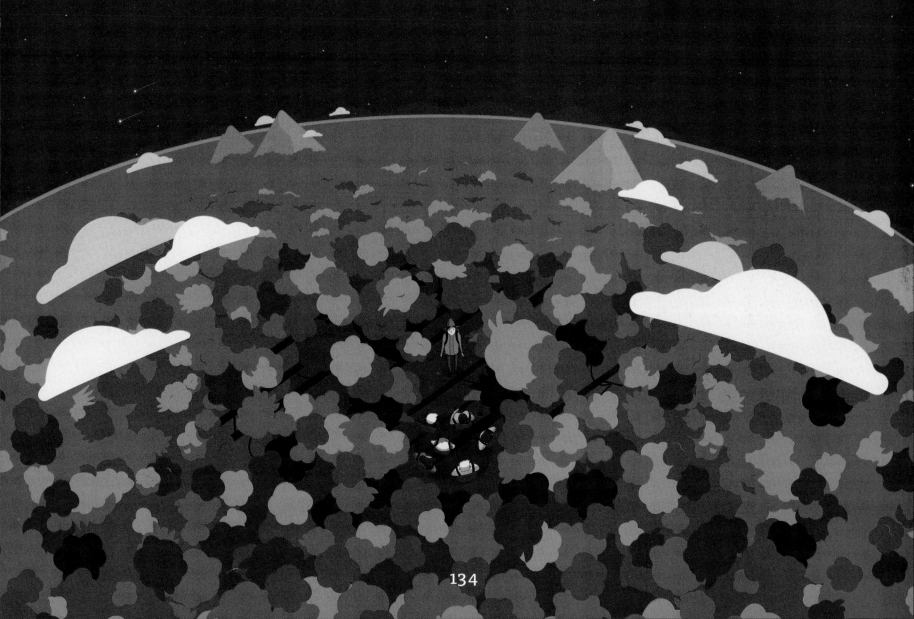

134

Looking back on my life I see that we all struggle with different things at different times in our lives until we become part of the larger evolutionary story.

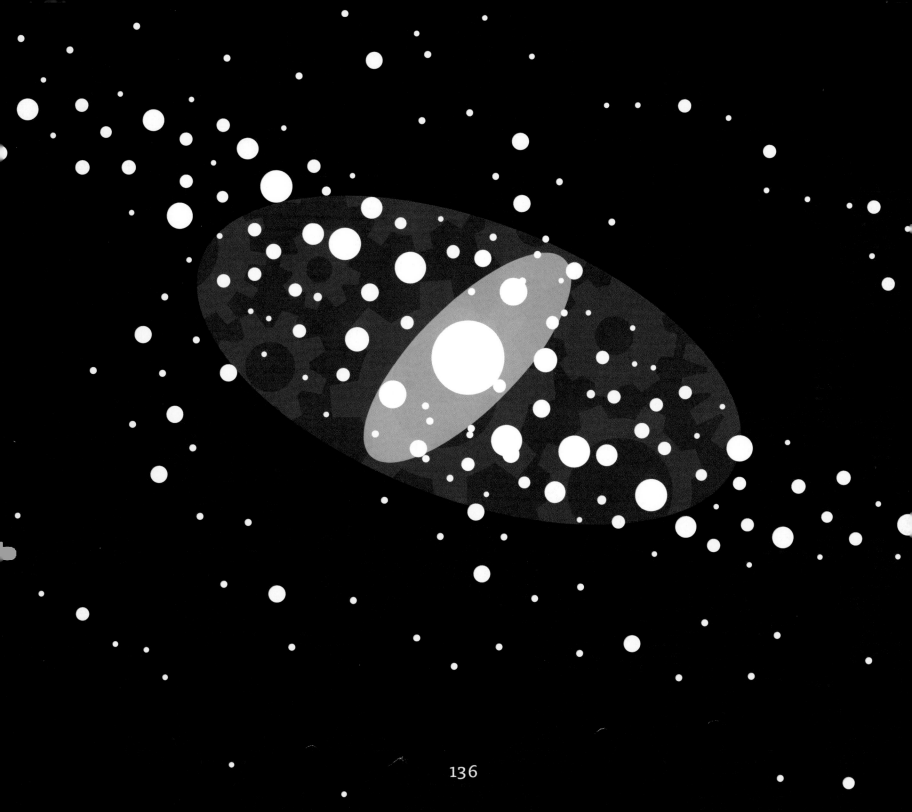

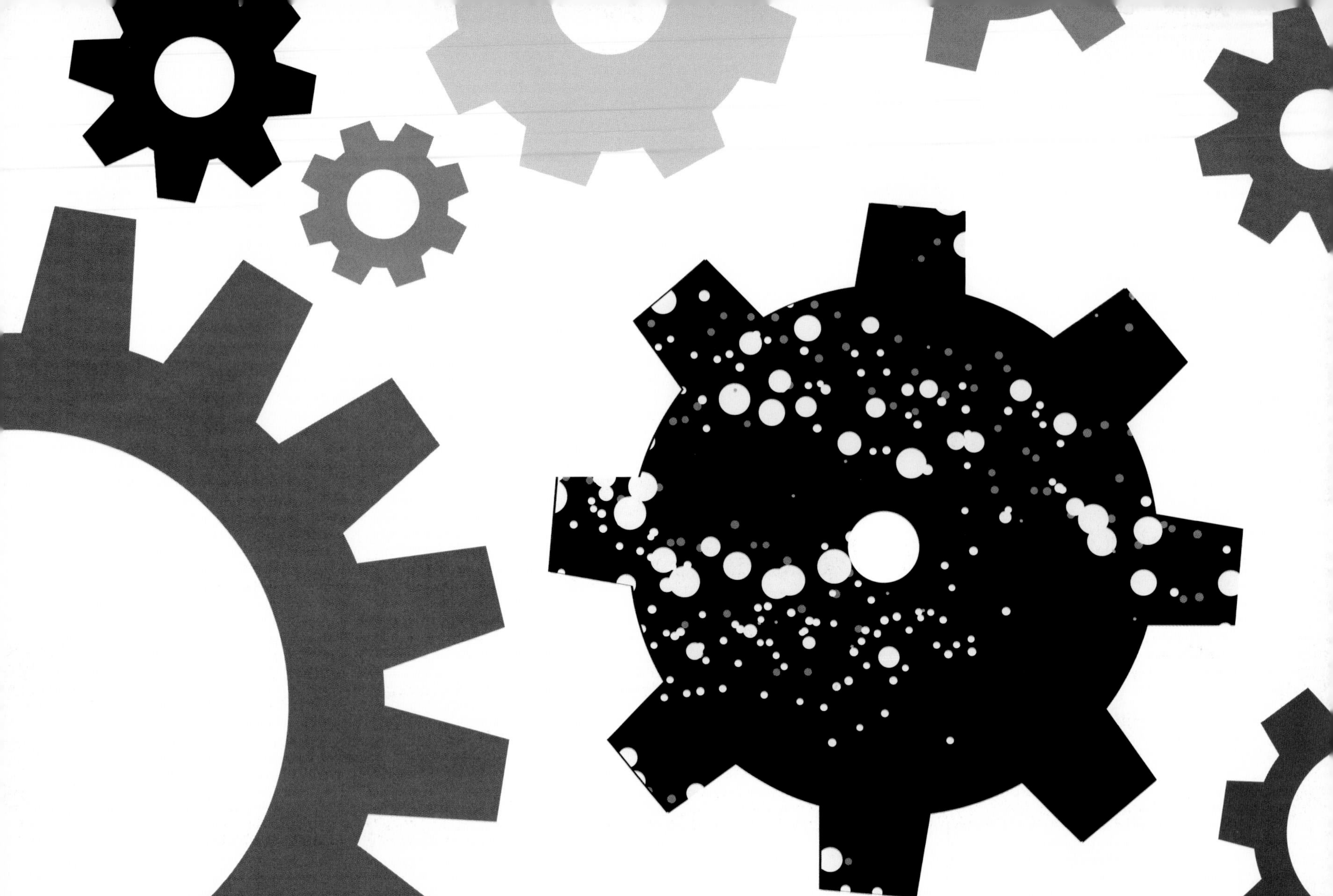

All machines eventually break down and their parts go back into the system to become parts of new machines.

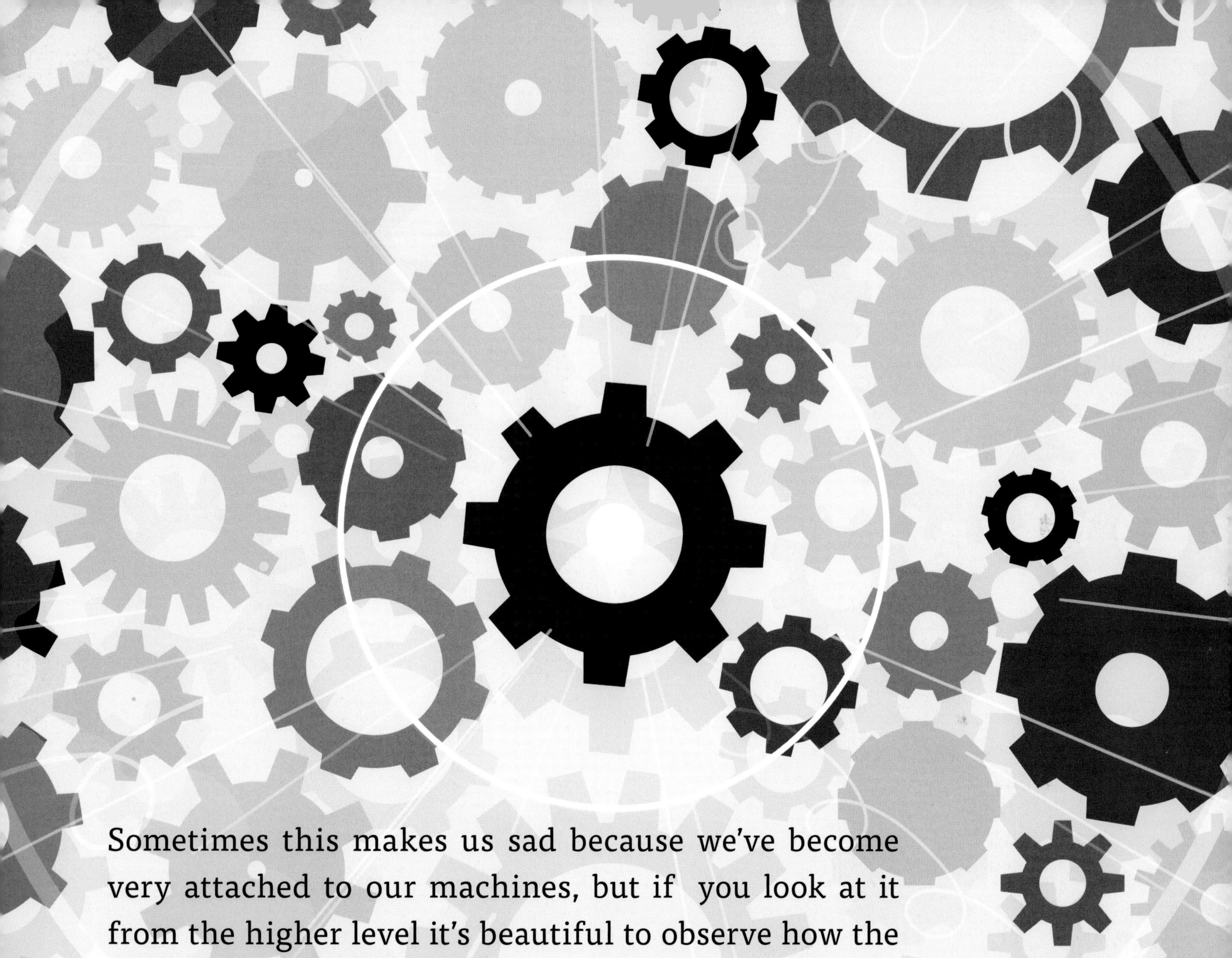

Sometimes this makes us sad because we've become very attached to our machines, but if you look at it from the higher level it's beautiful to observe how the machine of evolution works.

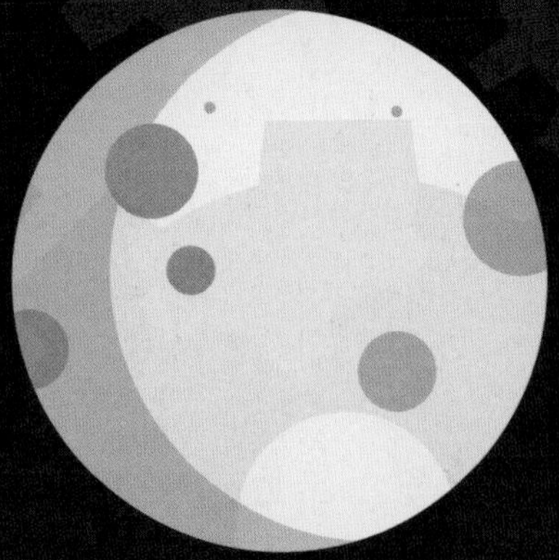

At this time, I'm most excited about you and your adventurous life journey.

Forget about where these principles came from. Just ask whether they are useful to you and evolve them to suit your own needs. And by all means, pick your own, write them down, and have them evolve with you.

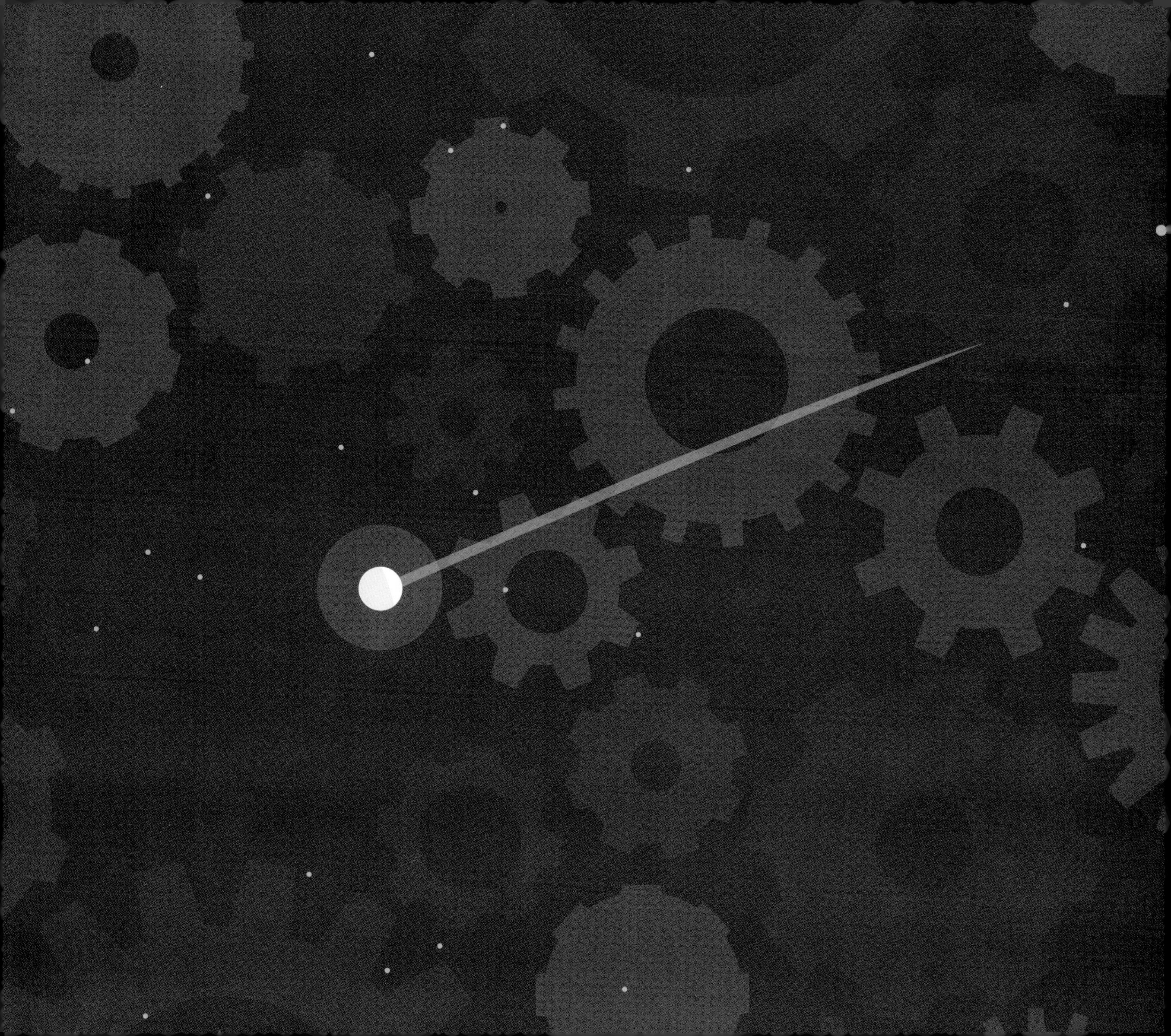

My only hope for you is that you will
live by your own good principles that
will help you decide what to do—and
give you the courage to do it.

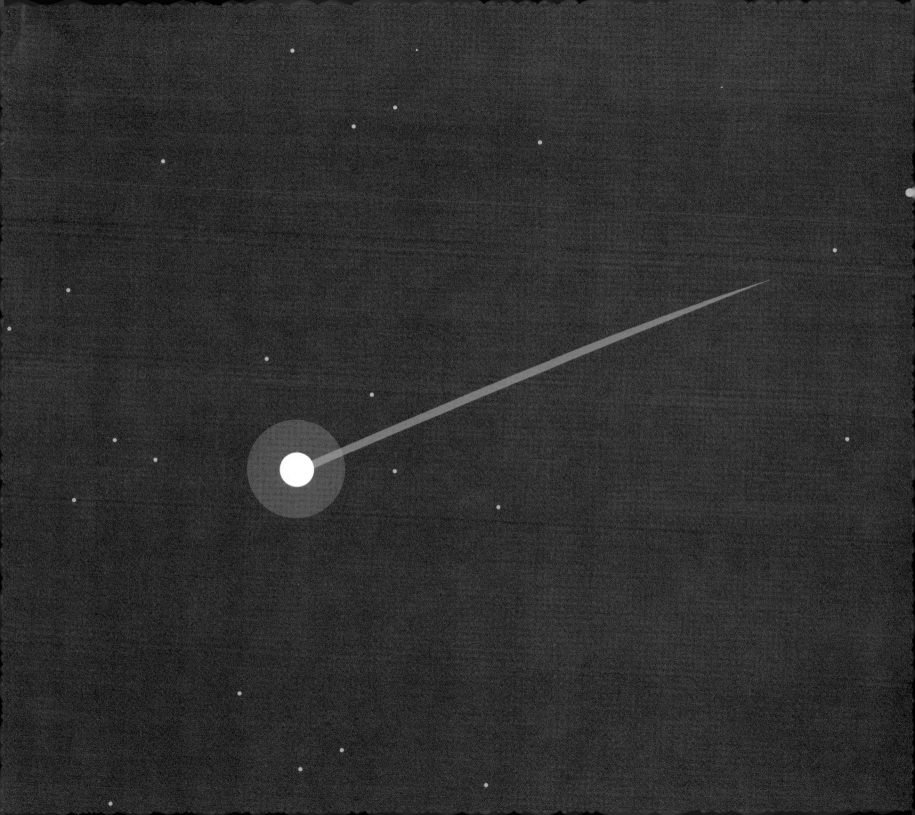

GOODBYE

TO KEEP EXPLORING PRINCIPLES:

REFLECTING ON YOUR PRINCIPLES

HAVING PRINCIPLES

Do you think having good principles is important?

Where are you going to get your
principles from?

Do you think it's a good idea to
write your principles down and
reflect on them over time? Do you
think you will do that?

UNDERSTANDING AND
EMBRACING REALITY

How good are you at embracing
reality as it is—not as you wish it
would be?

Do you agree that most everything
happens over and over again for
similar reasons?

Do you believe that by reflecting
on these patterns and considering

others' reflections on these
patterns, you can learn principles
for dealing with your realities
well, which will make you more
successful?

GETTING AROUND YOUR TWO
BIGGEST BARRIERS

How attached are you to having
the right answer yourself versus
discovering what's true?

Do you see how practicing
thoughtful disagreement can help
you find the best answer? Will you
do it?

How good are you at seeing things
through others' eyes so that you
can tap the best thinking available
to you?

Do you want to learn to struggle
well?

A COLLECTION OF RAY'S OTHER PRINCIPLES

If you are open-minded enough and determined enough you can get virtually anything you want.

Don't worry about looking good—worry about achieving your goals.

Pain + Reflection = Progress

Dreams + Embracing Reality + Determination = A Successful Life

Meaningful work and meaningful relationships are the greatest assets and the greatest rewards.

Create a culture in which it's OK to make mistakes and unacceptable not to learn from them.

Don't let your ego and blind spot barriers stand in your way.

Be open-minded and assertive at the same time.

Own your outcomes.

There is always a good path. If you don't see it, you just need to keep looking in a good way, with the help of others.

Find the most believable people who disagree with you and try to understand their reasoning.

Follow the 5-Step Process to achieving success: 1) know your goals, 2) identify and don't tolerate your problems, 3) diagnose your problems to get at their root causes, 4) design a plan to get around them, 5) implement your plan.

If you do this well over and over again with the help of others who are strong where you are weak, you will achieve success.

You can have virtually anything you want but not everything you want so you need to prioritize well.

Everyone has weaknesses as well as strengths.

The biggest mistake most people make is to not see themselves and others objectively, which leads them to bump into their own and others' weaknesses again and again.

Get around the weaknesses that are standing in your way by either 1) working well with people who are strong where you are weak or 2) working on getting strong where you are weak. Usually the first way is best.

Understand that people are wired very differently—so it's wise to see things through the eyes of smart people who see things differently from you.

Remember that great partnerships with mutual consideration and generosity are far more rewarding than money.

Remember that money is very important up to the point of having enough to take care of yourself and those you care about, and that the amount you need is more than you expect you will need because you will probably underestimate your needs and overestimate what you will end up with down the road. So

calculate carefully and then double what you estimate.

Make your work and your passion one and the same and do it with people you want to be with.

You can't compromise the uncompromisable and expect to be successful.

Be radically truthful and radically transparent.

Share the things that are hardest to share.

Never say anything about someone you wouldn't say to them directly and don't try people without accusing them to their face.

Remember that most people will pretend to operate in your interest while operating in their own.

Evolve or Die.

Understand where you and the people you care about are in your life arcs to put things in perspective and plan well for what's ahead.

YOUR LIFE JOURNEY EXERCISE

This exercise is meant to help you put your life and the lives of the people you care about in perspective and to plan for the future.

As I explained earlier in the book, most everything happens over and over again for pretty much the same reasons, so in order to understand anything it pays to understand how a typical case unfolds and to observe the cause-effect relationships that make it unfold that way. In this exercise I am going ask you to look at the typical journey through life and reflect on your own life and what will probably come at you.

On the following page is the typical life arc. It is chronological from birth to death. To get yourself oriented, estimate about where you are on that arc. You don't have to be precise because life isn't precise. While not all life journeys are the same, most are similar. They last about 80 years and evolve in three phases, with two roughly 5- to 10-year transition phases between them.

In the first phase you learn and are dependent on others. In the second phase, you work and others are dependent on you. That's when you try your hardest to be successful. In the third phase you want to help the people you care about be successful without you more than you want to be more successful yourself. That's because their being independently successful is best for them in their second phase, and you being free of worry and obligations is best for you in your third phase.

On the following pages we will look at each of these phases more closely. Then I will ask you to do some imagining of the future. In looking through these phases, see how the descriptions of what's happening to the typical person match up with your own experiences, especially at the critical junctures because choices then—like whether or not you graduate from high school or college, what career you pursue, whether you have children, etc.—will have big implications on the life that you will have.

PHASE ONE

In the first phase you are dependent on those who prepare you for the second phase in your life. How these early years go has a big effect on shaping your preferences and character and will give you your fundamental abilities and skills. Typically the early years of this phase are easier than the later high school years when you are striving to make the step to what comes next. In those high school years, you will naturally seek more independence and will experience more animal magnetism as your hormones kick in. As a result the high school years can be among the most fun for you and among the most challenging for you and your parents. Then, you either go to college or go straight into the second phase by going to work. If you go to college, you have much more freedom and fun with friends and will experience greater intellectual stimulation. During these college years you will be guided because your courses and most of your life are pretty much laid out for you. The next phase will begin when you end your school education by graduating and beginning to work.

Please take a moment now to check the boxes on the next page, noting the milestones that you have passed.

0

~80

YOUR NOTES AND REFLECTIONS

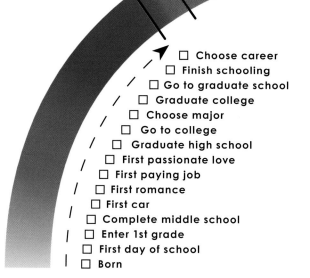

0

☐ Choose career
☐ Finish schooling
☐ Go to graduate school
☐ Graduate college
☐ Choose major
☐ Go to college
☐ Graduate high school
☐ First passionate love
☐ First paying job
☐ First romance
☐ First car
☐ Complete middle school
☐ Enter 1st grade
☐ First day of school
☐ Born

~80

PHASE TWO

In the second phase you will work to be successful and others will become dependent on you. In the early part of the second phase, you step off the track that you were guided on and are free to make your own choices, which are wide ranging. You can live anywhere in the world you want, work at any job you can get, and be with whoever you want to be with. In other words, you can do pretty much anything you want. The mid-20s is one of the happiest periods in life. You have romances and probably will find the partner you intend to spend your life with. As you progress deeper into this second phase you make more commitments and take on more responsibilities at work and in your love life, so your freedom to choose declines and your work-life balance becomes increasingly challenging. You might get divorced, which most commonly happens in the 25-40 age range and is not a happy experience. The years between 45 and 55 are especially challenging and are reported to be the least happy years. Most people transition in the 55-65 period, ending this second phase when they stop working full-time.

Please check the boxes of the milestones that you have passed.

0   ~80

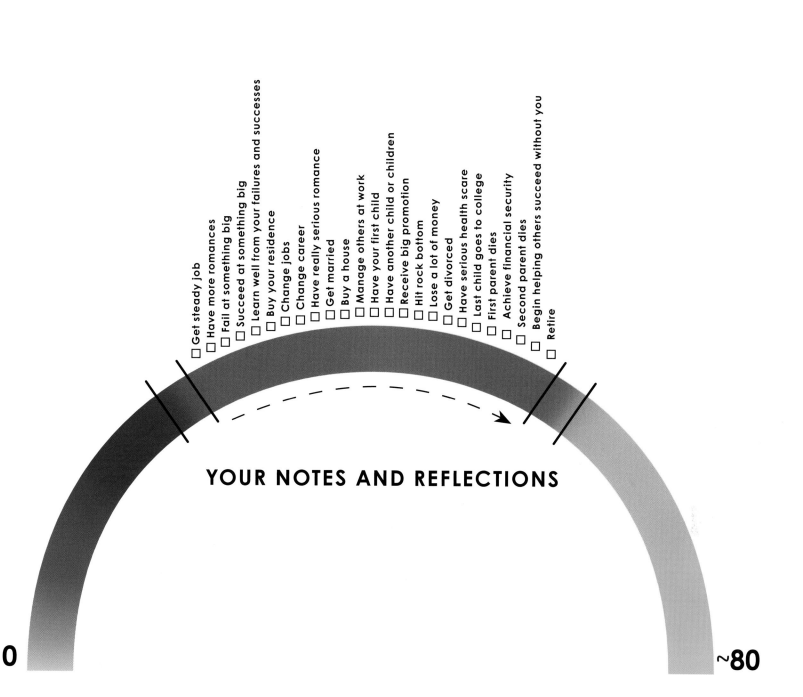

Get steady job
Have more romances
Fail at something big
Succeed at something big
Learn well from your failures and successes
Buy your residence
Change jobs
Change career
Have really serious romance
Get married
Buy a house
Manage others at work
Have your first child
Have another child or children
Receive big promotion
Hit rock bottom
Lose a lot of money
Get divorced
Have serious health scare
Last child goes to college
First parent dies
Achieve financial security
Second parent dies
Begin helping others succeed without you
Retire

YOUR NOTES AND REFLECTIONS

0

~80

PHASE THREE

In the third phase you gain much more freedom because you leave your work and parenting obligations behind, and you don't have to take care of your parents who are gone. You have plenty of free time to savor your family, your friends, and your favorite activities. It is typically early and throughout this phase that one has grandchildren, which is almost universally reported to be an exceptional joy. (I can attest to that.) The 70s are the happiest years in life, according to surveys. Late in this phase is more difficult as one starts to lose one's friends, perhaps lose one's spouse, and have more health problems. Surprisingly (to me at least), while happiness levels dip a bit in the last part of this last phase, they remain relatively high until the end, which is when wisdom and spirituality generally are high.

Please check the boxes of any remaining milestones that you have passed.

0

~80

YOUR NOTES AND REFLECTIONS

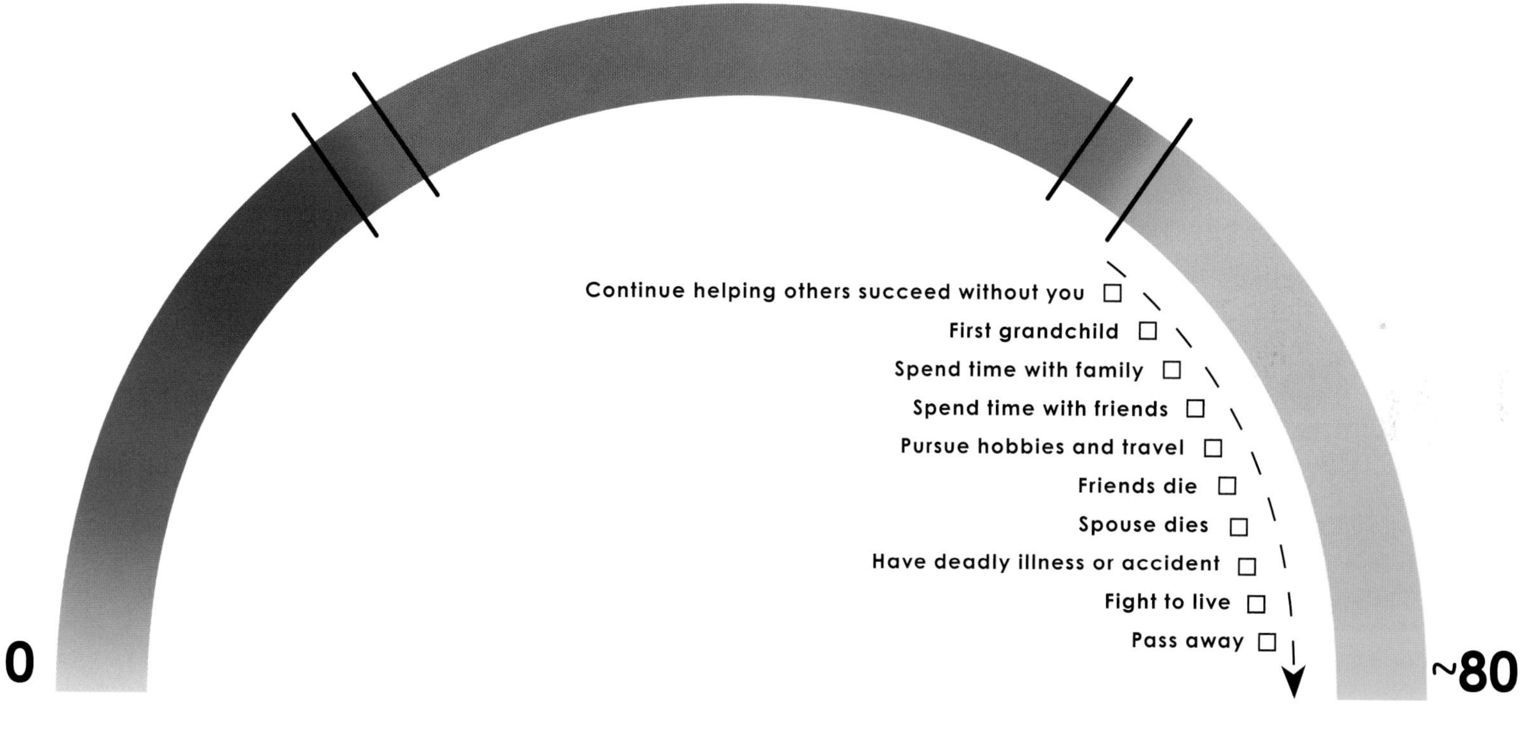

0
Continue helping others succeed without you ☐
First grandchild ☐
Spend time with family ☐
Spend time with friends ☐
Pursue hobbies and travel ☐
Friends die ☐
Spouse dies ☐
Have deadly illness or accident ☐
Fight to live ☐
Pass away ☐
~80

PLANNING YOUR LIFE ARC

Now that you've been through each of these phases in some detail, let's put things in perspective for you and the people you care about. Start by making a circle at the approximate spot on the arc where you are. Now put little marks where the people you care about are on their own arcs, designating who they are by putting their initials next to the marks.

Take a few minutes to try to imagine where you and they will be in 10 years and what is likely to happen between now and then, because what will happen to them will affect you and what will happen to you will affect you and them. For example, you might see that in 10 years your children (who are 25-40 years younger than you) will be leaving home and your parents (who are 25-40 years older than you) will likely be in their last years or passed away while you will be approaching the most challenging part of your career. By knowing what's ahead for you and them, you can start thinking about how to make these 10 years as good as they can be for both you and them. The more you visualize this next 10-year period in detail (e.g., how much money and time you will need for what) the better it will go.

Because it is hard to visualize what you haven't experienced yet, when you face new challenges ask others who have them ahead of you what they're like and what principles they have for facing them well. For example, if you are headed into a certain career, ask those people you respect in that career to describe what it is like, including how it evolves over time. Find those ahead of you who have been successful in the ways you want to be successful and find out the paths they took and principles they used to achieve that success. Make your notes on this diagram and if this diagram becomes complicated with your notes, draw another one or two arcs on other paper and use them.

You will appreciate referring to these notes and principles and refining them as the years go by. Then, when you are in your transition into your third phase and want to help people be successful without you, you can pass these principles along to them.

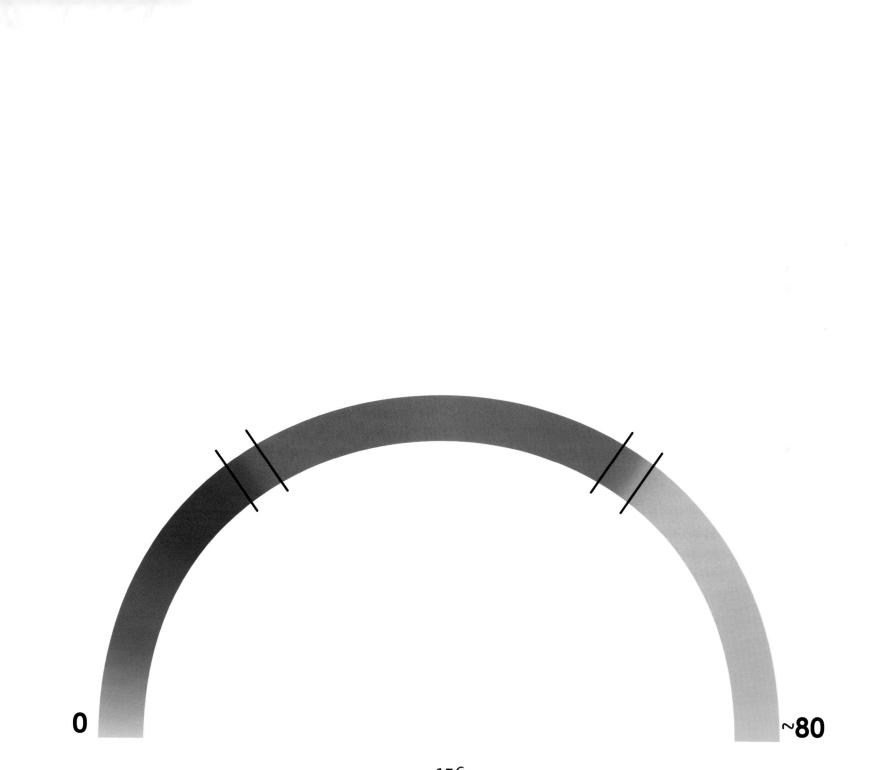

0

~80

WHERE TO FIND MORE ON PRINCIPLES

PRINCIPLES: LIFE & WORK

The original book offering the complete set of Ray's unique principles, which has sold more than 2 million copies worldwide.

PRINCIPLES FOR SUCCESS: AN ULTRA MINI-SERIES ADVENTURE

The 30-minute animated distillation of *Principles: Life & Work*, which this book is based on, available on YouTube and viewed 4 million times.

SOCIAL MEDIA

Follow @raydalio on Facebook, Instagram, Twitter, and LinkedIn, where he regularly answers questions about his principles.

PRINCIPLES IN ACTION APP

The complete text of *Principles: Life & Work*, along with case studies showing the principles in real life and a tool for writing your own principles. Available now in the U.S. Apple App Store and worldwide and on Android (in 2020).

ECONOMIC PRINCIPLES

If you're interested in economies and markets, visit www.economicprinciples.org for Ray's writing on those, including the free book *Principles for Navigating Big Debt Crises*.

Or find everything at www.principles.com